Whose God Rules?

To Toni and Gino:

Thank you for your love, support, friendship, and encouragement!

Joey
'11

Whose God Rules?

Is the United States a Secular Nation or a Theolegal Democracy?

Edited by
Nathan C. Walker and Edwin J. Greenlee
Foreword by Tony Blair

First published in 2011 by
PALGRAVE MACMILLAN® in the United States – a division of St. Martin's Press LLC, 175 Fifth Avenue, New York, NY 10010.

Where this book is distributed in the UK, Europe and the rest of the world, this is by Palgrave Macmillan, a division of Macmillan Publishers Limited, registered in England, company number 785998, of Houndmills, Basingstoke, Hampshire RG21 6XS.

Palgrave Macmillan is the global academic imprint of the above companies and has companies and representatives throughout the world.

Palgrave® and Macmillan® are registered trademarks in the United States, the United Kingdom, Europe and other countries.

ISBN 978–0–230–11783–9

Library of Congress Cataloging-in-Publication Data

Whose God rules? : is the United States a secular nation or a theolegal democracy? / edited by Nathan C. Walker and Edwin J. Greenlee ; foreword by Tony Blair.
    p. cm.
   Includes bibliographical references and index.
   ISBN 978–0–230–11783–9 (hardback)
  1. Religion and politics—United States. 2. United States—Politics and government.
3. Religion and state—United States. 4. Democracy—United States. 5. Democracy—Religious aspects. I. Walker, Nathan C., 1975– II. Greenlee, Edwin J., 1950–
    BL2525.W475 2011
    322'.10973—dc23   2011021591

A catalogue record of the book is available from the British Library.

Design by MPS Limited, A Macmillan Company.

First edition: December 2011

10 9 8 7 6 5 4 3 2 1

Printed in the United States of America.

Dedicated to the members and friends of
The First Unitarian Church of Philadelphia,
a Unitarian Universalist congregation established in 1796.

Contents

Foreword*

Tony Blair

After ten years as British prime minister, I decided to choose something easy. I became involved in the Middle East peace process.

There are many frustrations—that is evident. There is also one blessing. I spend much of my time in the Holy Land and in the Holy City. The other evening I climbed to the top of Notre Dame in Jerusalem. You look left and see the Garden of Gethsemane. You look right and see where the Last Supper was held. Straight ahead lies Golgotha. In the distance is where King David was crowned and still further where Abraham was laid to rest. And of course in the center of Jerusalem is the Al Aqsa Mosque, where according to the Qur'an, the Prophet was transported to commune with the prophets of the past. Rich in conflict, it is also sublime in history. The other month in Jericho, I visited the Mount of Temptation. I think they bring all the political leaders there. My guide—a Palestinian—was bemoaning the travails of his nation. Suddenly he stopped, looked heavenwards, and said "Moses, Jesus, Mohammed: why did they all have to come here?"

It is a good place to reflect on religion: a source of so much inspiration; an excuse for so much evil. Today, religion is under attack from without and from within. From within, it is corroded by extremists who use their faith as a means of excluding the other. *I am what I am in opposition to you. If you do not believe as I believe, you are a lesser human being.* From without, religious faith is assailed by an increasingly aggressive secularism, which derides faith as contrary to reason and defines faith by conflict. Thus, the extreme believers and the aggressive nonbelievers come together in unholy alliance.

And yet, faith will not be so easily cast. For billions of people, faith motivates, galvanizes, compels, and inspires, not to exclude but to embrace; not to provoke conflict but to try to do good. This is faith in action. You can

---

* Blair, Tony (2009). Reprinted from speech given at the U.S. National Prayer Breakfast, February 5, 2009, Washington, DC.

see it in countless local communities where those from churches, mosques, synagogues, and temples tend the sick, care for the afflicted, work long hours in bad conditions to bring hope to the despairing and salvation to the lost. You can see it in the arousing of the world's conscience to the plight of Africa. There are a million good deeds done every day by people of faith. These are those for whom, in the parable of the sower, the seed fell on good soil and yielded 60 or 100-fold. What inspires such people? Ritual or doctrine or the finer points of theology? No.

I remember my first spiritual awakening. I was 10 years old. That day my father—at the young age of 40—had suffered a serious stroke. His life hung in the balance. My mother, to keep some sense of normality in the crisis, sent me to school. My teacher knelt and prayed with me. Now my father was a militant atheist. Before we prayed, I thought I should confess this. "I'm afraid my father doesn't believe in God," I said. "That doesn't matter," my teacher replied, "God believes in him. He loves him without demanding or needing love in return." That is what inspires: the unconditional nature of God's love, a promise perpetually kept, a covenant never broken. And in surrendering to God, we become instruments of that love.

Rabbi Hillel was once challenged by a Pagan, who said, "If you can recite the whole of the Torah standing on one leg, I will convert to being a Jew." Rabbi Hillel stood on one leg and said, "That which is hateful to you, do it not unto your neighbour. That is the Torah. Everything else is commentary. Go and study it."

As the Qur'an states, "If anyone saves a person it will be as if he has saved the whole of humanity." We might also talk of the Hindu "Living beyond the reach of I and mine" or the words of Buddha "after practising enlightenment you must go back to practise compassion" or the Sikh scripture, "God's bounties are common to all. It is we who have created divisions." Each faith has its beliefs. Each is different. Yet at a certain point each is in communion with the other. Faith is not discovered in acting according to ritual but in acting according to God's will, and God's will is love.

Examine the impact of globalization. Forget for a moment its rights and wrongs. Just look at its effects. Its characteristic is that it pushes the world together. It is not only an economic force. The consequence is social, even cultural. The global community—"it takes a village" as someone once coined it—is upon us. Into it steps religious faith. If faith becomes the property of extremists, it will originate discord. But if, by contrast, different faiths can reach out to and have knowledge of one another, then instead of being reactionary, religious faith can be a force for progress.

The Foundation which bears my name is dedicated to achieving understanding, action, and reconciliation between the different faiths for the common good. It is not about the faith that looks inward; but the faith that resolutely turns us toward each other. Bringing the faith communities together fulfills an objective important to all of us, believers and non-believers. But as someone of faith, this is not enough. I believe restoring religious faith to its rightful place, as the guide to our world and its future, is itself of the essence. The twenty-first century will be poorer in spirit, meaner in ambition, less disciplined in conscience, if it is not under the guardianship of faith in God.

I do not mean by this to blur the correct distinction between the realms of religious and political authority. In Britain we are especially mindful of this. I recall giving an address to the country at a time of crisis. I wanted to end my words with "God bless the British people." This caused complete consternation. Emergency meetings were convened. The system was aghast. Finally, as I sat trying to defend my words, a senior civil servant said, with utter disdain: "Really, Prime Minister, this is not America you know."

Neither do I decry the work of humanists, who give gladly of themselves for others and who can often shame the avowedly religious. Those who do God's work are God's people. I only say that there are limits to humanism and beyond those limits God and only God can work. The phrase "fear of God" conjures up the vengeful God of parts of the Old Testament. But "fear of God" means really obedience to God; humility before God; acceptance through God that there is something bigger, better, and more important than you. It is that humbling of man's vanity, that stirring of conscience through God's prompting, that recognition of our limitations, that faith alone can bestow.

We can perform acts of mercy, but only God can lend them dignity. We can forgive, but only God forgives completely in the full knowledge of our sin. And only through God comes grace; and it is God's grace that is unique. John Newton, who had been that most obnoxious of things, a slave trader, wrote the hymn *Amazing Grace*: "'Twas Grace that taught my heart to fear and Grace my fears relieved." It is through faith, by the Grace of God, that we have the courage to live as we should and die as we must.

When I was prime minister I had cause often to reflect on leadership. Courage in leadership is not simply about having the nerve to make difficult decisions or even in doing the right thing since oftentimes God alone knows what the right thing is. It is to be in our natural state—which is one of nagging doubt, imperfect knowledge, and uncertain prediction—and to be prepared nonetheless to put on the mantle of responsibility and to stand up in full view of the world, to step out when others step back, to assume the loneliness of the final decision-maker, not sure of success but unsure of it. And it is in that "not knowing" that the courage lies. And when in that state of not knowing, our courage fails, our faith can support it, lift it up, keep it from stumbling.

I finish where I began: in the Holy Land, at Mount Nebo in Jordan, where Moses gazed on the Promised Land. There is a chapel there, built by pilgrims in the fourth century. The sermon was preached by an American, who spent his life as an airline pilot and then, after his wife's death, took holy orders. His words are the words of a Christian but they speak to all those of faith, who want God's grace to guide their life. He said this:

> While here on earth, we need to make a vital decision . . . whether to be mere spectators, or movers and shakers for the Kingdom of God . . . whether to stay among the curious, or take up a cross. And this means: no standing on the sidelines . . . We're either in the game or we're not. I sometimes ask myself the question: If I were to die today, what would my life have stood for . . . The answer can't be an impulsive one, and we all need to count the cost before we give an answer. Because to be able to say yes to one thing, means to say no to many others. But we must also remember, that the greatest danger is not impulsiveness, but inaction.

It is fitting at this extraordinary moment in your country's history that we hear that call to action; and we pray that, in acting, we do God's work and follow God's will. And by the way, God bless you all.

Acknowledgments

Whose God Rules? originated from a sermon offered by Reverend Nathan C. Walker on April 20, 2008, at the First Unitarian Church of Philadelphia entitled *Theolegal Democracy*. The sermon would not have become the basis for this book without the encouragement of members of the congregation, especially Edwin J. Greenlee, Anne Slater, Christine Carlson, Jennifer Zanck, Heather Speirs, and Dan and Christiane Geisler.

The editors are deeply grateful to the collegial support and encouragement of Howard Lesnick, Mark Rozel, Kim Scheppele, and Clyde Wilcox.

Special thanks is offered to Nate's mentors from Columbia University and Union Theological Seminary whose insights and kindness will never be forgotten: Jay Heubert, Janice Robinson, William Baldwin, Elana Sigall, Sharon Lynn Kagan, Alan Brinkley, Kathy Talvacchia, and Gabriella Lettini.

Introduction to Theolegal Theory

Nathan C. Walker

Humor can reveal truth. After Tony Blair closed a public speech with "God bless the British people," a senior civil servant replied, "Really, Prime Minister, this is not America, you know." Americans love this story. It not only arouses a giggle but also reveals a candid irony, best expressed in the form of a question. Does Mr. Blair's colleague, who serves a country with a national religion, consider the United States to improperly blur religion and political authority? His comment implies that U.S. citizens allow, if not reward, public officials who explicitly use God-talk in political discourse.

The United States is comprised of a religiously diverse citizenry, which leaves officials to balance the tension upheld by a constitution that simultaneously prevents the establishment of a national creed and yet preserves one's right to freedom *of* religion. In practice, officials in the United States cannot legislate theology, but they can, and do, use theology to legislate.

As a result, our government is not a secular democracy where laws guarantee freedom *from* religion and dismiss theological rhetoric in the political process; neither is it a theocracy, where a single religion prescribes all laws. The purpose of our book is to demonstrate that our country, whether we like it or not, is distinct from that of a secular democracy and a theocracy. The United States is a *theolegal democracy,* defined as a nation that simultaneously guarantees citizens the right to free expression of belief while preventing the establishment of a state religion. These guarantees allow officials to use theology as one of many resources in making, applying, or administering law because a theolegal democracy does not prevent citizens or officials from using their religious worldview in the public arena as seen in secular nations. Nor does a theolegal democracy permit officials to use their theology to deny civil rights to those who do not meet those creedal tests as seen in theocracies.

Our book is comprised of numerous examples of legislators, politicians, civil servants, and legal professionals using theology in their decision-making process. (For the purposes of our discussion, theology is defined as systematically developed beliefs affirmed by religious communities.) We do not classify these officials as theocrats because they do not govern in the context of a theocracy, where God's rule is executed by divinely guided leaders. Rather, they are defined as *theolegal officials* who govern within the tension found in a theolegal constitution that prevents them from establishing an official or a *de facto* state religion, yet affirms their right to freely express their beliefs. Some officials may try to adopt theocratic practices. However, the very nature of a *theolegal democracy* requires officials to exercise restraint by not allowing their particular religious worldview, or the religion of their constituents, to become the rule of the land. A theolegal democracy is also comprised of a plurality of citizens and interest groups that use the democratic process to remove aspiring theocrats from power. At the same time, this kind of government allows officials to freely express their theology and, to some extent, allows them to reference their beliefs during the legislative process.

As a result, *theolegal democracy* is a concept that can evoke at least three responses: it can be a pejorative term for those who believe in separating religion and government; an affirmative term for those who want to preserve one's rights to freely integrate their beliefs; and a candid term for those who value the active participation of a plurality of religious groups in their government. Tensions arise when officials with these varied perspectives govern a country comprised of diverse constituencies.

This sets the stage for our question, *whose God rules a theolegal democracy?* Depending on one's worldview this question may provoke fear, satisfaction, or curiosity as demonstrated in the following three schools of thought: separationists, integrationists, and pluralists. *Separationists* fear that the God of the majority will rule minorities who do not meet those creedal tests: separationists participate in the creation of a theolegal democracy by ensuring that officials do not establish a state religion. *Integrationists* are satisfied with officials' free expression of belief, aware that an official's beliefs are but one source of knowledge used by them to govern: integrationists participate in the creation of a theolegal democracy by promoting religious liberty. *Pluralists* are curious about how religious tyranny is preempted and democracy is strengthened by the engagement of diverse religious interest groups: pluralists participate in the creation of a theolegal democracy by encouraging a wide variety of religious and secular worldviews to be represented in our collective decision-making process. These three worldviews operate alongside one another as an interrelated unit that not only co-creates a theolegal democracy, but also prevents it from becoming either a secular democracy or a theocracy.

This introductory chapter is designed not only to explore these three worldviews, but also to analyze how these perspectives are manifested in the behaviors of citizens and legislators. These behaviors not only breed *theolegal* activities but, surprisingly, secular complacency. Before this conclusion is made, a discussion of these three worldviews is in order.

Separationists

Separationists are skeptical about officials infusing theology into legal rationale and seek to dissociate religion and the state, thereby ensuring that no God rules. From the critical perspective of this worldview, the very essence of our civil society is in danger of being governed from the shadow side of a theolegal democracy—when officials justify their legal decisions not on the preservation of the rights of the minority but on the religious views of the majority. A separationist is different from a pure secularist who rejects any form of religious discourse in civil society, but both agree that theolegal practices are problematic. Separationists believe in religious liberty, yet place a primary importance on the constitution's nonestablishment and no-religious-test clauses, and the jurisprudence derived from U.S. Supreme Court's interpretations that prevent government from enacting religious tests based on a legal creed.

Separationists are therefore critical about citizens' use of the media to probe the personal theology of political candidates, which creates a *de facto* religious test for office. Although aware of the complexities by which citizens vote, separationists worry they will elect representatives who will use their theology to enact laws in accordance with their beliefs. At best, such a government can pass laws that codify the widely accepted moral beliefs held by its citizens. At worst, the dominant theology goes unquestioned while minorities who do not meet those creedal tests experience a loss of rights. Separationists are most concerned about a negative byproduct of theolegal practices—the fortification of the majority's beliefs without instituting an official state religion. Separationists are dedicated to preserving justice and equality for all by preventing religious laws from becoming" so that it reads: Separationists are dedicated to preserving justice and equality for all by preventing religious laws from becoming civil laws. Although separationists recognize that religion plays a part in civil society, they are ultimately concerned that the God of the majority will be allowed to rule all.

Integrationists

Integrationists, sometimes referred to as *accommodationists*, also reject the establishment of a state religion but place greater emphasis on the constitutional guarantee of an individual's free exercise of religion and freedom of speech. They believe that the United States has always been, and should continue to be a theolegal democracy in order to prevent it from becoming a pure secular nation or a pure theocracy, with each extreme denying the inalienable human right to free expression. Integrationists make clear that citizens do not give up their civil rights when they dedicate themselves to public service. It is unrealistic to ask civil servants to separate their faith from their duty and to ask citizens to leave their beliefs at the voting booth door, whether religious or secular. Such a division, it is believed, would result in severe consequences to democracy. For example, some integrationists argue that if public officials were not allowed to authentically integrate their religious beliefs in their public life, they might be led to create a secret culture where officials might use theology covertly to undermine that necessary tenet of democracy, transparency. To censor a civil servant's application of beliefs in terms of job performance not only harms the individual, but also prevents voters from having full knowledge of the sincere beliefs held by the public official. To censor citizens' use of their religious worldviews is to regulate free expression, which could result in the use of covert theology in political mobilization. In order to thrive, democracy must be strengthened by the practice of transparency, wherein the beliefs of those elected are open to those they serve, and the people's beliefs are known to those who lead. Integrationists believe separationists oversimplify the complexity with which voters choose their representatives. They believe voters do not inquire about a candidate's faith in order to elect a power elite to legalize the beliefs of the majority. Instead, voters inquire to participate in a transparent political process that models religious freedom, affirms the constitution's Establishment Clause, all while contributing to an educated citizenry.

Subsets of integrationists urge officials to legitimate their professional status by exercising restraint and not using their religious worldview as the sole or predominant rationale in their decision-making. If and when an integrated theology is used to discuss law, it should involve a particular social issue that is inextricably theological. In such instances it is expected that there will be open and frank discussion, aware that faith is but one of the freely expressed lenses through which to examine issues.

An open democratic process permits individuals, including public officials and voters, to practice religious freedoms, while simultaneously preventing officials from establishing a state religion. In summary, integrationists believe an individual's theology is only one factor that informs one's decision-making: their God does not necessarily become the ultimate rule of law.

Pluralists

Pluralists believe that our theolegal nation was conceived out of the relative ecumenical diversity of the country's founders and their constituents, a supermajority of whom identified as Christians. Over time, religious pluralism became more complex as American society both influenced and was influenced by globalization. Therefore, in this book you will not find the historical term "separation of church and state" to describe a twenty-first-century theolegal democracy, but recognize the country's theological diversity by using the phrase "separation of *religion* and state."

To achieve a truly balanced democracy in a pluralist society, each world-view, whether derived from religious or secular beliefs, should have equal opportunity to participate in the political process thereby nurturing one of the country's greatest strengths, a diverse citizenry. The more belief systems represented, the more likely that a predominant religious view will not determine whose God rules. Pluralists believe the best way to achieve the goal of separation of religion and state is to increase the diversity of those participating in government. Diversity is honored when the state creates a public and transparent process through which officials and citizens can exercise their constitutional rights. This process is most effective when participants, first, express their views in universal terms; second, defend the rights of people other than themselves; and third, inspire a plurality of communities to participate in government.

Unlike separationists, pluralists do not assume that all Christians will vote for Christians to enact Christian values: there is a wide range of Christianities with divergent beliefs on a variety of topics. Despite the plurality in each religious tradition, some who come from the predominant Judeo-Christian worldview, for example, may feel uncomfortable voting for a minority candidate, such as an atheist or a Muslim or a Wiccan. This initial resistance is softened over time as the voting public diversifies. Multicultural countries that participate in the global political process find their citizens developing sophisticated sensitivities to a wide variety of worldviews. This diversification results in a lessening of the political power of historically predominant religions: their adherents have the option to choose from a wider pool of candidates and eventually cease from voting for only those whose religion traditions mirror their own. Pluralistic societies require diverse coalitions to form and to find common ground.

If an official fails to build a common good and appears to be religiously motivated to legalize their particular theology, resulting in the erosion of another's civil rights, pluralists believe it is the role of a multicultural democracy to counter that overt theology by building diverse coalitions who preserve justice and equality for all. Pluralists encourage citizens to bring a multitude of worldviews together to enact reasonable checks and balances, even if that results in removing the theolegal official from office. As a result, pluralists affirm a separationist perspective by promoting separation of religion and state.

Pluralists simultaneously affirm an integrationist standpoint. It is expected that public officials will be transparent about their beliefs and, if deemed rhetorically effective, will use their God-talk as merely one tool to motivate a wide range of religious interest groups to take collective responsibility for their government. Voters might be motivated by perceiving the theolegal language of the official to be either inspiring or offensive. Either way, pluralists consider democracy to be strengthened when there is increased participation. Pluralists therefore accept both the effectiveness and the consequences of officials' use of theology as one of many sources of knowledge to determine law. Faith is but one worldview used by those in power. Put simply, the God of the majority may inform the rules of yesterday, motivate citizens to act today, but will not necessarily be the ruling God of tomorrow. A pluralistic society is ruled by the belief *e pluribus unum*—out of many we are one.

Applying Theolegal Theory

Each of these three worldviews is situated within the context of a theolegal democracy where theology can become a political commodity. Public officials act on the religious faith of their constituents, or at least on the beliefs held by the majority, and use those beliefs to barter with voters and bargain for power. This process gives birth to a theolegal democracy, which is identified by examining the behavior of citizens, by observing the behavior of public officials, by studying the explicit and implicit theology found in legislation, and by appraising the rationales used by officials who apply theology to law. If religion is a factor in any of these arenas, then a theolegal democracy is co-created by the citizens themselves whether they identify as separationists, integrationists, and/or pluralists.

Theolegal Citizenry

One way a theolegal democracy forms is when religious interest groups elect officials based on theological principles. Their intent is to have their religious worldview somehow represented in legislative, judicial, and executive branches of government.

Take, for instance, the recent nationwide effort to replace Catholic members of Congress with "real Catholics." U.S. Senator Sam Brownback of Kansas served as the spokesman of the Catholic Advocates who sought to remove "so-called Catholics" from public office (specifically, Edward Kennedy, Nancy Pelosi, and John Kerry). In this example, a self-appointed group of Catholic voters wanted to elect officials to represent their particular form of Catholicism, which differed from the religious views of others within that particular religious tradition.

Separationists view such practices as a betrayal of the separation of religion and state and therefore support and enforce the constitution's Establishment Clause. Integrationists think it is inevitable for a group to express its beliefs and possibly take offense at those who believe differently and therefore promote the constitution's Free Exercise Clause. Pluralists consider this behavior a classic example of a religious interest-group engaging in political discourse and therefore emphasize the Equal Protection Clause. All three perspectives are critical foundations for a healthy democracy.

However, what happens when this theolegal interest-group behavior becomes a predominant practice, not necessarily based in a particular religious sect but in a larger theolegal worldview affirmed by many voters from a wide variety of similar traditions? The American public has a longstanding practice of upholding a theolegal democracy, often resulting in a *de facto* public religious test for office. It is common for U.S. voters to spend a great deal of time scrutinizing the beliefs of elected officials. For example, in the Saddleback Civil Forum on the Presidency, millions of voters watched Pastor Rick Warren interview senators John McCain and Barack Obama. Warren opened the forum by saying, "We believe in the separation of church and state. But we do not believe in the separation of faith in politics because faith is just a worldview and everybody has some kind of worldview." Warren made clear that, to the chagrin of separationists, citizens had the right to understand intimately the faith of those who were to take public office.

CNN's Democratic Candidates Compassion Forum with Campbell Brown and Jon Meacham had a similar intent. We might well ask whether the Democratic candidates themselves may have been theologically constrained by the public expectation that officials should believe in God. If so, whose God? An August 2008 Pew Foundation survey reported that 7 in 10 Americans believe that a president should have strong religious beliefs: 86 percent of Republicans agreed, whereas 68 percent of Democrats agreed.[1] Therefore, if Democratic presidential candidates are to win Republican votes, it may be a practical political strategy to be publicly pious. These polls highlight voters' motivations to inquire about the faith of presidential candidates and test the sincerity of their beliefs. Meanwhile, candidates recognize their audience and therefore seek to be overtly religious as a political strategy, which strengthens the free-expression pillar of a theolegal democracy.

Some integrationists are not concerned with such forums because reasonable transparency about one's theology is but one component in informing citizens about a candidate's character, choices, and values. Separationists, however, reply by asking what are the consequences of such behaviors? With good intentions, voters want to know what political candidates really believe. But what are the consequences of asking about a candidate's religious upbringing—is Barack Obama *really* a Christian? The media feeds on this desire and thoroughly investigates politicians' religious affiliations.

Take, for instance, the fury with which voters in the 2008 presidential election consumed information about Barack Obama's former pastor, Jeremiah Wright; or vice-presidential candidate Sarah Palin's Pentecostal rituals to "rebuke witchcraft in the name of Jesus"[2]; or the 2010 senatorial race in Delaware where candidate Christine O'Donnell was rebuked for saying, "I dabbled into witchcraft."[3] These statements were formative moments in their campaigns.

Citizens from various worldviews intentionally, and unintentionally, use this kind of information to shape their perception of candidates' characters, whether positive or negative. Separationists believe that these practices, coupled with public forums about candidates' faith, have become a way for the religious majority to enact implicit religious tests for office—a passing grade is granted to those who affirm the beliefs of the majority. Pluralists respond by granting a failing grade to candidates whose theology offends voters, which is also classified as theolegal behavior. Whether citizens vote for or against candidates because of their beliefs, all participate in a theolegal democracy, whether they intend to or not. Regardless of the election outcome, when a government allows freedom of expression and belief without establishing a state religion, it is expected that the beliefs of those running for office will in some way influence voters' perceptions. Voters in a theolegal democracy will act upon those impressions, whether pleased or offended by the official's beliefs.

Separationists criticize the way some citizens may base their votes for a candidate on the compatibility of their religious beliefs, while integrationists defend the complexity of voters' decisions, naming faith as but one factor. Pluralists, however, argue that faith may matter at the time for those particular constituents; however, in the long run it is likely the demographics will diversify, eventually making it possible for religious minorities and nonbelievers to hold office. Until then, pluralists believe laws should allow equal opportunity for all citizens to run for office, no matter the likelihood of their winning the race.

Theolegal Executives

Whether elected or appointed, citizens in a theolegal democracy continue to pay close attention to the God-talk of those in office. For instance, after Robert Bentley's 2011 inauguration as governor of Alabama, he proclaimed to the members of the Dexter Avenue King Memorial Baptist Church in Montgomery, "So anybody here today who has not accepted Jesus Christ as their savior, I'm telling you, you're not my brother and you're not my sister, and I want to be your brother."[4] After considerable criticism he issued a public apology.

Then there is Louisiana-born Governor Bobby Jindal who self-identifies as Catholic. Voters asked, how can a man whose Hindu parents emigrated from India *really* be Christian? Those who doubted may have found refuge in Jindal's professed faith in Jesus Christ, a belief statement more compatible with many Evangelicals than the views of mainline Catholics: ". . . our God wins . . . so let's recommit ourselves to go plant those seeds of the gospel so that others might come to have that gift of eternal life. It may be the most important thing we do."[5]

These theolegal statements made by Jindal and Bentley mirror that of Justice Roy Moore, who in 2003 protested the removal of the Ten Commandments from the Alabama state judicial building by denouncing: "We should be offended when elected representatives of this state, the governor, the attorney general, and the justices of this court fail to acknowledge God as the basis of our justice system."

A mere five decades ago it was legal for various states to enact religious tests for office, demonstrating the historic evidence of a trio of theolegal practices: the separationists who reject the establishment of a state religion by serving as watchdogs to theolegal behavior; the integrationists who require theolegal officials to exercise restraint; and the pluralists who affirm laws that honor a diversity of worldviews.

Theolegal Constitutions

Although it has not been exercised, to date the Arkansas Constitution disqualifies any person "who denies the being of God" from holding office and from testifying "as a witness in any court" (Article 19 §1). The North Carolina Constitution disqualifies from public office "any person who shall deny the being of Almighty God" (Article 6 §6). The South Carolina Constitution proclaims, "no person shall be eligible to the office of Governor who denies the existence of the Supreme Being" (Article IV §2). The Constitution of the State of Tennessee contradicts itself on this matter: Article I §4 confirms "that no religious test . . . shall ever be required as a qualification to any office"; however, Article IX §2 declares "No person who denies the being of God, or a future state of rewards and punishments, shall hold any office." It should be noted that Tennessee also denies "ministers of the Gospel" and "priests of any denomination" to be eligible to serve in either House of the Legislature (Article IX §1). The Texas Constitution is equally contradictory, "No religious test shall ever be required as a qualification to any office, or public trust . . . nor shall any one be excluded from holding office on account of his religious sentiments, provided he acknowledge the existence of a Supreme Being" (Article 1 §4). The Pennsylvania Declaration of Rights protects those who "acknowledge the being of God and a future state of rewards and punishment" from being disqualified from office (Article 1 §4), implying that those who do not believe in God, heaven, or hell will not receive protection based on their theological beliefs.

In the 1961 case *Torcaso v. Watkins*,[6] the U.S. Supreme Court found the Maryland Bill of Rights, Article 36, to violate the Establishment, Equal Protection, and No-Religious-Test clauses of the U.S. Constitution. Despite this ruling, the Maryland Constitution continues to read that no person will "be deemed incompetent as a witness, or juror, on account of his religious belief; provided, he believes in the existence of God, and that under His dispensation such person will be held morally accountable for his acts, and be rewarded or punished therefore either in this world or in the world to come." The U.S. Supreme Court ruled against theolegal officials in the state of Maryland and deemed that no State or Federal Government can require someone to express a belief or disbelief, which made moot the legitimacy of similar state constitutions. Justice Hugo Black, who authored the majority opinion, made clear that state legislatures cannot "constitutionally pass laws or impose requirements which aid all religions as against non-believers, and neither can they aid those religions based on a belief in the existence of God as against those religions founded on different beliefs."

Despite this ruling, the seven states listed have not yet repealed this language. Why? It may simply be a result of a failed legislative system that does not update its laws, or it could imply two factors related to our discussion. First, these articles provide historical evidence of the existence of a theolegal system. Such a system is not merely created by officials writing theology into law but by the jurisprudence that consistently affirms all three theolegal worldviews: the separationists who separate theology and law; the integrationists who believe officials must exercise restraint; and the pluralists who affirm diversity.

Second, the fact that these states still have these statements suggests an absence of political will to remove these laws. Why would that be the case?

Could it be that in a theolegal democracy, legislators consider it unimportant or politically risky to remove theolegal rhetoric from law? Maybe this is being too analytical, given that many states have laws on the books that were deemed unconstitutional decades ago; however, it is compelling to note that these statements continue to find their way into some legislative agendas.

Consider the proposed amendment sponsored by Arkansas State Representative Richard Carroll of North Little Rock, the Green Party's highest-ranking elected official in the United States. On February 11, 2009, Carroll filed a bill that would repeal the article that claims atheists are unworthy of holding office or testify as witnesses. In a telephone interview, Carroll explained to me, "this is a case of discrimination that goes against the values that the country was based on–freedom of belief."[7] Carroll makes clear that he is not trying to legally recognize atheism as a viable belief nor affirm the theology articulated in the state constitution, rather he is defending citizens' right to nondiscrimination. Carroll is finding that this religious test for office, which is outdated and cannot be legally enforced, is not so easily repealed. To date he has encountered two major obstacles: first, the amendment must be one of the top 3 of 15 current proposals to get out of committee; and second, he has to rally his colleagues who say that even though they support the bill they will vote against it because of pressure from the religious right. These officials are clearly constrained by the theology of their constituents who are determined that their legislators, in order to remain in office, hew to the majority's beliefs. This could easily result in no legislative action. If, as Tony Blair states in the Foreword, the greatest danger is inaction, then complacent legislators who are constrained by beliefs of the majority become theolegal officials, whether they intend it or not.

One of the most effective ways to prevent theolegal practices, integrationists claim, is to create professional peer-created and upheld codes of ethics in order to encourage theolegal restraint without necessarily denying officials the right to express their religious beliefs. The following examples illustrate the restraint many officials exercise in the context of theolegal decisions.

Theolegal Legislators

On February 11, 2008, Representative John Wright of the Oklahoma House of Representatives was deeply offended when Pastor Scott Jones, an openly gay United Church of Christ minister, acknowledged his male partner in a prayer from the legislative floor. This led Wright to move to strike the prayer from the record, a motion not affirmed by the majority of his colleagues. The very act of questioning the identity of a minister implies that legislators have the power to determine who is worthy of the free exercise of religion. Although Wright's religious beliefs were not used as public rationale, legislators need not explicitly exercise their beliefs to engage in theolegal practices. The very act of denying citizens the right to free expression of religion based on their identity is an example of theolegal behavior. For Representative Wright and those who voted against the prayer, the intention was to legally establish the God of the heterosexual as the only permissible expression of faith. Integrationists were pleased to hear that not all legislators followed suit, demonstrating that not all officials, many of them unabashedly religious, affirm Wright's theolegal practices. The pluralists celebrate this event as an exercise of diversity in the public square, an affirmation of how pluralism moderates the views of those elected to serve a diverse population. Separationists and secularists, on the other hand, clear their throats and ask, why is there public prayer in the state legislature?

They ask similar questions about school boards that mandate theolegal policy, such as the teaching of intelligent design. The landmark case *Kitzmiller v. Dover Area School District*[8] provides a powerful example of how local political officials used theology to determine policy. However, the judge found the attempt to teach creationism in Pennsylvania public schools to be religiously motivated. Judge Jones, appointed by President George W. Bush, was a known Lutheran and Republican whose integrated identity did not influence his decision. Similar to legislators in Oklahoma who did not vote with Representative Wright, Judge Jones chose not to act as a theolegal official. Judge Jones prevented this theolegal practice by deeming the actions of the school board to be religiously motivated, based on evidence that intelligent design was inherently theological, not scientific.

This case demonstrates how the God of these school board members was not allowed to rule, even in a theolegal democracy where free expression is affirmed. Neither, because of his ability to exercise theological restraint, was the God of the judge used to affirm the school board's theolegal practices. Likewise, citizens did not allow the God of the school board to reign: days before Judge Jones' ruling, the citizens of Dover elected nine new school board members, eight of whose campaigns were aligned with Judge Jones' eventual decision.

Pluralists celebrate the triumph of a diverse democracy when citizens form heterogeneous coalitions to ensure that those in power do not use the state to legislate their theology: more often than not these coalitions are comprised of religious individuals. This counters the claim made by secularists that religion is democracy's foe. Unfortunately, this point is often left unspoken when media provides a bullhorn for extremists, as demonstrated by the theolegal threat by evangelist Pat Robertson who responded, "I'd like to say to the good citizens of Dover, if there is a disaster in your area, don't turn to God, because you just rejected Him from your city."[9]

Separationists are infuriated by such remarks, as well as by the actions of the first Dover School Board. As a result they are religiously vigilant about preserving a strong separation of religion and state. However, it is often overlooked that religious conservatives, religious liberals, and even separationists, participate in creating a theolegal democracy, as noted in the following two theories: alternate theology and secular complacency.

Let us assume that religious conservatives are in the political majority and that they use theology in the public arena and lobby for laws to affirm their religious beliefs. This behavior lays the foundation for a theolegal democracy. Religious liberals, however, also partake in theolegal behavior by using *alternate theology* to counter those initiatives. Meanwhile, separationists are compelled to adopt secularists' views and to reject the use of theology in the public arena, resulting in *secular complacency*. This rejection dilutes their ability to mobilize a critical mass and unintentionally allows the beliefs of the religious majority to dominate. Together, these two terms—alternate theology and secular complacency—can be used to identify a theolegal democracy, demonstrating how all sides of the political spectrum, whether consciously or not, participate in its creation. Marriage, one of the most politically divisive religious issues of our time, serves as a compelling case study to make this point.

Alternate Theology

Liberals are quick to point fingers at religious conservatives who pervasively use theology in public discourse, but the truth is that religious liberals also contribute to a theolegal nation. The religious left is just as robust in numbers and resources as the religious right, and is often better poised to preserve the separation of religion and state than the secular left.[10] For example, it is commonly recognized that biblical references have been the primary source for legally defining conjugal marriage—a term used in conservative circles to define marriage as between one man and one woman. Yet coalitions of diverse Christian and Jewish clergy question the theolegal discourse on marriage, which narrowly represents a particular conservative theolegal worldview. In response, liberal religious coalitions formed around different interpretations of scripture and used alternate theology to promote marriage equality. Some of these groups are Unitarian Universalists, Reconstructionist and Reform Jews, the United Church of Christ, Episcopalians, Quakers, Methodists, Presbyterians, American Baptists, Western Buddhists, and independent Mormons and Catholics.

When religious minorities use theological language to contest the dominant belief system, they, too, contribute to the formation of a theolegal nation by using alternate theology. In both instances, faith is used to shape law in the name of freedom of religion and speech. The use of alternate theology becomes an essential political strategy in preventing a theolegal nation from becoming a *de facto* theocracy. The irony is that the very use of a plurality of theologies in the public arena prevents any one theology from dominating. Separationists warn us that a *de facto* theocracy is formed when a preponderance of theologies among religious groups is used to justify laws that reinforce the predominant beliefs of the majority to establish a covert state religion. Whether it is conservative or liberal use of theology, whether it is explicit or implicit use of God-talk in the public arena, these practices concern separationists. Strict separationists develop positions that unilaterally reject the use of theology in public discourse. This can result in strategies that, although laudable, lack political feasibility and, unfortunately, create *secular complacency.*

Secular Complacency

There is an emerging philosophy that separates *religious marriage* and *civil marriage:* a separationist system that divorces religious rites from civil rights. Both integrationists and pluralists agree with separationists about this legal strategy, but differ about the means by which the goal is achieved. By separating the sanctity of marriage from the civil rights associated with civil marriage, the state permits religious expression without requiring religious professionals to perform a religious rite of passage for those they deem unworthy of the sacrament. Put simply, the role of the state is to provide equal protection under the law. It is therefore in the best interest of those who believe in the current theolegal marriage system to divorce religion from the state. Religious conservatives would no longer need to fear government threatening their freedom of belief by forcing them to marry same-sex couples. Rather, religious communities will have the autonomy to define religious marriage according to their own theology, and the state alone will have the authority to legally define civil marriage. In this way, separationists deflate the political power of the religious majority by ensuring that equal protection based on legal arguments, not theological tenets, becomes the primary rationale for a legal definition of civil marriage.

In defense of the separation of religion and state, secularists delegitimize the use of theology in the public square and unintentionally empower the theolegal position of the majority. In a highly religious country, separationists, unlike those in purely secular democracies, lack the ability to organize a critical mass. Although praiseworthy, it is unlikely that a secularist agenda will motivate masses of couples to demand that the state grant them a civil marriage. Why? This rationale does not motivate those benefiting from a theolegal marriage system to act on behalf of those without such privileges. In fact they may perceive it as threatening their own civil rights and therefore continue to choose to do nothing. In the absence of a political context where such an argument would win in the next election cycle, secularists and strict separationists unintentionally contribute to *secular complacency*. As years go by, those who disregard the majority's theolegal practices remain unorganized, while the theology of the majority continues to dominate. Separationists believe religious and civil marriages should be distinct, but the belief itself does not necessarily motivate citizens. Ironically, the accountability rests with religious professionals and religious citizens to overthrow the one-sided religious system of theolegal marriage.

It is the civic responsibility of religious minorities to articulate alternate theologies and lobby on behalf of those without equal protection under the law. It is the responsibility of clergy to refuse to play the role of *de facto* civil servants—religious professionals mandated by the state to sign civil marriage licenses. In other words, in a theolegal democracy the duty rests with religious citizens to use alternate theology in the public arena to ensure that a dominant theology is not established as a *de facto* state religion. Religious professionals need to exercise restraint to ensure that the dominant theological worldview of the day does not become the law of the land.

While it may have become "tradition" for clergy to authenticate marriage licenses, all three theolegal worldviews—separationists, integrationists, and pluralists—urge clergy to exercise restraint by denouncing their state-mandated *de facto* civil servant status. Clergy can choose not to be the sole legal authority to sanction civil marriage licenses, thereby teaching fellow citizens about their decision not to be theolegal officials. Religious professionals can reclaim their authority in several ways.

First, they can educate those who intend to marry, and their communities, about the difference between religious marriage and civil marriage. This would empower the community to take seriously their understanding of religious marriage as a sacramental rite distinct from civil marriage being a civil right. Second, clergy can ask those who are seeking legal recognition to go directly to a civil servant to confer the state-issued licenses, which is custom in numerous countries throughout the world. This would mean a judge or a county official would issue a civil marriage license. Or third, clergy can advocate for their states to duplicate the legal practice upheld in most counties in the state of Pennsylvania: the *self-uniting marriage license*. This allows any two witnesses to sign along with the betrothed, which relieves clergy of the obligation of serving as public officials. If clergy do sign a self-uniting license, they do so as a witnessing citizen as compared to a civil servant. Pluralists encourage this third option so that clergy can serve as one of several witnesses to sign the document. This honors the longstanding tradition of clergy conferring a civil license, choosing not to serve as a theolegal official but rather as an equal to all citizens.

Any of these three options makes a distinction between civil marriage and religious marriage and therefore preserves the separation of religion and state. Why is this not the predominant practice? There are several answers to consider.

First, most clergy take tradition at face value and remain uncritical of the contradiction of serving simultaneously as a religious professional and as a theolegal civil servant. Separationists urge clergy to consider the consequences of the state imposing a legal definition of a religious sacrament and to evaluate the repercussions of when the God of the majority is used to rule all.

Second, most clergy defer their religious authority to the state's legal definitions of marriage, rather than take the responsibility to articulate their own theology of marriage. For example, even clergy who affirm marriage equality continue to use terms such as "union" or "commitment ceremony" instead of "religious marriage." This diminishes the authority of the religious professional and affirms the state's role in determining which sacramental rites come with legal privileges. Integrationists urge clergy to practice transparency by making a public statement about their theology of marriage and to practice restraint by choosing either to be a witness to a judge signing the marriage license, or as pluralists advise, to serve as one of many witnesses who collectively sanction the document as a community of equals.

Third, some clergy still deeply believe in the dual role of wedding officiant and civil servant: they believe the United States should regulate a unified religious/legal definition of marriage. This theolegal position, however, would create a law that restricts freedom of belief and establishes a state religion for all legal marriages. Pluralists urge such clergy to recognize that they are merely one of many religious citizens who deserve equal protection under the law.

In each of these three examples, the power lies with the religious professional to choose whether or not to marry theology and law. It is the responsibility of religious leaders and their constituents to preserve their right to freedom of belief by being vigilant about guarding the wall of justice that stands between religion and the state. This practice, although it prevents the establishment of a theocracy, does still contribute to a theolegal democracy because alternate theology, not secularism, is the predominant tool to counter those who want their God to rule.

Conclusion

All three theolegal worldviews—separationism, integrationism, and pluralism—decline to adopt the intentions of a theocracy or of a purely secular democracy. Rather, each seeks to strengthen the two constitutional pillars of a theolegal nation, as articulated in the Free Exercise and Establishment clauses of the constitution.

Separationists warn us about legal practices that fortify the beliefs of the religious majority, which not only establishes a *de facto* state religion but also erodes the civil rights of religious minorities. They differ from secularists by distinguishing between freedom *of* religion and freedom *from* religion.

Integrationists also emphasize the importance of religious liberty as a fundamental human right. If used responsibly, the private theology of civil servants becomes public so as to preserve a transparent legal process; without it, covert and secretive theolegal practices could be used to rule. They value authenticity in public life and warn against censorship that unintentionally encourages covert theolegal behavior. In addition to transparency, integrationists require religious officials to practice restraint and not fall into secularist or theocratic behavior. They are motivated to do so because integrationists know that by preventing the establishment of a state religion they guarantee the human right to religious freedom.

Pluralists highlight the multiplicity within and among religious traditions and emphasize citizens' rights to equal opportunity and equal protection under the law, aware that one of the great strengths of the United States is its diverse citizenry.

Diversity is a threat to both a theocracy and a purely secular government, neither of which accurately describes the complex political system of the United States. Our nation is comprised of three unlikely collaborators whose wisdom is likely to thrive for centuries to come: the separationists who counsel us to heed the guidance of separation of religion and the state; the integrationists who counsel us about the wisdom of freedom of belief; and the pluralists who counsel us to self-govern with the belief that—*e pluribus unum*—out of many we are one.

Each of these worldviews is necessary to describe the unique intricacies of our theolegal democracy, a nation that simultaneously guarantees citizens the right of free expression while prohibiting the establishment of a state religion. These laws allow officials to use theology as one of many sources of knowledge in making, applying, and administering law; however, they are not allowed to use their theology to deny civil rights to those who do not meet creedal tests. These theolegal practices may displease some and satisfy others, but many appreciate the contradictory yet necessary qualities of our theolegal democracy.

If we agree that the theology of one should not be used to rule all, as seen in theocracies, and that freedom of belief is a fundamental human right denied in secular nations, then we might agree that the United States is, whether we like it or not, a theolegal democracy.

Notes

1. Although the Pew Forum survey mentions that half of Americans are bothered when politicians talk about how religious they are, they overwhelmingly affirm that a president have strong religious beliefs. See http://pewforum.org/docs/?DocID=337.
2. Tube2HA (2008) Pastor Thomas Muthee's blessing of Sarah Palin, as accessed on YouTube on September 24, 2008, http://www.youtube.com/watch?v=iwkb9_zB2Pg.
3. O'Donnell, Christine (1999) *Politically Incorrect with Bill Maher*, HBO, replayed on Bill Maher's HBO show "Real Time" on September, 17, 2010.
4. Fausset, Richard and Abby Sewell (2011) Alabama Governor's Remarks on Non-Christians Raise Eyebrows. *Los Angeles Times*, January 19, 2011.
5. Jindal, B. (2009) Sermon offered by Governor Bobby Jindal at the New Chapel Hill Baptist Church, West Monroe, Louisiana, July 5, 2009, as filmed at http://www.youtube.com/watch?v=0zdl4snoIBE&feature=related. Also see Millhollon, Michelle (2009) *Governor's Sunday Helicopter Travels Have Come at Taxpayers' Expense.* Advocate Capital News Bureau, August 30, 2009.
6. *Torcaso v. Watkins*, 367 U.S. 488 (1961).
7. Personal communication with Arkansas State Representative Richard Carroll of North Little Rock on Sunday, March 8, 2009.
8. *Kitzmiller v. Dover Area Sch. Dist.*, 400 F. Supp. 2d 707 (M.D. Pa. 2005).
9. Robertson, Pat (2005) "Robertson To Pa. Town: 'You Voted God Out Of your City' Religious Broadcaster Warns of Wrath of God." Distributed by the Internet Broadcasting Systems, Inc with contributions by Associated Press, November 10, 2005.
10. Shiffrin, Steven (2009) *The Religious Left and Church-State Relations,* Princeton, Princeton University Press.

Part I

A Theolegal Nation

Ark
by Katie Ford

We love the stories of flood and the few
told to prepare in advance by their god.
In that story, the saved are
always us, meaning:
whoever holds the book.

Editorial Preface

Whose God rules a theolegal nation? The one who holds the book. Which book? Some claim it should be a sacred text. Others hold in esteem the text of the U.S. Constitution that permits one to interpret and apply religious tenets and yet prevents religion from being enshrined in the laws of the country. The tension in these questions serve as a metaphor for the tension between the Free Exercise and Establishment Clauses in the U.S. Constitution, both of which are necessary to achieve religious liberty and to preserve the separation of religion and state.

For this reason we begin the book with Kent Greenawalt's discussion of the role of citizens and officials within the context of a religiously diverse society. His chapter reflects the interests and rhetoric of both separationists and integrationists in a theolegal democracy. He provides legal guidelines for officials to responsibly exercise self-restraint without denying their own religious views, a classic integrationist/accommodationist concern. We consider Greenawalt to rightfully reflect separationist sentiments when he makes clear the types of cases that would violate the constitution, particularly laws that are influenced by religion-based morality to restrict behavior on a theological tenet such as sin. Greenawalt describes the complex nature of a theolegal democracy in the United States, highlighting the legitimate uses of religious reasoning in legal decision-making as compared to theocratic practices. His highlighting of integrationist views demonstrates the way that officials can balance the two essential principles, freedom of belief and nonestablishment. Greenawalt's discussion is founded upon political philosophy and constitutional law, disciplines also used by Martha Nussbaum in Chapter 2.

The "fixed star" of the constitution is religious fairness, Nussbaum explains. The United States has seen many covert and overt attempts to legalize a particular religious orthodoxy, but on the whole religious fairness has triumphed. In her book *Liberty of Conscience: In Defense of America's Tradition of Religious Fairness*, she analyzes trends that threaten this constitutional principle. Various theolegal practices result from officials determining which religion is and is not worthy of legal protection. She argues that the courts are reliable guardians in those times by protecting religious fairness; however, she offers multiple examples that we interpret to describe the *theolegal official*. Theolegal officials are elected, appointed, or hired government employees who draw upon their own religious beliefs or those held by their constituents to make, apply, or administer law. This term is the premise for the second unit of the book, which is foreshadowed with Nussbaum's reference to the use of theology in the executive, judicial, and legislative branches of government. For example, Nussbaum describes the historical origins of the inscription "In God We Trust" on U.S. currency, when the Secretary of the Treasury in 1861 was persuaded by a Baptist clergyman to do so. She also examines how Congress legislated a belief in God during the 1950's McCarthy era when God's name was added to paper money and to the Pledge of Allegiance. In addition, Nussbaum examines justices who believe that local governments have the right to establish a state religion or a religious test for office. These are but some examples that substantiate the theolegal analysis, as set out in the introduction and critiqued in Chapter 3.

Paula Cooey notes the Protestant bias underlying the theolegal theory and demonstrates that the absence of theolegal practices does not separate the state from religiosity. We agree with her analysis that the state is not a neutral arbitrator mediating the power struggles of a pious citizenry. For instance, officials in all branches and levels of government are theologically bound by their own religious worldview and, therefore, consciously or unconsciously, enact laws that reinforce their beliefs or those held by the electorate. Cooey argues that laws espousing religious neutrality form a façade that reinforces the state's own religiosity through secular practices while maintaining its sole authority to define what is and what is not religious, which she defines as religious secularism. Cooey astutely demonstrates that a theodemocracy is the State's religion under the pretense of religious neutrality.

The first three chapters are designed to contextualize the theolegal theory and lay the conceptual foundation for analyzing the words and deeds of *theolegal officials*, the subject of the second section. The third examines the behavior of citizens and the media when contributing to a *theolegal democracy*. The final section discusses the international significance of *theodiplomacy*.

1

Religious Premises in Politics and Law[1]

Kent Greenawalt

My two-volume publication entitled *Religion and the Constitution* concentrates on two main pillars in the U.S. Constitution's treatment of religion as stated in the First Amendment: "Congress shall make no law respecting an establishment of religion, or prohibiting the free exercise thereof."[2] This chapter which bears a relation to Nathan Walker's theory of *theolegal democracy*, asks whether officials and citizens violate desirable principles of liberal democracy or the Establishment Clause when the law enforces a moral judgment that is grounded squarely on religious sentiments or when laws and policies rest on religious premises.

No one doubts that laws against killing and stealing are all right, although *one reason* that some people think these acts are wrong is because the Ten Commandments forbid them. But what of laws that lack a plausible secular justification or would not have been adopted except for religious sentiments? Some think one or both of these characterizations are true about laws limiting marriage of persons of different genders, laws restricting sexual acts among consenting adults, laws (or administrative decisions) forbidding government assistance for embryonic stem cell research, and laws prohibiting abortions. Occasional judicial opinions and more extensive writings by scholars have suggested that certain exercises in the enforcement of a morality that is grounded in religious premises are unconstitutional. This chapter will explain to what extent this thesis has support in the existing law and to what extent it represents a wise understanding of the Establishment Clause. In that endeavor, we will look carefully at exactly which kinds of laws and government policies might be singled out as depending on religious sentiments.

The controversy over legal enforcement of morality is one aspect of a wider discussion about the role of religion in U.S. political life, and in the political life of liberal democracies more generally. This discussion, which is often cast as one about "public reasons," definitely reaches beyond *constitutional law*, but one can, as I shall explain, think of it as concerning concepts of nonestablishment and free exercise in the realm of political philosophy. It thus merits our consideration for its own sake, but it is also a needed backdrop for the specifically legal discussion in this chapter. Because I have written on this subject extensively,[3] my treatment here will be highly summary, but it does sketch the basic positions and competing claims.

Before we begin, a caution about the relation among the competing claims in the political philosophy and their relevance for constitutional law may help. For the most part I assume that when a government violates the Free Exercise Clause or the Establishment Clause, a court presented with a case involving a violation will say so. That, I have noted, is an over-simplification, one that is particularly relevant to this chapter. One might believe that a fair amount of legislation enforcing morality violates the Establishment Clause, but not in a way a court can declare. One might believe that individual legislators violate the Establishment Clause, or some spirit of it, even though the official action to which they contribute does not do so. The characterizations of such actions tie to the broader question of when should people feel constrained by public reasons, not relying on specifically religious grounds?

Advocacy, Justification, and Judgment

Most proponents of public reasons have assumed that any constraint applies in the same manner to officials and citizens, and in the same manner to grounds of judgment and public discourse.[4] My position differs from most public reasons theorists and from Walker in distinguishing between advocacy and justification, on the one hand, and grounds of judgment, on the other, and between officials and ordinary citizens.

When we think about how we make up our minds and how we discuss issues, we realize that monitoring our discourse is a lot easier than restricting our bases for decision. Moreover, while other people hear our discourse, they cannot know our full grounds of decision. These truths matter.

Most people would be hard put to *try* to carry out a program of excluding their deepest religious convictions from their political judgments. They could not disentangle what they believe because of underlying religious convictions from what they would believe if they relied only on premises of liberal democracy and shared techniques of understanding.

Speaking without reference to religious convictions is not difficult. Members of our law faculty share an assumption that school problems are to be resolved in terms of values that are not explicitly connected to particular comprehensive views. I have yet to hear a specifically Jewish, Christian, atheist, or Benthamite argument for a faculty decision. Yet, when decisions involve the point of legal education, I doubt that colleagues try rigorously to remove the threads of their religious understandings about the nature of society and education for a profession.

If it is working, a constraint of public reasons is reciprocal. People can tell easily whether arguments are being made from explicit religious premises; they will know if restraint on their part is matched. If they try to purge their silent deliberations of religious influence, they cannot be sure if others are similarly motivated. And once someone realizes just how arduous this purging exercise is, he will question the success of others, even if he thinks they are trying. Such uncertainties are a poor basis for reciprocity.

Consider some differences between officials and ordinary citizens. Officials have a lot more to do with the law that gets made and applied than do citizens; there are a lot more citizens than officials. Officials are used to making judgments and offering reasons that do not include all that is relevant in their personal lives. Citizens are less used to practicing such restraint. Perhaps a highly educated, participating citizenry could learn to draw distinctions between what matters for most aspects of life and what matters for politics. But that is not our citizenry. When officials practice restraint, it impinges much less on a population's religious liberty than when citizens do so. Official restraint more greatly affects the quality of political life. These basic distinctions—between advocacy and judgment and between officials and citizens—suggest that if any self-exclusion is justified, it is mainly self-exclusion for officials in their public statements.

Among officials we can divide roughly between those who apply law and those who make law or exercise ordinary discretionary judgment. Among those who apply law, judges and quasi-judicial officials often provide reasoned justifications for their decisions. At this stage of American history, one does not often find explicitly religious grounding in opinions, even when courts reach beyond standard legal sources to comment on the social benefits or harms of a possible ruling. By an explicitly religious grounding, I mean reasoning in this form: "Given a true religious proposition, these conclusions about social good follow." Some examination of religious sources might be acceptable to show the community's attitudes toward a practice or its deep moral assumptions, and judges might employ familiar religious stories to illustrate a point; but none of these is a reliance on religious grounds in the sense I mean. Although judicial opinions are rarely completely candid about the strength of competing arguments, one expects judges to rely on arguments they believe should have force for all judges. In our culture, this excludes arguments based on particular religious premises.

When we turn to legislators, we may start with the proposition that if an explicit religious grounding were placed in the preamble to a statute, it should be viewed as a promotion of religion that would violate the Establishment Clause. Although the use of religious language increased among legislators and executive officials during the second Bush administration, it is still true that members of Congress typically do not make religious arguments on the floor of Congress or before their constituents. There is, however, no accepted understanding that they should avoid giving any weight to their own religious convictions, and to those of constituents in arriving at positions. I believe legislators should give greater weight to reasons that are generally available than to those they understand are not; but some reliance on religious and similar reasons is appropriate, especially since the generally available reasons are radically indecisive about some crucial social problems.

If legislators rely on religious understandings more than their public advocacy reflects, are they not lacking in candor? Does restraint impoverish discourse and leave voters less well informed than they might be? Realism counsels that much legislators say is far from fully candid, so self-restraint about religious grounds is hardly a *major* contributor to lack of candor. In any event the value of self-restraint overrides this drawback and whatever reduction in information voters suffer. Legislators should not deny religious bases that motivate them, but they should not develop public arguments in these terms.

Because citizens are not used to practicing self-restraint of this kind, and because most citizens have little involvement in the political process, I do not think they should regard themselves as constrained to avoid relying on religious grounds *or* to avoid stating those grounds. Some citizens, however, such as university and corporation presidents, and individuals consistently engaged in political life, have a much more public role. For them, something like the constraints for legislators is appropriate.

Religious leaders and organizations have a special place. They properly develop religious grounds as these relate to political problems, and they also properly take part in direct efforts to win support for particular positions, although it is usually unfortunate when religious leaders endorse parties or candidates.

Much of the theorizing about public reasons and religious reasons has been cast in terms of liberal democracies in general, or as what the Establishment Clause of our constitution actually requires. Neither of these approaches answers the most central practical questions. The Establishment

Clause, in its direct forces, has modest implications. It is mainly about what laws do, not why they are enacted. What of liberal democracies and theories of legitimacy? Democratic theorists argue persuasively that in a liberal society people will adopt many different comprehensive views. This condition will not change. The history of Western liberal democracies, forged out of religious division, shows that differences in religious views can be a source of intense conflict; but we can imagine people of various religious views who seek to learn from one another and who trust each other's social judgments. These people might welcome religious perspectives in political discourse. On the other hand, one might not recommend an explicitly religious politics as the most fruitful approach for a newly constituted Northern Ireland or for the fledgling, fragile union that may emerge in Bosnia. Much depends on history, culture, the religious and other broad views that people hold, and their degree of mutual tolerance and respect. Specific principles of self-restraint should be offered for particular political orders, not in gross. If this is true about religious discourse and public reason, it is also true about many other practical issues to which political philosophers speak.[5]

The United States is a country of great diversity in culture and religion. The percentage of our people that is neither Christian nor Jewish increases steadily, with immigration policies that no longer discriminate egregiously against Asians. Outright religious conflict is rare, but religious differences remain a source of distrust and tension. Religious convictions are intense and widespread enough to influence politics and to disturb people with their influence. That is partly why some restraint may be needed.

What Count as Public Reasons?

A general degree of acceptance cannot alone be the test of what reasons are public. Were that the only standard, Christians could rely on the New Testament in a country that was mainly Christian; Muslims could rely on the Quran in a Muslim society. This evident inequality for what happen to be minority perspectives conflicts with the ideals of a liberal democracy. General acceptance might play some role in whether reasons are relevantly public, but cannot be the exclusive or primary standard.[6]

Sometimes it is suggested that particular ideas of the good, or controversial ideas of the good, are what are excluded by public reasons.[7] People have various convictions about what makes life good, and they should be able to pursue them within a framework of just social relations and mutual respect.[8] This position, to be clear, is not that the government should avoid all moral questions, but that it should limit itself to moral questions that concern justice and mutual respect, not resolving moral questions about the kinds of activities people should value in their lives.[9]

This constraint alone leaves untouched much that proponents of public reasons believe should be excluded. Most notably, it does not exclude much that religions have to say about just social relations.[10] Here, the subject of stem cell research is illuminating. Whether embryonic stem cells should be used for medical purposes is *not* an issue about the good life; it is an issue of justice and respect for the embryo that may be a human being. If the only public-reasons constraint concerned claims about the good life, an argument that a papal encyclical condemns stem cell research would be within the realm of public reasons. But that sort of argument is just the kind that the public-reasons filter is designed to exclude. So a constraint of public reasons cannot be limited to questions of the good life.

Should it at least include all such questions, whatever else it may also contain? The answer is no. We expect public schools to educate children about desirable ways to live, about the importance of physical and mental health, about the dangers of addictions, about the benefits of culture, and about the value of activity as contrasted with indolence. All these aspects of what schools do cannot be summarized fully as helping to make children into good citizens and aiding them to realize whatever goals they set for themselves; they encourage students to live according to our society's ideas of what a good life contains. State support of arts and literature and high taxes on alcohol and cigarettes show that the government's involvement in questions of the good life extends to adults. Laws against the use of drugs are controversial, but few object to laws that forbid human beings from having sex with animals. These cannot be defended as consistent with neutrality about the good life, unless one (implausibly) regards them as mainly protecting animals who would be potential sexual partners.

It is at least a defensible position that the state should not coerce people in respect to *controversial* judgments about the good life;[11] but the basis for such a position seems to be more a judgment that individuals should have autonomy in this realm than a judgment that the reasons for coercion could never be sufficiently public.

Another possibility for grounds that do not qualify as public is reasons that do not rest on rational grounds. Here, roughly, the idea is that people should be able to rely on reasoned arguments that other people can understand and accept, not on faith or intuition that others do not share.[12] Notice, for instance, how Robert George's chapter on stem cell research does not depend on controversial religious premises but on "the scientific facts." One difficulty with the "rational grounds" approach is drawing the line between rational grounds and nonrational bases for judgment.[13] In much of what we believe, rational understanding, however that is conceived, intertwines with other assumptions.

Insofar as a constraint conceived in terms of rational grounds privileges on a particular way of understanding, some people object that it unfairly discriminates against other modes of apprehension; but a more troubling practical worry arises out of divergent opinions about what can be established rationally. A good many people believe that the existence of a beneficent God can be established rationally. Years ago, one of my sons had me read a book that claimed that by proof of miracles and accurate prophecies, the Bible established itself as the infallible word of God and showed that Jesus was the Son of God. Any constraint of public reasons is to operate as a self-restraint. If people agreed that they should rely only on rational grounds, they would still disagree vigorously about what rational grounds could establish. The author who thought that he could rationally establish the infallibility of the Bible would feel free to rely on biblical passages; others who believed that recognition of biblical truth depends on faith could not rely on the same passages, though they might be no less certain the passages represent God's true word.

The most appealing single category of claims that do not count as ones of public reasons are those based on comprehensive views, overarching philosophies of life.[14] According to John Rawls, people resolving constitutional essentials and basic questions of justice should rely neither on religious perspectives nor on secular philosophies, such as utilitarianism or the view that human autonomy is the most fundamental good.[15]

To recapitulate, what are not public reasons? We have looked at grounds that are not widely accepted, conceptions of the good, grounds that are not rational, and comprehensive views. Although the most plausible single criterion for what reasons are public is that they do not rest on comprehensive views, we should be open to the possibility that more than one of these criteria may count for whether a reason is public. We should also be open to the possibility that some reasons may be more or less public, rather than public or not.

Our treatment of reasons may seem to have wandered far from the constitutional principle that no law should be adopted that establishes religion. The crucial connection is that whatever other reasons may be *non*public, it is widely assumed that religious reasons fall within that amorphous category. According to a theory of public reasons, if laws are adopted based mainly on the religious convictions of citizens and officials, something has gone wrong from the standpoint of liberal political philosophy, and that impropriety may well be considered a kind of establishment of religion. No one thinks that because *some* citizens and officials have relied upon religious convictions, resulting laws actually violate the

Establishment Clause as a matter of law. But conceivably if officials rely mainly on their religious convictions or those of their constituents, laws are invalid, and should be so declared by courts.

The part of this chapter devoted to the uncertain boundaries of public reasons does not directly touch the status of reliance on the Bible or on church authority—those are not public in the relevant sense—but it affects that reliance in a more complicated way. Any minimally fair theory of public reasons cannot touch religious reasons and no other reasons. If religious reasons are to be "excluded," then other reasons that are similarly not rational or based on comprehensive views must also be excluded. If one is hard put to explain just what other reasons are not public, that casts doubt on whether it is fair to insist that good citizens and officials not rely on religious reasons.

The earlier part of the chapter summarizing my own limited, "intermediate," account of the constraints of public reasons provides a more decisive response to extravagant claims about the relevance of the Establishment Clause for this subject. It has never been widely assumed in the course of the country's history that people should refrain from relying on their religious convictions when they consider the wisdom of proposed legislation. Among other movements, arguments for abolition of slavery, for Prohibition, and for civil rights were substantially religious. Neither widespread reliance on religious premises nor the active involvement of religious groups should, alone, be regarded as marking laws that violate the Establishment Clause, much less as marking laws that courts should declare to violate the Establishment Clause. What remains is consideration whether certain narrower connections of religion to laws that are adopted might render the laws unconstitutional.

Legal Enforcement of Religion-Based Morality

In this context, this closing section explores the implications for constitutional law of the broader subject we previously discussed—legislative and executive policies that are grounded in religious premises. At the end of the day, these implications are very slight if one is interested in what measures courts should hold invalid, or so I shall argue. The analysis leading to this conclusion can help dispel confusion about the relation between political rhetoric and judicially enforceable constitutional law. It can also enable those who would like the courts to play a more active role to see exactly how they differ from those who reject such a role.

The overarching question for us is which laws and policies violate the Establishment Clause *because* they rest on religious premises. The question mainly has cogency in respect to legally enforced morality; but to understand why this is so, we need to clear away various matters that are not at issue.

Most of my second volume of *Religion and the Constitution* is about tangible assistance to religious groups and about government sponsorship of religious ideas; it examines a number of topics and the major constitutional approaches for dealing with them. Government assistance can be open, as with financial aid to religious charities, or covert, as with the hypothetical example of a highway route chosen because it will benefit a particular church. Government sponsorship of religion can be undeniable, as with devotional Bible reading in public schools and the hiring of army chaplains, or it can be more subtle or debatable, as with moments of silence and "under God" in the Pledge of Allegiance. If the obvious and dominant purpose or a "primary" effect is to aid religion, legislation is invalid under the Establishment Clause.

As far as purpose is concerned, the Supreme Court has declared invalid only those laws whose overriding objective was to promote religion. One can certainly imagine stricter approaches, ones under which more legislation would fail a purpose test. A court might ask whether a religious aim was influential or whether a statute would have been adopted in the absence of religious objectives. Take for instance a highway board whose deliberations were open to the public. Two of the five-member board voted for Route C, which would have gone 30 miles from the Baptist church (thus inconveniencing churchgoers), one member who voted for Route A said she would have voted for Route C except that she wanted to aid the church and its members, and that two other members said they preferred A on a number of grounds, one of which was that it would aid the Baptists. In these circumstances, we could say that the religious aim was influential *and* that the decision would (almost certainly) have been different without it. In deciding whether a worker had been improperly fired because of his race or religion, a court might employ such an approach, not allowing the firing to stand if it probably was a consequence of discrimination.[16] And I have suggested that if an individual legislator votes for a bill only for a religious reason that would have rendered a statute invalid if it had been the reason of every legislator, the individual legislator has violated the Establishment Clause.[17] But the Supreme Court has been very clear that it will not engage in such nuanced inquiries. On the understanding that courts should accord deference to legislatures, it has required that promoting religion be the evident dominant purpose if legislation is to fail the purpose test.

The legislative measures we are considering in this chapter do not mainly promote religious groups or religious perspectives. They do not give religions tangible aid and they do not encourage people to adopt any particular view about religion. What most do, to put it starkly, is to force nonadherents to behave in ways that those with particular religious views think they should behave. Thus, laws that forbade people from engaging in sexual acts with others of the same gender were not intended to convert to a religious view; rather, they were aimed at making people comply with a moral standard, or, to put it differently, at preventing people from falling into sin.

For analytical purposes, it helps initially to assume that every legislator has the same attitude about a law and that this shared attitude is spread on the record for all to see. What attitudes run counter to the Establishment Clause? Religious convictions that underlie reasons to vote might function in one of at least five different ways. (1) Among entities that undoubtedly deserve the protection of the state, religious convictions are the basis for determining what a just distribution of resources, privileges, and penalties is. Into this category could fall laws regarding welfare for the poor and autho-rizing, or not authorizing, capital punishment. (2) The crucial question is whether entities of some kind deserve serious protection, and religious convictions determine the answer. Arguments based on religious authority for a law against use of embryonic stem cells (because embryos are human beings) or against scientific experimentation with animals fall into this category. (3) Religious convictions determine judgments whether actions will harm persons other than consenting adults who are most directly involved. One argument against incestuous marriage is that the knowledge that such marriage is possible among adults will have a detrimental effect on family relations while children are still minors (e.g., a brother and sister may relate differently to each other, and in a less healthy way, if they realize they can marry each other when they are old enough). A person might believe this argument is persuasive *only* because a sacred text condemns incest. (4) Religious convictions are the basis to decide that actions will harm the adults who chose to perform them. A person's religious beliefs might lead him to think that homosexual relations are bound to be psychologically damaging to participants, damaging according to ordinary assessments of psychological health. (5) Religious convictions are a basis to judge acts as wrongful, though without any harm as conceived by nonreligious standards. A person might oppose homosexual acts on the basis that they constitute sins in the eyes of God (perhaps to be punished in some form of afterlife), even though there is powerful evidence that such acts do not cause ordinary physical or psychological damage.

Distribution, Protection, and Harm

We should not be surprised that argument about this topic tends to focus mainly on my last two categories, usually without a distinction being drawn between them. I shall concentrate on these as well, but I initially explain why the first three categories are also important and yet different. Normative questions about what entities deserve protection and about what justice requires for these entities are not matters of simple fact. In a liberal democratic society, there will be wide agreement about some of these questions. All or virtually all human beings who have been born and are now alive warrant protection, and justice for people within a society requires some form of equal treatment. At the edges of which entities deserve protection and to what degree, there is controversy. What protection, if any, should be given to animals, to the environment (for its own sake), and to embryos and fetuses? How far should the state assist the less fortunate? Should capital punishment be available as penalty? As to these matters, disagreements hardly fall out with religious opinions lined up neatly on one side and secular opinions on the opposite side. Various religious people have different views. It would be hard to trace any particular position a legislature might adopt directly to religious convictions. It is true that most people in the United States now who want to protect embryos are people of religious faith, but, as we see with Robert George's argument against stem cell research, many of these people also believe that one need not rely on religious premises to justify that protection.

Two other aspects about issues of justice and the borders of protection strike me as very important. For many of these issues, rational analysis is highly indecisive.[18] In making up their minds about whether to protect higher mammals, everybody will rely to an extent on nonrational (I do not say irrational) intuitions. Were citizens and officials permitted to rely on nonreligious intuitions but not permitted to rely on religious convictions, that would constitute a form of implicit discrimination against religious perspectives. Moreover, any religious individual would have a hard time saying where his religious convictions leave off and what his intuitions would tell him apart from these convictions.

The other crucial aspect of our first two categories concerns the rationale for regulating behavior. Suppose it were true that only those with particular religious convictions believed that the state should protect dolphins, and they manage to get a law adopted that prohibited the killing of dolphins. Their *aim* would not be to promote a religion or even to prevent sin, but to protect entities that deserve protection. It would be odd to think that it should be impermissible for society to protect dolphins, even if the great majority of its members hold the religious view that they deserve that protection.[19] When the issue is the distribution of benefits and burdens, the analysis of legislative aims is typically similar. It is not that those adopting a law particularly want to control behavior to make sure it is moral; rather, they want to see that people (and other protected entities) get the benefits they deserve and share burdens fairly.

Although arguments against restrictive abortion laws are often cast as ones about immoral behavior, and thus not so different from arguments about laws restricting sexual behavior, in fact the most powerful argument *for* a restrictive law is quite different. It involves, first, a claim that at the moment of conception, or at some later stage, the embryo, or fetus, deserves protection. (Often this point is put in terms that the fetus is a human being, implying that the fetus deserves as much protection as a full human being, but someone might believe a fetus deserves significant protection from the state though less than does a full human being.) The protection afforded to it by a restrictive law is of the kind that would benefit the fetus from any point of view. It concerns physical survival. The second part of the argument against abortion is one about justice, about burdens and benefits. The innocent fetus should be protected even if the cost is that the pregnant woman must carry the fetus against her wishes and give birth to a baby she would rather not have. Because the basic issues about abortion concern disagreements about entities deserving protection and about the degree to which fetuses should be protected if that impinges severely on the liberty of persons who undoubtedly deserve protection (i.e., pregnant women), any assertion that restrictive laws about abortion violate the Establishment Clause is less promising than similar assertions about laws more easily classifiable as aimed at sin.

Our third category (like the fourth and fifth categories) mainly involves laws that are directly addressed at people who together wish to perform a forbidden act. There is no immediate innocent victim, in the way that the fetus is an innocent victim in the eyes of those who want restrictions on abortions. Often with respect to such laws, people disagree about indirect harms. I have used the example of incest. If we put aside the concern about the genetic effects of inbreeding, which rest on a solid scientific base but would not apply to incestuous marriages of couples unable to conceive children together, we face a concern about the effect on minor children within families who knew that they might someday be eligible to marry a parent or sibling. Perhaps legal permission would have extremely little effect, especially if social taboos about incest remained strong. Were social scientists to study the effect of the repeal of laws against incest on typical family life, changes in attitudes would take time, and claimed casual relations would be disputable. And, of course, all anyone could do in advance of such a legal change would be to make an educated guess. A person might respond to this inevitable uncertainty from the standpoint of social science by reasoning as follows: "My religion firmly condemns incest. That is a strong basis to conclude that legal acceptance of incest would harm family life more broadly."

As I have put the point so far, the exact chain of inference from religious basis to harm for families is inexact. Here are two oversimplified stark alternatives. (1) "My religion condemns incest. So also, I believe, do most other religions. Whatever the theological truth of my religion, the rejection of incest probably reflects a sound moral sense that it is destructive of family life." (2) "My religion condemns incest. I believe my religion accurately understands God's will. Since God forbids incest, that probably means it is destructive of family life." Were someone to rely on the first chain of inference, that could hardly present a problem for liberal political philosophy or the Establishment Clause. If one looks to past societies to provide *some evidence* of what kinds of restrictions promote healthy social life, one could hardly disregard what religious traditions have to say.[20] The second chain of inference, relying on the truth of a particular religion, is more questionable, but, *if* social science evidence is substantially indeterminate, people should be able to rely on religious convictions as well as nonreligious institutions to fill in their sense of the broad effects of proposed laws.[21] *If* one believed, contrary to my view, that in some way the Establishment Clause *was* at odds with officials' relying on the second kind of inference, that would still not provide a workable principle for courts to invalidate laws under the Establishment Clause.

Restrictions on Behavior

This leaves us with our last two categories, involving laws that restrict behavior just because it is immoral or because it is thought to harm the very people who choose to engage in it. In moving to these last two categories, we already are practicing deceptive oversimplification, because those who want to restrict behavior as immoral almost always believe that behavior does have corrosive effects on the broader society. But for clarity of analysis, we can put claims about those effects aside.

Laws restricting sexual conduct among consenting adults provide the main examples for these last two categories. We can focus on laws against homosexual acts and on restrictions on marriage between persons of the same gender. The Establishment Clause argument against such laws is that they would not be adopted if not for people's religious convictions and therefore, they amount to an establishment of religion. At least so long as the proponents of the restrictions do not rely heavily on claimed harm to innocent third parties, these laws differ from ones we have yet considered. They are not about borderlines of status or about distributive justice;[22] they *are* efforts to control behavior because that behavior is regarded as intrinsically wrongful.

One constitutional argument against restrictive laws about sexual behavior is equal protection, which is cast in terms of oppressed groups.[23] The idea is that regulation violates equal protection of the law. Laws against interracial marriage violate equal protection;[24] laws against intragender marriage could be similarly viewed, since homosexuals as a group have long suffered discrimination by the majority. For this alternative argument, one needs to find a group that has suffered historical discrimination, something easily done with abortion laws and limits on the privileges of gay couples. This discussion is a caution that Establishment Clause challenges to laws in our last two categories are only one kind of constitutional claim against their validity, and perhaps far from the most promising.

Our two crucial inquiries for Establishment Clause analysis are (1) whether laws that are directed against behavior just because it is immoral promote or endorse religion; and (2) what connection would be needed between religious premises and a law's enactment to generate an invalid establishment of religion. On the question of promotion or endorsement, we need to assume that the reason legislators prohibit behavior is not because it bears a close relation to what they consider to be distinctive and desirable religious practices. Arnold Loewy has hypothesized a law requiring attendance at Methodist church on Sunday because it is immoral not to go to that church[25] and a law forbidding all members of society from driving vehicles during the Jewish Sabbath.[26] The first of these is obviously unconstitutional because it requires attendance at particular worship services; the connection of the second law to Sabbath observance is also probably strong enough to make it a promotion of that religious practice.[27] Laws against homosexual acts are not quite like this. The legislators regard the behavior as wrongful whenever it is engaged in, and refraining from the behavior does not, in itself, involve any strong connection to anyone's religious practices.[28]

The two contrasting positions about law that forbid behavior just because it is immoral, according to a religious view, are that (1) to enforce the morality of a religion *is* to promote and endorse that religion[29] and (2) to enforce morality is different from promoting religion, and it has always been assumed that legislatures can enforce the dominant majority in society.[30] I think a more discriminating analysis is needed.[31] Let us suppose that the overwhelming basis for a restriction is a religious view that behavior is wrong. So long as it is clear that all legislators want to do is to stop the behavior, their aim is not to promote the religious practices of a particular religion. Whether citizens will take the law as expressing approval of a particular religion may depend on circumstances, and particularly whether the religious perspective about morality that wins enforcement is sharply at odds with the moral views of others. Whether a particular religion is or is not implicitly approved, I believe that requiring people to comply with the moral code of a religion, absent any belief about ordinary harm to entities deserving protection, is a kind of imposition of that religious view on others. Thus, as a matter of theoretical principle, I think enactment of a religious morality could violate the Establishment Clause, even if the religion, as a set of beliefs and religious practices, is not promoted or endorsed in the more direct sense.

Three Standards

In this context, we can roughly sketch out three possible standards for judicial application of the Establishment Clause.[32] (1) A law violates the Establishment Clause if religious convictions were influential in its adoption. (2) A law violates the Establishment Clause if "a substantial number of religious skeptics would not have supported it."[33] (3) A law violates the Establishment Clause if the ascertainable dominant reason for its passage was a view that acts are immoral, based on a religious point of view and detached from any perspective about harm in this life that would be sufficient to justify a prohibition or regulation. The third position is my own. Given all the other ways religious judgments can figure in legislative choice, given the mixture of religious and nonreligious reasons individuals may have, given the mixture of reasons different legislators bring to bear, and given the deference courts do and should show to legislative decisions, this approach will rarely, if ever, lead a court to invalidate a law.

The first approach is much too broad. Religious convictions figure in many appropriate ways in the judgments of citizens and legislators. For that reason and because of considerations of deference, too much legislation would be held invalid, were religious influence sufficient to render laws invalid.

The second approach may seem more promising. If a court asks whether a substantial number of skeptics would support the legislation, that action seems reasonably deferential to the legislature. The court is not applying a fine-tooth comb to the legislative process or trying to pry apart mixed motives. If few skeptics would support legislation, is not that a sure indication that religious convictions underlie it? This approach, however, founders on three objections. The first objection is that it will not be easy to decide whether the number of skeptics would be substantial, or to decide what number counts as "substantial." The second objection involves the connection between religious grounds and nonreligious ones. Suppose it were determined that the number of skeptics who would restrict embryonic stem cell research is not substantial. Suppose it was also determined that many serious Roman Catholics believe with Robert George that the wrongness of research need not depend on religious convictions. Are we to label these citizens as dishonest or deluded, to say that their self-consciously nonreligious understanding does not count because they have a religious understanding with the same import for legal regulation and *we know* that the latter drives the former? That is not an approach that is very respectful of fellow citizens, and it is not the kind of judgment a court should be essaying.

The third objection takes us back to the various ways religious convictions can figure. Professor Loewy puts forward the test about skeptics as an application of a principle that the legislature cannot simply condemn an activity because it is immoral. That sounds like our fifth category. But it is possible that many people with religious convictions will believe, reasonably or not, that an activity (such as marriage of people of the same gender) will have harmful enough consequences to justify a prohibition, although few skeptics will agree. In their minds, these religious people would not be forbidding the activity simply because it is immoral; they think they would be protecting people from harm.

Having argued that many reliances on religious convictions are appropriate, I do not accept the standard that would render laws invalid if few skeptics would support them. I have resisted the idea that all legislation of religious morality is constitutional, but, as far as courts are concerned, and apart from situations in which a religion or a specific religious outlook is promoted or endorsed, the limits on appropriate grounds for laws are too narrow to have much practical significance.

Conclusion

My survey of the constitutional principles of the Establishment Clause is designed to bring a deeper understanding of the relation between religion and government in our society. More broadly, I claim that in political philosophy, as well as constitutional law, much depends on a country's history and culture and on the identities and activities of its citizens. Whether, and how far, citizens and officials should try to stick "to public reasons" in their political judgments and discourse depends a good deal on a country's religious makeup and the level of mutual tolerance and respect that it enjoys. My conclusions about what now makes most sense in the United States are not intended to be generalizations for all liberal democratic political orders.

Principles of free exercise and nonestablishment are fundamental aspects of our country's legal and political orders. We understand that avoiding establishment of religion can sometimes seem to be in conflict with promoting free exercise, but that across most of the coverage of the two clauses, the free exercise of religion is fully compatible with nonestablishment; and that nonestablishment is strongly conducive to religious liberty. People differ sharply over the proper boundaries of constitutional rights under the religion clauses. I have both defended the broad strokes of the Supreme

Court's "no hindrance–no aid" approach to the clauses against proposals that would radically shift the constitutional focus, and have sharply criticized some recent Court decisions as insensitive to the basic values underlying the conceptions of free exercise and nonestablishment.

It is in this nature of fundamental constitutional principles that their full content is never settled once and for all. One aspect of our culture, in which religious liberty greatly matters, is that scholars, lawyers, and laypersons ask themselves from time to time just how the religion clauses of our constitution should best be understood.

Notes

1. Excerpts from *Religion and the Constitution, Vol. 2: Establishment and Fairness,* chapters 23 and 24 and the conclusion (Princeton: Princeton University Press, 2008).
2. U.S. Constitution, amend. 1.
3. *Religious Convictions and Political Choice* (New York: Oxford University Press, 1988); *Private Consciences and Public Reasons* (New York: Oxford University Press, 1995).
4. For a discussion of various arguments about how public reasons apply to citizens, see Paul J. Weithman, "Citizenship and Public Reason," in Robert P. George and Christopher Wolfe, eds., *Natural Law and Public Reason* 125 (Washington, DC: Georgetown University Press, 2000).
5. One may analyze the problem of public reason and the closely related problem of religion and politics from a particular religious or other "comprehensive" view, say Roman Catholicism, Orthodox Judaism, liberal Protestantism, or Kantianism, and see what implications follow, or one may try to do "detached" political philosophy, not relying on any particular comprehensive view. Both exercises are valuable. What I do summarily in this chapter is the latter, "detached" political philosophy, although readers will not be surprised that my conclusions fit my own comprehensive view, a variety of liberal Protestantism. The hope is that the analysis will appeal to those who hold different comprehensive views.
6. For one claim about general acceptance, see Mario M. Cuomo, "Religious Belief and Public Morality: A Catholic Governor's Perspective," 1 *Notre Dame Journal of Law Ethics and Public Policy* 13, 18 (1984).
7. See generally Charles E. Larmore, *Patterns of Moral Complexity* (New York: Cambridge University Press, 1987).
8. See ibid. pp. 118–135.
9. See ibid. p. 133 (stating that "the ideal of neutrality must always take precedence over disputed ideals of the good life").
10. More precisely, it does not exclude religious conclusions about just relations that do not depend on claims about what is a good life.
11. See Jeffrey Reiman, "Abortion, Natural Law, and Liberal Discourse: A Response to John Finnis," in George and Wolfe, supra note 19, pp. 107, 109, 110 ("What

is ruled out is forcing people to live this way or that, beyond what is needed to protect every sane adult's chances of living as he or she see fit").

12. See Thomas Nagel, "Moral Conflict and Political Legitimacy," 16 *Philosophy and Public Affairs* pp. 215, 230 (1987) (referring to grounds of decisions that "can be shown to be justifiable from a more impersonal standpoint").

13. See my discussion on Natural Law on pages 511–523 of *Religion and the Constitution: Vol. 2 Establishment and Fairness.*

14. See Rawls, supra note 2, p. 62 ("There is no reason . . . why any citizen, or association of citizens, should have the right to use the state's police power to decide constitutional essentials or basic questions of justice as that person's, or that association's, comprehensive doctrine directs").

15. If someone's comprehensive view reflects his overarching approach to life, how can he possibly be expected not to rely on it? Rawls's answer to this question is a two-level approach. People with a variety of comprehensive views will coalesce around the premise that liberal democracy is a desirable form of government. A feature of liberal democracy is resolving political questions in a way that is detached from people's comprehensive view. Thus, a person's comprehensive view calls on him to accept a political arrangement in which issues are resolved without direct reference to comprehensive views. There is nothing illogical about this arrangement, as we can see clearly if we imagine people of different religious convictions who agree upon principles of religious liberty and separation of religion and state, including a principle that officials will not resolve issues based on their own understanding of religious truth.

16. *Emmel v. Coca-Cola Bottling Co.*, 95 F.3d 627 (7th Cir. 1996); *Venters v. City of Delphi*, 123 F.3d 956, 972 (7th Cir. 1996).

17. One might fairly resist this conclusion and say the legislator has violated only the spirit of the clause.

18. In *Religious Convictions and Political Choice* (New York: Oxford University Press, 1988), I make an extended argument along these lines about animals, the environment, the status of a fetus, and some issues of just distribution.

19. One *might* take a different view if the reasons for protection are actually *at odds* with what rational, secular morality might indicate—if, for example, the species that received special protection had much lower capacities than some other species but was thought by some to be favored by God. I discuss this possibility in ibid., pp. 204–207.

20. However, were one to rely on that first approach, one would need to be open to moral assumptions of other religions, to evidence not from religious traditions, *and* to the possibility that various restrictions have reflected indefensible oppression or outright ignorance.

21. As a matter of liberal political philosophy, I am inclined to think they should not rely in politics on factual judgments (grounded in religion) that are strongly opposed to what the evidence of science and social science establishes. Thus, people who believe the world will end five years from now should not press for government policies based on that assumption. Supra note 18, pp. 204–211.

22. I am here assuming that the argument that the majority should be protected against behavior that affronts it is not an appropriate claim of justice in a liberal society.
23. For a complete discussion of a second constitutional argument against restrictive laws about sexual behavior, see my discussion of due process in *Religion and the Constitution Vol. 2*, pp. 531–532.
24. *Loving v. Virginia*, 388 U.S. 1 (1967).
25. Arnold H. Loewy, "Morals Legislation and the Establishment Clause," 55 *Alabama Law Review* 159, 166 (2003).
26. Ibid. p. 164.
27. Loewy thinks that the strongest permissible argument for the ordinance would be to protect the safety of the larger than usual number of pedestrians.
28. Of course, one *might* view refraining from sinful acts as part of religious practice.
29. Loewy, supra note 16, p. 161, concludes that a law should be held to violate the Establishment Clause if it "simply condemns the activities because it is immoral."
30. See Michael Perry, "Why Political Reliance on Religiously Grounded Morality Does Not Violate the Establishment Clause," 42 *William and Mary Law Review* 633 (2001); Scoett L. Idleman, "Religious Premises, Legislative Judgments, and the Establishment Clause," 12 *Cornell Journal of Law and Public Policy* 1 (2002). Professor Idleman provides an extensive review of relevant cases and competing scholarly opinions.
31. See Greenawalt, supra note 18, pp. 87–95.
32. I put aside here fact-sensitive appraisals that a particular law strongly, if indirectly, endorses some religion.
33. Lowey, supra note 25.

2

Religious Fairness[1]

Martha Nussbaum

Every year, at Thanksgiving, thousands of small American children dress up like Pilgrims. Grave in tall hats and buckled shoes, or starched bonnets and aprons, they proudly act out the story of that courageous band of settlers who fled religious persecution in Europe, braving a perilous ocean voyage and the harsh conditions of a Massachusetts winter—all in order to be able to worship God freely in their own way. Those who survived feasted with the native inhabitants and gave thanks to God.

We cherish and celebrate this story, but we too rarely reflect on its real meaning: that religious liberty is very important to people, and that is often very unequally distributed. The dominant majority in England did not have to run risks to worship God according to their consciences. They established an orthodoxy, an official church, that favored them and subordinated others. In the England from which the Pilgrims fled, people were not equal citizens, because their rights were not equally respected by the government under which they lived. The Pilgrims were not expelled from England, as the Jews had earlier been expelled, but they were living in a condition of subordination. Something very precious had been withheld from them, and it was to recover that space of both liberty and equality that they crossed the ocean in three small vessels.

The lesson of the first Thanksgiving is easy to forget. Indeed, the early settlers themselves soon forgot it, establishing their own repressive orthodoxy, from which others fled in turn. People like exclusive clubs that rank them above others. My mother's ancestors came over on the *Mayflower*, and some of my relatives were obsessed with triumphal genealogizing, as they marshaled the evidence that they belonged in the exclusive and socially prominent Mayflower Society, while others did not. The Pilgrims' quest for freedom, centuries later, had become elite

Americans' quest for superiority. Nor was religious toleration in a healthy state among the Pilgrims' descendants, as the exclusion of Jews (and, often, Roman Catholics) from local private schools, country clubs, law firms, and prestigious social events indicated. When I later married a Jew and converted to Judaism, the Pilgrims' descendants did not applaud my choice to worship God according to my own conscience.

People love in-groups that give their members special rights. Equality and respect for equality are difficult for human beings to sustain. Particularly in the area of religion, which seems so vital to the salvation of individuals and the health of the nation, it is very tempting to think that orthodoxy is a good thing and that those who do not accept it are dangerous subversives. This sort of in-group favoritism, however, is what the laws and traditions of our country utterly reject. This is a country that respects people's committed search for a way of life according to their consciences. This is also a country that has long understood that liberty of conscience is worth nothing if it is not equal liberty. Liberty of conscience is not equal, however, if government announces a religious orthodoxy, saying that this, and not that, is the religious view that defines us as a nation. Even if such an orthodoxy is not coercively imposed, it is a statement that creates an in-group and an out-group. It says that we do not all enter the public square on the same basis: one religion is the American religion and others are not. It means, in effect, that minorities have religious liberty at the sufferance of the majority and must acknowledge that their views are subordinate, in the public sphere, to majority views.

The dominant American political tradition repudiates this style of thinking, so common in the world's history. Citizens, we believe, are in fact all equal. We have not just rights, but equal rights. The state may not create a two-tiered system of citizenship by establishing a religious orthodoxy that gives rights to nonorthodox on unequal terms. As Justice Jackson put it in a famous opinion holding that Jehovah's Witnesses may not be compelled to recite the Pledge of Allegiance in school (which their religion forbids, as a form of idolatry): "If there is any fixed star in our constitutional constellation, it is that no official, high or petty, can prescribe what shall be orthodox in politics, nationalism, religion, or other matters of opinion or force citizens to confess by word or act their faith therein. If there are any circumstances which permit an exception, they do not now occur to us."[2]

Our commitment to religious equality did not emerge immediately or easily. The colonial period saw intense and painful differences about religious matters, and much intolerance. Gradually, however, the sheer experience of living together with people who differed in belief and practice gave rise to a consensus: the future constitutional order must be dedicated to fair treatment for people's deeply held religious beliefs. The framers of our constitution reflected long and well about these matters, and they carefully wrote protections for religious fairness into the document they framed. The constitution as a whole makes no reference to God, not even the vague and general reference to a Creator that Jefferson thought acceptable in the Declaration of Independence. Article VI states that "no religious Test shall ever be required as Qualification to any office or public Trust under the United States." And the First Amendment states: "Congress shall make no law respecting an establishment of religion, or prohibiting the free exercise thereof." The freedom of religion and a prohibition against setting up any religion as the national orthodoxy are the first two protections for citizen's rights mentioned in that all-important amendment.

Throughout America's history, those clauses have been understood to guarantee all citizens both religious liberty and religious equality: no religion will become an orthodoxy that undercuts any citizen's claim to equal rights. Many difficult questions of interpretation have arisen, but on the whole Justice Jackson is right: a shared understanding of religious fairness has been a "fixed star" of our tradition.

To say that there is a shared understanding and that noble tradition has on the whole prevailed is not to say that it has not often been assailed. Religious fairness has periodically endured challenges throughout our history, some subtle and some less subtle, some apparently benign and some violent. People aren't always content to live with others on terms of mutual respect. So the story of the tradition is also a story of the attacks upon it, as difficult groups jockey for superiority. What has kept the tradition alive and healthy is continual vigilance against these attacks, which in each new era take a different concrete form.

My book *Liberty of Conscience: In Defense of America's Tradition of Religious Equality* concerns both the tradition and these periodic attacks, and its purpose is both to clarify and to warn. Without vigilance, our "fixed star" may not be fixed for much longer. Religious fairness has always encountered temporary threats. No doubt it will encounter others in the future—because the tendency to exalt one's own group as the good, orthodox group and to demote others is lamentably common in human life. Fear of strangers, demonization of new or unpopular groups, panics about the future of the nation—all these, from time to time, have caused Americans to diverge temporarily from our fundamental constitutional commitment to equal citizenship and equal liberty in religious matters. It was one of those panics that led several states to mandate the recital of the pledge, expelling children who refused to recite it for religious reasons. For a time, even the U.S. Supreme Court went along. Jews, Mormons, Jehovah's Witnesses, Seventh-Day Adventists, atheists, members of nontheistic religions such as Buddhism or Taoism, Native Americans, Santeria worshipers—all these have suffered religious disabilities at the hands of the majority. Constant watchfulness has been required to protect liberty and equality from various social pressures. Many of these threats, however, were local rather than nationwide, and many were short-lived. On the whole, despite such lapses our judiciary has been a reliable guardian.

The current threat to religious fairness is not local, and it is not likely to be short-lived. In that way, it is less like the temporary uproar over Jehovah's Witnesses and the pledge and more like the long sad history of anti-Catholicism that is the ugliest blot on our national commitment to religious fairness. Anti-Catholicism was violent, and the current threat is not, or not yet, violent. We are not beating small children because they refuse to say the Protestant version of the Ten Commandments in public schools, as happened in the mid-nineteenth century, and we seem to have reached a shared understanding that government-orchestrated sectarian religious observances in the schools are utterly unacceptable. Nonetheless, watchfulness is needed. An organized, highly funded, and widespread political movement wants the values of a particular brand of conservative evangelical Christianity to define the United States. Its members seek public recognition that the Christian God is our nation's guardian. Such an agenda threatens to create, once again, in-groups and out-groups, defining some citizens as dominant members of the political community and others as second-class citizens. It threatens to undermine the very idea that all citizens, no matter what they believe about the ultimate meaning of life, can live together in full equality.

We are living in an area of unprecedented religious diversity in America. The two most rapidly growing religions in our nation are Hinduism and Buddhism, the former through immigration from India, the latter through a combination of immigration and conversion. An increasing number of Americans, moreover, define their religion as eclectic and do not attach themselves to a particular conventional denomination. (Such was the case, as well, at the time of the Founding: only between 8 and 17 percent of the colonists belonged to a recognized church.[3]) Propositions that might have seemed the common ground of all the religions (the singleness of God, the concern of God for human beings, the very existence of a deity) are now newly divisive—not simply dividing religious people from atheists and agnostics, but dividing monotheists from polytheists, and theists from members of nontheistic religions (Buddhism, Taoism, Confucianism, and in some interpretations Unitarian Universalism). Fairness is a tall order among so much diversity, and sensitive thought about apparently unproblematic statements is badly needed.

Instead, we all too often have a push in the opposite direction, a push to institutionalize Christian evangelical fundamentalism and its near relatives as our state religion. It is alarming when a justice of the U.S. Supreme Court argues, as Justice Scalia recently did, that it is perfectly all right for government to endorse monotheism publicly, giving polytheism and nontheism a secondary status.[4]

Equally shocking are the many ways in which the rhetoric of important political officials highlights Christianity, implicitly suggesting the inequality of non-Christians. Examples abound. Here are just a few of the more disturbing:

- John Ashcroft, former attorney general, regularly asked his staff to sing Christian songs before work began in the morning.
- While he was a sitting U.S. senator, Ashcroft characterized America as "a culture that has no king but Jesus."
- The "faith-based initiatives" program, a major conduit for federal welfare funding, permits the religious institutions (most of them Christian) that dispense federal funds to refuse aid to people of a different religion *even in programs* (like health care and job training) *that have a purely secular purpose.*
- The idea that we are a holy nation with a divine mission has been omnipresent in the second Bush administration's rhetoric on the war in Iraq. A typical example is President Bush's statement that "the author of freedom is not indifferent to the fate of freedom," a comment that not only seeks to wrap controversial policies in a mantle of sanctity, but also neglects the fact that many Americans do not believe in an anthropomorphic God who is the "author" of freedom.
- Lt. General William Boykin, a former head of U.S. Army Special forces who is involved in the search for Osama bin Laden, said in a speech in June 2003 that radical Muslims hate the United States "because we're a Christian nation, because our foundation and roots are Judeo-Christian and the enemy is a guy named Satan."
- Alan Keyes, Republican candidate for Senate in 2004 in the state of Illinois, claimed in a televised debate that voters should choose him because Jesus opposes his opponent, Barack Obama (who won the election). (Obama's appropriate riposte was that he was running to be senator from Illinois, not the minister from Illinois.) After his loss, Keyes refused to make a concession speech or to speak to Obama, characterizing the contest as one of "good" versus "evil."
- President Bush endorsed the move to require the teaching of "Intelligent Design," a view of the universe with sectarian religious roots, in science classrooms alongside the theory of evolution.[5]

The effect of all this is to suggest that those who do not share the particular religious values of the current administration are less than fully American and less than fully equal.

The Supreme Court remains in a relatively healthy state where issues of religious liberty are concerned. Indeed, we can see clear signs of progress in the court's ability to understand the strange and initially alarming rulings on religious matters, although there remain difficult issues about the level of protection that religious minorities deserve from the courts. Where the public establishment of a state religion is concerned, our recent tradition has been more tumultuous, and the court at present is deeply divided. Particularly worrying is the stance recently taken by Justice Thomas concerning the all-important Establishment Clause of the First Amendment.[6] He holds that it applies only to acts of the federal government, thus freeing the states to adopt policies that favor some religions over others, and religion over nonreligion. The doctrine that the Bill of Rights applies to state as well as federal government had its origin after the Civil War. Called "incorporation," it is the view that the Fourteenth Amendment applied key provisions of Bill of Rights to the states. (Prior to that time citizens were protected from tyranny at the hands of state government only by individual state constitutions.) At the time, the doctrine of "incorporation" was controversial, and some history scholars contest that history today. Incorporation, however, is settled law. For many years Americans have relied on the fact that the Bill of Rights protects us against abuses at the hands of state as well as federal government. When, in 1960, the state of Maryland revoked the appointment of a state official because he refused to declare his belief in God, both the public and the Supreme Court were very clear: this is a shocking violation of a basic constitutional guarantee.[7] Thomas's view, however, implies that a state can, with no constitutional barrier, call itself a "Christian state," order Christian prayer in state-run schools, require Christian oaths of state officials, and even decide to fund only Christian schools. His radical doctrine removes vital protections for equal rights on which Americans rely every day.

Justice Thomas, while denying that the Establishment Clause applies to the acts of state government, at least accepts "incorporation" for the Free Exercise Clause (as well as the speech and press clauses of the First Amendment). In other words, he still believes that it would be constitutionally impermissible for a state to deny Jews, or Muslims, or Buddhists the right to practice their religion freely. Even that deeply traditional idea, however, has been denied by another judge whom the Bush administration has made a linchpin of its program for remaking the federal judiciary. Janice Rogers Brown was recently confirmed to a seat on the Federal Court of Appeals for the District of Columbia Circuit—a court second only to the

Supreme Court in influence and prestige—as a result of the deal through which Democrats made concessions to Republicans in order to avoid the "nuclear option" (removal of the traditional right to filibuster). Janice Rogers Brown is radical in many areas, but on the "incorporation" of the Bill of Rights she is a true extremist. In a 1999 speech, she said that the arguments against the idea that the Bill of Rights applies to the states are "overwhelming," and that the Bill of Rights is "probably not incorporated"—contrary to a century and more of Supreme Court precedents. At her hearing before the Senate Judiciary Committee, she hedged, saying that she had spoken hastily and would now give the matter further study. But she still called incorporation "anomalous."[8] Judge Brown did not invent these radical notions. They have been marked aggressively by the religious right, and there are many younger thinkers like her out there.

The religious right has been active for many years, at least since the 1980s. Recently, however, the threat posed to our tradition has, for several reasons, become more acute. First, the growing religious diversity of the United States raises new issues of fairness, making statements endorsing monotheism, for example, more evidently problematic than they were before. To endorse monotheism in the face of this diversity is to make a statement that was not intended by many eighteenth-century references to a monotheistic God. Second, the efforts of the religious right to "mainstream" some of their chosen doctrines have taken time, and have only recently begun to bear fruit at the level of appellate adjudication, as years of subsidized scholarship has finally succeeded in moving positions that were once considered marginal to the center of the political spectrum.

The distressing change in our recent political life is further spurred, as bad changes so often are, by fear. When people feel fear and insecurity, it is easy for them to demonize those who are different, seeking safety in solidarity. This search often takes the form of seeking to define the nation as one under God's protection. After great national trauma of the Civil War, in 1861, a Baptist minister wrote to the Secretary of the Treasury, Salmon B. Chase, saying that the war had been caused by God's anger because He was not recognized on our currency. The Secretary of the Treasury agreed, as did Congress in 1864. As a result, the words "In God We Trust" were added to our coins. (They did not appear on paper money until 1957.) During the Cold War, Americans terrified by the threat of communism and nuclear war rallied around the idea that we ought to add the words "under God" to the Pledge of Allegiance. Prior to 1954, the pledge had read simply, "one nation, indivisible, with liberty and justice for all." The political debate surrounding that addition focused on the importance of distinguishing the United States from "godless communism."

Now we are in the midst of another war that inspires great fear and that appears to have no end: the "war on terror." This time the enemy has been linked in the public mind with an extremist interpretation of Islam. As more and more Muslims enter the United States, the rhetoric of war makes people wonder whether they are trustworthy citizens. Fear makes people ask whether all religions should really be treated equally. Other fears concern the future of the family in an era of change. As women's growing economic independence makes many less dependent on traditional marriage, as many people choose to live together without the benefit of marriage, as gays and lesbians live openly in our communities and raise children, people fear that society is losing its moorings and seek to return it to traditional religious values. As always, fear makes people ask whether equal treatment should really apply to all citizens—or only to citizens who hold religious and moral views similar to their own. The current eagerness to declare religious foundations for our nation is an understandable reaction to more general global and domestic insecurities, but it is also dangerous, threatening the commitment to equality that holds us together. It has been greatly fueled by the rhetoric of the Bush administration. It is difficult to say whether our judicial tradition will respond appropriately now, as it has in the past.

Many citizens of goodwill, who would be horrified by the representation of minority religion or by the very suggestion that all citizens do not have equal rights, see the trend toward public endorsement of a religious national identity as innocuous, or even good—because they do not see the way in which it is connected with unequal liberty and unequal standing in the public domain. Many, if not most, Americans think that religion is enormously important and precious, and they do not like being told by intellectuals that they should not bring their religious commitments into the public square. Even "separation of church and state" sounds to them like an idea that marginalizes or subordinates religion, asking it to take a backseat, when people think that it should be in the driver's seat. Many people think, then, that defenders of the continued separation of church and state are people who have contempt for religion.

These people are right about something: religion is enormously important and precious. Not every American believes this personally, but all ought to be prepared to see, and respect, the importance of religion for many, if not most, of their fellow citizens. I myself believe religion important personally as well: I am a committed Jew whose membership in a Reform Jewish congregation is an important part of my life and my search for meaning. It is certainly supremely annoying when intellectuals talk down to religious people, speaking as if all smart people are atheists. Philosopher Daniel Dennett is particularly guilty of this. In an op-ed piece in the *New York Times,* he coined the term "brights" for nonbelievers, suggesting very clearly that the right name for believers was "dummies."[9] In his popular new book *Breaking the Spell*[10]—whose very title drips contempt—he contrasts religious people with philosophers, as if there were no such thing as a religious philosopher. I am a philosopher, but I and many of my professional colleagues disagree with Dennett personally: we are ourselves religious people. Almost all, furthermore, would disagree with Dennett about respect for others: we think that people's religious commitments should be respected, and that is simply not respectful to imply that religion is a "spell" or that people who accept such beliefs are dummies. Michael Newdow, the plaintiff in the Pledge of Allegiance case[11] (and in a new similar case recently decided in California) is similar to Dennett: a proud atheist who has evident contempt for religious beliefs and religious people. Many Americans of goodwill associate the very idea of the "separation of church and state" with this sort of smug atheism. They therefore prefer the idea that we are a godly nation; at least they see nothing wrong with public statements of this idea. I sympathize with them up to a point, sharing their reaction to arrogant public atheism and with some people's use of the language of separation to express it.

Indeed, the story told in *Liberty of Conscience* is one in which religious fairness faces threats from both the "right" and the "left," from arrogant secularism as well as from aggressively insular forms of Christianity. Particularly during the second phase of intense anti-Catholicism, in the period after World War II, leftwing intellectuals played a key role in denigrating Catholics as bad citizens and in promoting an approach to the legal tradition that was, in its extreme form, deeply unfair both to Catholics and to other people committed to educating their children in religious schools. The phrase "separation of church and state," which does not appear in our constitution and plays no role in our early tradition of religious fairness, attained currency during the first wave of anti-Catholicism in the nineteenth century, and was resurrected during the second, to express a doctrine that denied the religious schools some forms of protection from the state that ultimately seemed to most Americans both fair and decent. The issue of aid to religious schools is a profoundly difficult one, but we can say with confidence that it is one on which some parts of the left went wrong, and we can also conclude that leading figures on the left, at that time, used the idea of "separation" in a way that went astray from the tradition's central commitment to fairness and equal respect. It seems to me that there is little point in simply adding to the swelling chorus of alarm over "the religious right." The helpful thing is to produce a good analysis of religious fairness. But any such good analysis entails, I believe, that there are errors on the left as well, and that we should be, and remain, vigilant about them.

Insofar as "separation of church and state" is a good idea, it is good because of the way it supports equal respect, preventing the public realm from establishing a religious doctrine that denigrates or marginalizes some group of citizens. Nobody really believes in separation taken literally across the board. The modern state is ubiquitous in people's lives, and if we really tried to separate church from state all the way, this would lead to a situation of profound unfairness. Imagine what it would be like if the fire department refused to aid a burning church, if churches didn't have access to the public water supply or the sewer system, if the police would not investigate crimes on church property, or if clergy could not vote or run for office. Such proposals seem horribly unfair, because the state is providing all these forms of support for everyone else. So, we can't use the bare idea of separation to guide us: we need other guiding ideas to tell us how far and when separation is a good thing.

Our legal and judicial tradition, on the whole, knows these things well, although there was a brief era when the separation idea acquired a momentum of its own and things became unbalanced. Discussion in the general public realm seems to me more confused on this question. Liberals of good faith attach themselves to the rhetoric of separation, without asking seriously why and how much separation really is good or fair. Meanwhile, there are some leading figures who speak on these matters and seem animated by the same aversion to religion that motivated the leftwing intellectuals of the 1950s, when they tried to convince people that the United States was facing a Catholic takeover that would destroy our democratic traditions. We hear something like this hysteria today, and it is important for liberal intellectuals to eschew it.

Seen in its right relation to the idea of fairness, the idea of separation of church and state does not express what the left sometimes uses it to express, namely contempt for, and the desire to marginalize, religion. Our tradition has sought to put religion in a place apart from government, in some ways and with some limits, *not* because we think that it has no importance for the conduct of our lives or the choices we make as citizens, but for a very different reason. Insofar as it is a good, defensible value, the separation of church and state is, fundamentally, about equality, about the idea that no religion will be set up as *the* religion of our nation, an act that immediately makes outsiders unequal. Hence separation is also about protecting religion—minority religion, whose liberties and equalities are always under pressure from the zeal of majorities. Protecting minority equality in religious matters is very important because religion is very important to people, a way they have of seeking ultimate meaning in their lives. If religion were trivial, it would not be so vitally important to forestall hierarchies of status and freedom in religious matters.

Americans disagree about how much separation is required by a commitment to equality. Nobody thinks that the fire department should not help the burning church, and most people agree that, on the other side, the state should not subsidize religious instruction or introduce sectarian religious observances. Both in the funding area and in the area of public displays and ceremonies, however, there is much disagreement about how much separation is constitutionally required. Such dispute must be settled by values other than the bare value of separation.

To be sure, there are and have been since the Founding other plausible arguments in favor of the separation of church and state. Separation is partly sheer insulation, since the founders thought that the machinery of government would be likely to corrupt true religion, producing lifeless bureaucratic established churches, such as those they had observed in Europe. They believed, furthermore, that churches ought to be free to manage their own affairs, and that they would not be free if they were deeply involved with government. On the other side, they also thought that the machinery of government needed to be insulated from the divisive influence of religious bickering. They had seen that in Europe too. These arguments have merit: in many nations with an established church we do see religion becoming a lifeless bureaucracy, and we also sometimes see government impeded by bickering among religious factions. More basically, however, separation is about equality and equal respect.

Still, why should we really find it objectionable to speak of America as a nation protected by God? We might grant that there should be no hierarchies *among* the different religions and yet believe that a general reference to God is totally fine, excluding nobody. There are, however, subtle difficulties here. First of all, we should remember that even an apparently nonsectarian reference to God is in fact sectarian and excludes many people. Most obviously, it excludes atheists. More subtly, it excludes polytheists and members of nontheistic religions. More subtly yet, it includes many believing members of monotheist religions who do not hold that God offers special protection to favored nations. Maybe these people believe that God is remote and not personally involved in human affairs. Maybe they believe that God's primary way of being involved is to look for justice and righteousness, not to take a particular flawed group of humans under a protective wing.

Long ago, people did not notice some of these exclusions, because very few members of nontheistic and polytheistic religions were in America—apart from the Native Americans, whose religious concepts few Americans took very seriously, since most of them, culpably, had contempt for Native Americans. Judaism, Islam, and the various forms of Christianity were all people thought they had to deal with. New immigration—and new recognition of the equal dignity of Native Americans—has brought new demands for respect and equal treatment.

But nonetheless, can't public, governmental references to faith, or event to a particular faith, go hand in hand with toleration and protection of minorities? Yes, perhaps—but only in a country where people do not care very much about religion or the values that divide people among religious lines. Some of the established churches of Europe create few troublesome inequalities because people do not pay very much attention to them and because they are few religious differences that inspire real passion. This is especially likely to be true in nations that allow little immigration—not a particularly admirable policy in a world in which so many people are fleeing persecution and starvation. In most other European countries, moreover, recent immigration, especially from Muslim countries, has challenged the toleration that goes with benign establishment, and has shown it to be, in many cases, a thin veneer, undergirded by insufficient respect for people who have nonmajoritarian practices and ways. Used to the idea that citizens are all alike, many Europeans have thought little about how to live with people who are different. I have had frustrating conversations with entirely admirable Italians who find nothing problematic in the presence of a crucifix at the front of a public school classroom, with French colleagues who defend the ban on the Muslim headscarf and the Jewish yarmulke in French public schools, with Dutch journalists who favor banning the wearing of the Muslim burqa in public places.

The American constitutional tradition offers insight into these cases—insights not only helpful to Americans seeking self-understanding, but helpful as well, to European nations newly grappling with religious difference. This tradition suggests that the Italian crucifix represents a dangerous form of religious establishment, dangerous because it announces to young impressionable children from minority religions (including Protestant Christianity) that they do not enter society on equal conditions so long as they cling to their religion. The legal banning of the burqa (if the law passes) would be a similar subordinating establishment.[12] Our tradition also suggests that the French law is an unjustified incursion into an area of religious self-expression that the law ought to protect for all citizens. Once again, this restriction of liberty also threatens equality, since it bears more heavily on Muslims and Jews (whose religions require articles of apparel that the new French law forbids) than on Christians (who are not required to wear the large crosses that the law also forbids, and who are permitted to wear small crosses). The French tradition of coercive assimilation (as earlier, in policies concerning the assimilation of the Jews) neglects the insight expressed in George Washington's letter to the Quakers, when he said, "I assure you very explicitly, that in my opinion the conscientious scruples of all men should be treated with great delicacy and tenderness: and it is my wish and desire, that the laws may always be as extensively accommodated to them, as a due regard for the protection and essential interests of the nation may justify and permit."[13] No essential state interests are at stake in the headscarf controversy. If Washington was prepared to allow Quakers to refuse military service, a very important public function, why are the French so unwilling to allow Muslims and Jews to wear religious articles of dress? The French policy seems to express a refusal of the "delicacy and tenderness" that is owed to other people's "conscientious scruples."

When I contemplate these cases, I feel considerable pride in the U.S. tradition, which seems to me to have struck basically the right balance between the need for neutral institutions and the needs of people of faith. How terrible it would be, then, if that admirable American tradition were undermined in a time of widespread public uncertainty and fear.

Like many Americans, I have seen these questions from the perspective of the dominant majority. As a girl I went to church on Sunday, celebrated Christmas, and never had to worry about missing school when I did. Like many other Americans, however, I have also seen things from the side of the minority.[14] As a convert to Judaism, I found that I suddenly had to wrestle with questions about whether to attend (or, later, to hold) classes on Jewish holidays, since those were never public holidays. As a Reform Jew, I also understood the more difficult struggles that Orthodox students and faculty routinely face, since their rules for holiday observance are stricter. It is not surprising that my temple, among the oldest Jewish congregations in Chicago (about 160 years old), has an ongoing project to study, and support, the separation of church and state—under the leadership of congregation member Abner Mikva, a distinguished retired federal judge. Religious minorities know what the denial of that separation usually leads to: the imposition of the ways of the majority on all—or, at least, the public statement that the majority is orthodox, who "we" are, and that the minority are outsiders.

As a scholar whose work concerns issues of economic development, focusing on India, I also have an acute awareness of the struggle of much newer minorities, Hindu, Buddhist, and Muslim, in the U.S. political context. I understand that for many Hindus the words "under God" in the Pledge of Allegiance are problematic because, as polytheists, they do not like the implication that a single god presides over the fate of the nation. Polytheism has so often been denigrated as a low-level or barbarous type of religion that this exclusion carries a particular connotation of inequality. (One of the great acts of the late Pope was his public recognition that Hinduism, as well as Judaism and Islam, offers a legitimate route to salvation.) Hindus are even more troubled by public displays of the Ten Commandments, a sacred text that is shared (though in different forms) by Judaism, Christianity, and Islam. A Hindu group submitted an amicus brief asking the Supreme Court to declare one of these public displays unconstitutional. Muslim citizens have their own, more obvious struggles. Although anti-Muslim feeling in the United States has not caused as great an assault on civil liberties as might have been feared after 9/11, and though President Bush as made numerous commendable efforts to express respect for Islam and to distinguish Islam from terrorism, the danger of intolerance is there, increased by Americans' considerable ignorance of Islam, even though it is a religion on the rise here.

I approach these questions as a scholar of constitutional law, but also, and more fundamentally, as a philosopher. Philosophical ideas were important to the Founding, and thinking about some of the philosophical texts that formed its backdrop helps to clarify the underlying issues. I take an independent interest in these philosophical ideas as good ideas to think with, not just ideas that had a certain historical and political influence. But I will also argue that the constitutional tradition is best read as embodying at least some of these ideas, in some form.

Law is more piecemeal than philosophy, and it is constrained by many things other than the philosophical truth: by the facts of the case at hand, by the legal precedents (which may or may not be clear or well argued), by the fact that a court is always a plurality of people with different views, and a majority opinion has to seek consensus among these views. Often, too, there are both majority (or plurality) and concurring opinions that offer different reasons for the outcome, so even respect for precedent is a highly complex matter. We should, therefore, not expect the legal tradition to be tidy, and, in this area above all, it certainly is not. Philosophical ideas can mislead if they make us think that there is more unity than there is, or ignore important strands of reasoning that diverge from the one that seems most philosophically interesting. Judiciously used, however, philosophical reconstruction can illuminate some of the grand themes of a tradition in ways that help us see what has been accomplished, and what still remains to be done.

Why do I claim that both of the "religion clauses"—the so-called Free Exercise Clause ("Congress shall make no law . . . prohibiting the free exercise [of religion]") and the so-called Establishment Clause ("Congress shall make no law respecting an establishment of religion") are centrally about equality? Consider these two cases, one decided under the Free Exercise Clause and one under the Establishment Clause.

Adell Sherbert worked in a textile factory in South Carolina. All the employers in her town had similar policies for working hours. After Mrs. Sherbert had been a good employee for many years, the policy changed, during a time of economic stress and competition. Instead of working five-day weeks, employees were now expected to work six-day weeks. Saturday was the added day, and that was true of all employers in the area. Mrs. Sherbert, however, was a Seventh-Day Adventist, for whom it was religiously forbidden to work on Saturday. She tried to find similar work elsewhere in the region, but all employers required Saturday work. Not surprising, there was none who chose to close on Saturday and to remain open on Sunday, because most workers and managers were Christian. Mrs. Sherbert resigned and sought unemployment compensation. She was denied by the state of South Carolina on the grounds that she had refused "suitable work." She went to court, arguing that the state had impermissibly impeded her free exercise of religion.

In a famous judgment in 1963, the U.S. Supreme Court agreed.[15] They held that benefits could not be made conditional on a violation of a person's religious scruples: this was just like fining someone for Saturday worship. In other words, the denial of benefits was a violation of Mrs. Sherbert's *equal* freedom, as a citizen, to worship in her own way. Free exercise does not mean simply that nobody can come up and put Mrs. Sherbert in jail for her nonstandard religious practices. It means, as well, that the conditions of liberty must be the same for all. The court held that no person may suffer a "substantial burden" to their religious liberty without a "compelling state interest"—which clearly did not exist in this case.

Workplace arrangements are always made for the benefit of the majority. The holiday observed, the workdays chosen—all are tailored to suit the local majority, in this case Christians who worship on Sundays. There is nothing inherently wrong with this—*so long as* care is taken to prevent this convenient arrangement from turning into a fundamental inequality in freedom and respect. The Free Exercise Clause, the court held, guarantees that equal freedom.

The Allegheny County Courthouse stands on public property in downtown Pittsburgh. In the late 1980s, the county set up two holiday season displays. The first, inside the courthouse, consisted of a crèche (Nativity scene), donated by a local Roman Catholic organization, and labeled to that effect. Placed on the grand staircase of the courthouse, with no other displays around it, the Nativity scene bore a sign—carried by an angel above the manger—saying "Gloria in Excelsis Deo," Glory to God in the highest.

The second display was outside on the courthouse lawn. It consisted of a Hanukkah menorah 18 feet tall, standing next to the city's 45-foot decorated Christmas tree. At the foot of the tree was a message from the mayor saying that the display was a "salute to liberty." (In fact, the menorah is a symbol of liberty, since the holiday Hanukkah commemorates the Maccabees' courageous rebellion against oppression. It is difficult to say whether a Christmas tree represents liberty, but it is such an all-purpose symbol that the majority can probably declare this without implausibility.) Local residents took both displays to court, charging that they violated the Establishment Clause.

The court obviously considered this a very difficult case.[16] Ultimately a split court judged that the first display violated the Establishment Clause and the second did not. The crucial question they asked was whether each display communicated the message that the country was giving its endorsement to a particular set of religious beliefs and practices, thus threatening equality. The first display seemed to the majority to communicate such an endorsement: the religious Christian display stood alone, in a position of special prominence and honor. The second display was different: the fact that more than one religion was honored, and that the theme connecting the tree with the menorah was that of liberty, a theme that could include all citizens, whatever their religion or nonreligion, meant to at least the court's center that the people of Pittsburgh would not be likely "to perceive the combined display of the tree, the sign, and the menorah as an 'endorsement' or 'disapproval . . . of their individual religious choices.'"

We can grant this a difficult case to decide, and we can even differ about whether it was correctly decided, while yet agreeing about the immense importance of the principle involved. What my Italian friends don't understand about the message sent by a crucifix in front of a public school classroom is what the court sees very clearly in *Allegheny:* some religious symbols, set up by government, threaten the equal standing of citizens in the public realm. They attach the imprimatur of orthodoxy to Christian observance, while demoting the beliefs and practices of others. Our "fixed star" is that no such orthodoxies are admissible.

The Free Exercise Clause and the Establishment Clause are difficult to interpret and even more difficult to relate to one another. But a central thread that connects them, directing some of their most important applications, is this idea of a government that does not play favorites.

Notes

1. Nussbuam, Martha (2008) *Liberty of Conscience: In Defense of America's Tradition of Religious Equality,* excerpts from chapter 1, sections I and II, "A Tradition of Fairness" and "Two Cases: Mrs. Sherbert and the Pittsburgh Courthouse," pp. 2–18. (New York, NY: Basic Books.)

2. *Board of Education v. Barnette*, 319 U.S. 624 (1943).

3. For references, see Chapter 3.

4. *McCreary County, Kentucky v. ACLU*, 545 U.S. (2005), Scalia, J. dissenting.

5. *Washington Post* online, Tuesday, August 2, 2006.

6. *Elk Grove Unified School Dist. V. Newdow*, 542 U.S. 1, 49–54 (2004). See detailed discussion in Chapters 3 and 4 of *Liberty of Conscience*.

7. *Torcaso v. Watkins*, 367 U.S. 488 (1961).

8. "Committee Hearing Reinforces Case Against Confirmation of Janice Rogers Brown," http://www.pfaw.org.pfaw.dfiles/file_257.pdf.

9. Dennett, "The Bright Stuff," *New York Times*, July 12, 2003, op-ed.

10. Daniel Dennett, *Breaking the Spell: Religion as a Natural Phenomenon* (New York: Viking, 2006).

11. *Elk Grove v. Newdow*, above.

12. See Chapter 8 of *Liberty of Conscience*.

13. Letter of 1989, quoted in *Religion and the Constitution*, ed. Michael W. McConnell, John H. Garvey, and Thomas C. Berg, 1st ed. (New York: Aspen, 2002), p. 54.

14. A full discussion of my religious conversion, and my views, can be found in Nussbaum, "Judaism and the Love of Reason," in *Philosophy, Feminism, Faith*, ed. Ruth E. Groenhout and Marya Bower (Bloomington: Indiana University Press, 2003), pp. 9–39.

15. *Sherbert v. Verner*, 374 U.S. 398 (1963).

16. *County of Allegheny v. ACLU*, 492 U.S. 573 (1989).

3

Religious Secularism

Paula M. Cooey

Can justice be blind regarding religion in the United States? The short answer, in my opinion, is no. Not as long as the authority of the law services the State's best interest over all others, even as the State is the law's chief legislator, arbiter, and administrator.[1] Not as long as the State reinstates itself as an entity among its people through religious and quasi-religious practices. The concept *theolegal* rightly confronts what it regards as the ongoing use of theological arguments and rhetoric to make law and to manipulate democratic political processes in favor of Protestant Christianity, or the majority religion. I propose, however, that the theory does not go far enough. By this I mean that when Nathan C. Walker proposes in the introduction that the United States is a theolegal democracy with particular attention to a more robust participation of minority clergy to counter majority religions, he needs to be cognizant of some of the pitfalls of his assumptions regarding his conceptions of secularism, the law, religion, and power that underlie the concept *theolegal* itself. The problem is that theodemocracy *is* the State's religion under the guise of religious neutrality.

The concept *theolegal* suggests that the United States is becoming or has become a theodemocracy. As Walker articulates, *theodemocracy* is a nation-state, in this case, the United States, in which lawyers and politicians among others, use theological and religious rhetoric with varying degrees of success, to authorize and validate legislative, executive, and judicial power. This rhetoric is also used in everyday practice in the courts and in the realm of politics. One piece of evidence in favor of applying the concept of a theolegal democracy would be, according to Walker, the frequent practice of referring to religious scriptures and the often-employed rhetorical device of using theological language that has characterized and continues to characterize American public discourse in and out of the courtrooms. At bottom, the concept *theolegal* attempts to grapple with an ongoing historical dilemma: potential and actual conflict between the authority and interests of the State and religious authority as central to individual and communal identity. In regard to individual and communal identity, this conflict with State authority results from an irresolvable, arguably healthy, even necessary tension between the interests of the State as embodied in the law as the arbiter, partial producer, and regulator of secularism and what religious practitioners (themselves often legislators, lawyers, and judges) understand to be the ultimate authority for their values, practices, and beliefs, namely God and scripture understood as divine revelation—distinctively monotheist and most often Christian loyalties.

Some legal theorists have argued that this tension is a good thing that sustains the First Amendment distinction between religion and state through the First Amendment free expression and prohibition clauses; for them, the use of religious discourse in the public square is acceptable, even encouraged. Others have countered that the State's separation from religion and its espoused secularism (by which it means, among other things, religious neutrality) require the absence of religion altogether from public space.[2] Though Walker tilts toward the first position, from his perspective the concept *theolegal* prescribes neither, carving out instead a third possibility—theodemocracy—a middle ground between secularism, which he defines as religious neutrality, and theocracy. In short, he assumes a categorical opposition between religious and secular practices and beliefs. I think that the assumption of religion and secularism as a logical dichotomy is a conceptual flaw underlying all three positions. However, I find the concept *theolegal* promising, particularly its understanding of the kind of secularism practiced by the United States as a theolegal democracy. Its promise lies chiefly in unmasking the attribution of religious neutrality to secularism.

As presently articulated, the concept is limited by its own inherent, unintentional Protestant bias. It seeks to detect, monitor, and engage in theological arguments for political and legal authority in the public domain as if the absence of these arguments would evidence secular neutrality without respect to scrutinizing the State's practices more widely. In addition, the concept's assumed definition of religion is insufficiently broad enough to track the appeal to religious authority outside revelation-based, text-oriented traditions.

In my opinion, the concept *theolegal* needs to be expanded, its central issues reframed. The concept rightly points out that the United States is a society where monotheistic theology, and by implication, religion in general, have become political commodities that produce a theodemocracy. I propose to demonstrate, however, that by situating theodemocracy between secular states and theocracy, the concept itself presupposes a masked Protestantism in both its own historical development and in its underlying assumptions about what constitutes religion and secularism. *Theolegal* thus exemplifies the inherent Protestant bias already characteristic of U.S. secularism with respect to the relation between religion and politics, a secularism of which theodemocracy is its primary form. Without clarity here, genuine religious pluralism is most unlikely to be achieved.

By Protestant bias, I mean that Protestant theology assumes the priority of right belief or faith in a single God over practice (i.e., ritual and ethical) as the defining characteristic of Christian identity and as the determining factor of what defines religion. It further privileges the authority of text, as divine revelation, over the authority of tradition or institution in determining right teaching and belief as these inform or construct identity. In short, text alone (*sola scriptura*), as determined by faith alone (*sola fidei*), sets up the framework for posing secularism as the antithesis of religion and for masking secularism, as practiced in the United States, as religiously neutral. *Theolegal* as a concept does not sufficiently interrogate this supposed conceptual polarity; rather it assumes it and thereby inadvertently reinstates it. In other words, Walker does not grasp the religious features and functions inherent in secularism itself, what I call the religiosity of secularism. It poses theodemocracy as a middle ground or third alternative, when in fact it is the form secularism takes in this country.

Walker thus inadvertently takes on the wrong issue when he proposes that the United States is moving toward or has become a theodemocracy. Rather than posing theodemocracy as a middle way between theocracy and secularism, he needs to confront the implicit Protestantism of secularism itself and ask more broadly how public discursive practices, both in the courtroom and in the wider political arena, reflect an ongoing tension between the interests of the State and the interests of formally acknowledged religious institutions and individuals. For neither the State, regardless of how secular, nor religion, however spiritual or ethical, escapes functioning in religious capacities that reinstate each other. He should consider to what extent the notion of religious neutrality is not actually neutral, itself not absent of religiosity. It is rather a rhetorical strategy by which the State imposes its authority paradoxically on religious grounds. He should address why some non-Christian, indeed, non-Protestant traditions can find justice in the United States and some cannot and what the State has to gain or lose in withholding or granting justice. In short, Walker should consider U.S. theodemocracy, a system that has been dominant throughout most, if not all, of the country's history, a form of secularism, because secularism is itself a system of religiosity that in turn defines what does and does not count as religious and how designated religious traditions will be treated before the law.

This recognition of theodemocracy as the from of secularism practiced in the United States rather than having one foot in secularism and the other in Protestantism may sound like splitting hairs, merely an argument over finding the right word, but it is not. Once it is clear that theodemocracy *is* this country's form of secularism, then the issue of how the State, which, after all, ostensibly represents its citizens' corporate will in a democracy, exercises and sustains its power, sometimes for better and more often for worse, can be addressed. Then one may raise normative questions as to how it is that religious and antireligious dissenters often use the same rhetorical practices and strategies, as representatives of the State, to challenge statist authority. One may also ask and begin to answer how to tell the difference between what religious dissenters' view as their authority from God and the State's claims to enacting God's authority. This distinction in authority is of special significance to foreign policy and the exercise of warfare, most recently the invasions of Iraq and Afghanistan, but it holds implications for domestic issues as well, for example, civil rights protests of the 1960s.

My argument is largely analytical and critical. My point is neither to attack U.S. theodemocratic secularism nor to defend appeals to religious authority in public discourse in and out of the courtroom and the state house. Rather, I seek simply to reflect critically on the concept *theolegal*, its assumptions, and its use as a hypothesis for the further possibility of developing a more robust critique and application of the nature and use of religious argumentation in the public square. I will proceed by demonstrating that secularism, as exercised in the United States, does not and cannot stand in opposition to religion or to theology. Rather, it is the religion of the State, the arbiter, through the law, of now subordinated religions including the dominant traditions, and a participant in their commodification—precisely what Walker dubs theodemocracy. To do this I will look briefly at the historical role played by Protestantism in the production of secularism; the religious, including theological, functions performed by secularism; and the authority of the State over religion. I will conclude by suggesting briefly additional avenues that those who wish to apply the concept *theolegal* might pursue for a more robust pursuit of theodemocracy.

Historical Development of Secularism

Until the sixteenth century, *secular* referred largely to the realm of "this world" in European rhetorical practice. Sometimes interchangeable with lay, as in laity, it also signified the Catholic orders concerned with the management of these worldly concerns from within Christian institutions. In this context, it stood in contrast with the religious orders, those communities of men and women who separated from this world and its concerns, not religion *per se*. Initially then, *religious* was a narrowly restricted category, paired with *secular*, both of which were positioned within the institutional structures of Catholicism within the Holy Roman Empire and later its remnants. The sixteenth century, commonly known as the Protestant Reformation, marked the redefinition of both terms in relation to one another.

The sixteenth century bore witness in actuality to several religious reformations within European Christian traditions. In addition to the Protestant Reformation, these included the radical reform movements of Anabaptists and Unitarians, among others, and the reform efforts within the Roman Catholic Church culminating in the Council of Trent (1564) and the founding of the Jesuit Order. Without question the upheaval of the times resulted from a variety of material conditions including new technologies, colonial expansion, and disrupted patterns of labor due to emerging capitalism. At the same time, this period also saw great public theological debates over human salvation in relation to human freedom. Are humans free to choose between good and evil, a freedom that makes sin inevitable and requires a human role in salvation? Or, is the inevitable sinfulness of such choices the very antithesis of freedom? Does salvation lie instead in release from the bondage of bad choices, a release that depends on God's grace alone? What are the origin, status, and role of ethical actions or works within the drama of sin and salvation? What is the significance of ritual and spiritual formation in the economy of salvation? Wherein lies the ultimate authority for adjudicating doctrine and practice? Is it in the structures of the Church or revelation received through scripture? Posing and addressing such questions shifted how humans came to understand their ethical, political, and spiritual agency. This shift redefined their relations to their immediate communities, to external authority, to the cosmos, and to God. We live today with the legacy of this redefinition. Furthermore, the processes of redefinition continue. Indeed, we may well be in the middle of another historical shift of at least the same magnitude of what we now call the Reformation.

This period of history registered the growth, if not the birth, of both capitalism and socialism, of democracy, of individualism, and of literacy among laity in the midst of colonial expansion, institutional deterioration and corruption, fanatical apocalypticism, and torture and massacre. At a more conceptual level, the theologies of both reformed Protestants and radicals redefined the concept *religion*, to refer more widely to belief and the practices associated with it, though subordinated to it, both of which depended for authority on texts (*Bible* in the case of religion and, later, some form of *Constitution* in the case of the political realm). The Radicals in particular attributed much more intentionality to individual persons. Concomitantly the concept *secular* became more restricted to the political arena, exclusive of religion, giving rise to the polarity we now take for granted between religion and secularity. Nevertheless, both orders—religious and secular—were subordinated to God as theologically expounded.

Sixteenth-century theological debate thus actually marks a turning point in the historical development of the concepts. The works of Luther, Calvin, and most especially Zwingli argued for the separation of church and government, though all of them saw the political realm as ultimately dependent upon biblical interpretation for its authority. Their various arguments marked a tendency on the part of Reformed Protestants in particular to distinguish a something called "religion" that, although it stands at the heart of identity or one's soul, exists in a meaningful way separately from one's political obligations and activities.[3] Thus, the popular concept of religion as a system of belief, without *necessary* reference to ritual or even ethical practice, or to material reality, in short, a concept now altogether distinguishable from civic life, began to evolve.

The Treaty of Westphali (1648), which sought to end nearly a century of violence over theological differences (that often masked economical and political manipulations), formalized the polarity of the religious and secular. It also reversed the authority and power of the two orders by granting self-determination and sovereignty to the nation-state over religious institutions and in relation to other States. Both concepts to this day nevertheless hold in common that they receive their different authority from written documents. Their polarity in its asymmetrical relation and its dependence on texts continues to underlie what constitutes ultimate authority. An example of this is judicial decision-making on First Amendment issues at the highest levels in this country—a particularly Protestant spin pervading an ostensibly religiously neutral branch of government, designated secular. Though this arrangement sometimes succeeds as a strategy for negotiating what are now designated more narrowly to be religious differences within the nation-state, it does so by ultimately shifting regulatory control over religion to the State by subordinating institutional, communal, and individual religious interests to the State's interests in its own self-preservation. In this respect, one could say of the United States that all its religions are secularized. While this appears to have decreased the level of violence authorized on religious grounds within States most of the time, violence legitimated by appeal to authority of State interests in relation to other States or to entities recognized as having no "legitimate" State continues to run rampant.

One might suggest that the grounds have merely shifted from one set of discursive practices and institutions to others for their authority.

Whereas *secular*[4] simply refers to this world or this age, *secularism* refers to a loose system or set of related, ongoing processes, that produces and sustains the State as a transempirical reality (like God or the Market). In the European-American West, various secularisms perform many of the functions of religion, that is, they represent loosely defined worldviews, grounded in certain doctrines and beliefs made real by various disciplines and practices (ritual and ethical).[5] The effect is to authorize these world-views (now recognized as scientific, political, and economic, though not grasped as religious) as "just the way things are."[6] The State is a product, co-producer, and exporter of secularism.

Secularism can take many forms. Consider French *laicite* (dependent on residual Catholicism[7]) or Turkish Kemalism (dependent on the cult of Ataturk[8]). Though polity may vary across States, in a contemporary context secularism will seek to construct human identity in relation to the nation-state, including the possibility of its empire-building intentions. Secularism as practiced in the United States is distinctively a theodemo-cracy, as described by Walker, though its theology, embodied in the law, is masked as religiously neutral, as separate from and final arbiter of religious concerns and activities. Its purpose is to produce "America" and "Americans," just as various Christian traditions produce Christianity and Christians.

So, for example, the ongoing production and preservation of America depend on discipline. By *discipline* I mean everything from the informal cues or lessons in life that we continually receive from the circumstances within which we find ourselves, to the distinctive symbols, the central nar-ratives, the formal teachings, and the ritual, ethical, and legal practices of our political, economic, and religious traditions. *Discipline* refers to how these various, often conflicting, events and forces configure through the cultivation of particular sensibilities and attitudes to establish the habits of daily life that make us who we are as ever-changing beings. Discipline produces desire. Grounded in an economy of scarcity (one of the bedrock assumptions of capitalism), the disciplines of various modern secularisms, particularly U.S. secularism, produce narrowly defined desires that seek to align individual self-interest with the interests of the State.[9]

U.S. secular disciplines abound. While they may be contested implicitly by other traditions, for example, the Jehovah's Witnesses or the Quakers, or explicitly resisted by protest in the streets, by parents in the home, or in a number of other possible ways, their practice begins early and runs deep. They may appear more or less transparently religious or, to use Walker's term, theodemocratic. They register multiple forms of patriotism that play to different audiences and shape multiple, sometimes deeply conflicting, national identities or kinds of Americans. While we as citizens are not automatons, we do receive our identity as citizens either by way of practice of them or resistance to them, often some configuration of both. One can track the differences through the different desires they instantiate. Whereas one community sings "This Land Is Your Land," another prefers "God Bless the USA." Whereas one community dances to the strains of "War, What Is It Good for? Absolutely Nothin'" and "Born in the USA," another gathering listens raptly to the narrative of "The Green Beret." Differences notwithstanding, God is, one way or another, as Bob Dylan satirically chanted, on "our" side, and theodemocratic secularism is at work.

The children from these diverse communities, unless they are Jehovah's Witnesses, will stand together daily in their public or private classrooms and repeat the Pledge of Allegiance to the United Sates of America, understood, however tenuously, as "one nation under God, indivisible . . . ." With their families or perhaps as students, sponsored by their schools, they may make pilgrimage to various historical sites and monuments located throughout the country to pay homage to their historical forbearers, irrespective of which side these ancestors represent in whatever historical conflict commemorated. These pilgrims can witness their elected officials take their oaths of office by swearing to serve their country on the Christian Bible (though in rare cases, a Jewish Bible and in one case a *Quran*[10] may be substituted).

These officials, if elected to a legislature, will likely begin each session of their work with a prayer to a monotheistic God, sometimes authorized expressly in the name of Jesus. From daily practice to the holy days of theodemocratic secularism that attempt to narrate U.S. history—Columbus Day, Thanksgiving Day, Independence Day, Emancipation Day, Veteran's Day, Memorial Day, Labor Day, Victory in Europe Day, Victory over Japan Day, Presidents' Day, Martin Luther King, Jr. Day—we are taught and disciplined to love the country, to want what is good for it, to seek its good in terms of our own, and to seek our own good in terms of its good. In effect, the State, albeit an abstraction, assumes the role of God, also an abstraction, as a center of trust and loyalty.[11]

Children and adults alike transact and perform their material desires through the exchange of goods for coins and cash, economic artifacts, marked distinctly by reference to God, connected directly to national heroes, especially the presidents of the past. This embellishment has gone by the wayside with the use of checks, credit and debit cards, and electric transfer, perhaps signifying a shift in identity from worker and citizen to consumer. Through money, the God in whom we are to trust conjoins directly with the national trust and financial trusts to integrate religious, political, and economic desires into a single national identity as Americans in a theodemocratic society designated as secular.

The symbols of American identity are not restricted to the explicitly religious, though these symbols nevertheless perform recognizably religious functions to discipline desire to a national good or goods. Children and adults alike will learn through secular educational systems and other secular media the defining narratives of the United States told from various, sometimes conflicting perspectives, but most often told in terms of winners and losers or insiders and outsiders populating a drama portrayed as destiny. The national destiny, as if singular, is marked by progress, aimed toward a glorious end, a drama for which God, sometimes disguised as nature or the market, is the ironic, unnamed playwright. By some accounts, in this drama the losers will eventually become winners and outsiders will be taken in, if governed by the right desires defined by the right ends.

These historical narratives serve in their telling to orient desire, in order to produce specific virtues and to regulate certain practices. From the simplicity of never telling a lie, to tolerating differences, to lifting oneself up by one's own bootstraps, to dying for honor of God and country as a soldier, to spending the country's way out of an economic recession or depression, these virtues and their associated practices register deep desires to seek good over evil and to do the right thing. Theodemocratic disciplines of ritual, pilgrimage, economic practice, legal practice, and narrative, sometimes but not always saturated with explicit religious and theological valence, teach desire, molding it interactively in accordance with the desires of the State, regardless of whether one is docile or resistant in relation to the State itself.

Within theodemocratic secularism, the law serves as primary enforcer of the disciplines that produce national identity. Its extraordinary effectiveness as enforcer depends in part on how successfully its disciplines mask its statist agenda. These disciplines require entanglement with the dominant religious traditions with which the State engages even as they mask theodemocracy's own political and philosophical particularism. These disciplines must disguise themselves in order to validate the State's economic exploitation of its own workers, as well as foreign workers, in the interest of multinational corporations. Theodemocratic disciplines must hide overt and covert forms of violence exercised upon others both at home and abroad to secure the State's control of its environment, perceived under theodemocracy as global.

The most elegant way to enforce the State's control through the disciplines of theodemocratic secularism, however, is to universalize finite self-interested desire—either by appeal to the authority of the laws of God or of nature. Whether self-interest be god-given or natural, it is projected through some form of lawfulness as universally shared. Theologians may attribute it negatively to a sinful nature. Scientists may neutrally ascribe self-interest to a socio-biological nature that is selfish and competitive (traits that are actually positively valued as long as they are restricted to straight, white males). Policy makers may positively construe self-interest as being in the best interest of all humanity in ways that obligate us to extend our self-interests beyond ourselves. In any case, both God and nature authorize the projection that all humanity wants freedom, understood as individual self-determination, grounded in self-interest, best accomplished by Western democracy and free-market capitalism. Nature, if not always God, ordains that self-determination take the form of active, competitive participation as a worker-consumer in free-market capitalism, naturalized as "market forces" or "the Market." In the case of economic desire, socially constructed desires for highly specific goods transmute into a universal human nature, grounded in the so-called science or discipline of Economics, currently practiced in U.S. institutions of higher education as the theology of capitalism. Individualism, freedom, and competition become naturalized as "the way things are." Religion, now redefined largely through the legal system in terms of belief and further privatized as a matter of individual choice, relocates as a commodity to the marketplace of ideas.

These social processes, like all other society and culture-building processes, including those that we call religious, are neither arbitrarily fabricated nor the product of some kind of conspiracy. They occur neither by the hindsight of necessity nor by the foresight of chance. Nor are they immutable. These systems are networks of power that operate like hydroelectricity. Produced through human effort exercised on water, electric power courses through nodes, transported by webs of wiring to numerous destinations, simultaneously fueling all kinds of related and unrelated human activity, and dependent on rain from the heavens. Human beings working as individuals and groups produce and are produced by these systems through their reciprocal relations as participants in the daily work of social and individual life. As individuals and groups they may circulate or resist within these systems. They may be conscious of power or oblivious to it; they may seek it or eschew it; their motives may be good or evil, their actions ethical or unethical, masked to themselves or transparent. In other words, we make the disciplines that in turn produce the desires that define us.[12]

When, due to resistance, the more benign disciplines fail to produce a cooperative and complicit citizenry, the State often resorts directly to violence through foreign wars, domestic military occupation, and the criminal justice system. For example, the removal of visible religious symbols notwithstanding, and regardless of the distinction between legality and morality, the legal system provides, through the court-room, theaters where morality plays dramatize successful and failed attempts to socialize desire, arenas of confession and penance, systems of judgment that may bestow or withhold redemption. Failed attempts merit further schooling through imprisonment where, particularly if the punishment is execution, theater becomes the performance of a lifetime, summed up by an injection ritually administered, to be witnessed through the communications media as further instruction, a warning to be heeded by the public at large.[13]

Religion, posed in contrast to secularism, like secularism, in this case theodemocratic secularism, carries a multitude of different meanings, but for purposes of this discussion refers to loosely organized systems that structure and order desire and identity through belief and practice in relation to transempirical realities symbolically projected (e.g., God, Goddess, a pantheon of deities, Nature, Nothingness, the State, or the Market). For the most part, formal religious traditions as we convention-ally think of them depend on teachings and disciplines that cultivate or produce desires beyond the confines of self-interest. By this definition of religion, the State is ambiguous, and secularism as a system distinguished from religion is ironic. On the one hand, secularism is a religion, in this case, theodemocracy, in that it orients identity through appeal to a tran-sempirical reality, namely the State. On the other hand, insofar that it depends on a capitalist economy, the self is constructed by self-interest. The self-interest of the individual is aligned through the law to the self-interest of the State, a linkage that has severely broken down with the rise of global or free-market capitalism. One could say that theodemocracy, as a form of secularism, is ironically a religion of self-interest. Its God or Higher Power is the State itself.

Modern theodemocracy cannot formally recognize authority beyond its own as its equal. At the same time, however, because secularism in the West grew out of and depends on Christian traditions, it draws upon these very traditions to perform, produce, and sustain human desires commensurate with the desires of the nation-state. In other words, U.S. theodemocratic secularism extends itself in the interest of the Sate through the figure of Jesus and by direct reference to the Christian Bible, implicitly if not always explicitly, to discipline the desires that produce individual and corporate identity as American. The appropriation of Christian teach-ings and disciplines for State interest is certainly neither new nor unique to the United States. In virtually any form, even the purportedly most atheistic, the State has historically appropriated what we now separate out and call religion and religious disciplines to produce and sustain itself.

In the case of Christian religions, this process can be traced at least as far back as Constantine.

Common parlance has mistakenly confused the separation of church and State with the separation of religion and secularism. While governmental and clerical institutions may be legally separated from one another, religion and politics are inseparable. Today, insofar as the Christian Churches must submit to the authority of the U.S. government as regulated by the Supreme Court, the Christian denominations are virtually all secularized, often precisely when they take a dissenting stand.

As many scholars have noted, chief among them Robert Bellah, secularism as practiced in the United States, far from religiously neutral, reflects specifically Reformed Protestant virtues, practices, and desires, though often stripped of their specific theological content so that their religious functions remain masked.[14] U.S. polity is structured as a representative, bicameral democracy, influenced heavily by the bicameral structure of the Presbyterian Church as reflected in the Presbyterian *Book of Order*. U.S. economics grew in part out of a Calvinist, ascetic work ethic necessary to accumulating and investing capital. U.S. political ideologies of individualism and manifest destiny echo, albeit faintly, the solitary nature of human-divine relations and the communal sense of the people of God that are trademarks of a Calvinist doctrine of election. Stripped to some extent of explicitly theological content and stretched to accommodate other forms of monotheism such as Deism, Anabaptist traditions, Lutheranism, Methodism, and Anglicanism, U.S. theodemocratic secularism eventually absorbed Judaism and Catholicism as well, insofar as Jews and Catholics assimilated to secular, implicitly Protestant practices. Absorption of non-Protestant traditions taken into consideration, theodemocratic secularism stands directly in symbiotic, albeit morally ambiguous, relationship with what were once the mainline Protestant churches. While to some extent tolerant of extremely diverse religious traditions, theodemocracy has, for the most part, reflected privileged white mainline Protestant attitudes, values, and practices both politically and economically. In other words, U.S. secularism is religious, indeed a theodemocracy.

Implications for Theolegal Theory

Secularism is this-worldly religiosity in the service of this-worldly transempirical realities (the State, the Market) by appeal to otherworldly (often better-worldly) ones (God, Goddess, a pantheon of deities, a cult figure invested with supernatural qualities, but in any case, the majority religious tradition of whatever State in which it finds itself). If secularism is understood as a genus that includes many different species depending on the history and the self-interest of the State it supports, several reconceptualizations follow for the secularist State's relation to the designated religions over which it becomes authority and arbiter. First it becomes clearer that theodemocracy as practiced in the United States cannot accept other religions within its domain as equal to itself or to each other in status, power, and authority. The State's power through the law must have final authority in those cases where its own authority is challenged; it will default to the majority religious beliefs and practices, albeit in faded form, to justify its actions. One corollary to this is that to sustain this power and authority the State will, and does, reconfigure what "religion" is by separating the political and economic from the religious as if the three were minimally related at best. The State, in this country as theodemocracy, will and does further employ an ideology of universal individualism before a universal law to privatize and spiritualize traditions formally recognized as religious. One effect, among others, is that the putative religions become commodified, that is, competitors in a marketplace of "ideas" (note the absence of reference to practices). As commodities, religious traditions, choices, beliefs, and acts become trivialized, decentralized, and destabilized as determinants of individual identity, in short, subordinated to national identity. Though both national and religious identities are socially constructed, national identity assumes the status of a given (as with gender, race, and ethnicity) in contrast to a religious identity of "choice" (analogous to choice of political party). In other words, it is a given that one is an American; it is one choice among many possibilities that one is a Presbyterian.

Given these reconceptualizations, it becomes more transparent the extent to which *theolegal* as a concept needs to be rearticulated more clearly and directly with respect to power and its distribution in a theodemocracy—with special attention to the law as the State's regulator on behalf of the State's interests. Of course, a theodemocracy will privilege those formal religious traditions to which it owes its partial historical origins and constitutive similarities. Theodemocracy will further not easily recognize that it does so, because it assumes that its own categories of construction are natural (i.e., "just the way things are"). Theodemocracy further cannot concede that what is natural to it is, as with all claims to "natural," constructed through the exercises of its power, as this power disperses throughout its most cherished institutions and values—most especially in the structuring and practice of the law. Religious neutrality is one of the primary rhetorical devices deployed to accomplish this task.

The critical burden of the concept *theolegal* and its usages in regard to the United States (theolegal democracy, theodemocracy, theolegal nation) becomes, then, vigilance with respect to the State, not as if the State could be neutral in regard to religion, but in the exercise of State's own religiosity through its secularist beliefs and practices; its strategies for masking its religiosity while determining what counts as religious; and its ranking of what counts as "legitimately" religious according to its own partialities and blindness.

The concept has a constructive role to play as well. What ultimately protects the State from its own worse impulses (tyranny) is the resistance produced by the plurality and diversity of traditions, as well as the dissent of citizens from *across* the spectrum of theist, nontheist, atheist, and agnostic traditions, particularly those for whom their traditions, whether one or many, hold centrality in determining communal and individual identity. Those who find it useful to understand the United States as a theodemocracy should concern themselves with discerning where such resistances occur and to what end, for no State can permanently and totally control all differences; change is inevitable, one way or another. In order to accomplish this task of vigilance, scholars and practitioners alike need to be more alert to the fluidity of the categories of religion and secularism and their relation to each other as deployed in public discourse, as measures of the State's exercise of its power and authority.

Given these circumstances, assumptions, and reconceptualizations, scholars of the theolegal need to consider *how* it is that people use shared traditional rhetoric for conflicting, even opposing ends, both to support the State and to challenge it. To do this, Walker needs to shift focus beyond the formally theistic and theological. He needs to focus on the various concepts *religion*, *religions*, and *religious*, now understood as contextualized, rather than having a fixed definition throughout all times and places. In other words, these are fluid terms that gain their meaning from their histories, their immediate contexts, and their relations to the equally fluid conceptions of the *secular* and *secularism*, now understood in terms of religious and quasi-religious strategies deployed to govern multiple religions rather than as religiously neutral. It will thus become clearer that *religion* at the hands of a secularist State in the twenty-first century will often mean those structures and disciplines of belief and practice that constitute the potential to challenge the authority of the State (for ill as well as for good), now corralled and redefined through the law to minimize the possibilities for political challenge.

The State's chief rhetorical strategy in this deployment is to designate itself as secular, as in religiously neutral; meanwhile, the success with which the State pulls off this charade will depend ironically on the use of religious rhetoric and the exercise of essentially religious disciplines to authorize its actions. Note that Rick Warren of the Saddleback Church ushered in our most recent presidential inauguration by praying that we are "not a nation bound by race, religion, or blood," but "Americans bound by a commitment to freedom and liberty." Quoting Hebrew scripture, he prayed to the God of Judaism, Christianity, and Islam in the name of Jesus, whom he clarified carefully as the one who had brought him to pray, as opposed to the savior over all: commitments that have authorized both noble and heinous deeds. Our newly elected president, in his inaugural address, subsequently urged us, quoting Christian scripture (1 Corinthians 13), to give up childish things and to choose "our better history." President Obama went on to point out that we do this as "a nation of Christians and Muslims, Jews and Hindus, non-believers. . . ." The inclusion of Muslims, Hindus, and nonbelievers is stunning for its normative absence from U.S. political discourse, even at its most inclusive. Nevertheless, that Obama included Muslims, Hindus, and nonbelievers ironically reasserts the Protestant primacy of belief and in no way guarantees that nonmonotheistic and atheistic practices will receive equal justice before the law. There are numerous other traditions noteworthy for their absence as well.

Can justice be blind when it comes to religion? Justice herself crosses (no pun intended) several religious boundaries and religious histories. This endows her with a built-in capacity for resistance to serving solely the interests of any State. For this reason, I prefer that she be alert, discerning, and self-critical.

Notes

1. I capitalize the term *state* to emphasize that it is a reification of a specific, usually geographically moored, political abstraction that takes on a transempirical reality, an ideality, not unlike God or any other abstraction or reification (Nature, or the Market, for example). The State, like God, is personalized or anthropomorphized and elicits among its citizens a faith (a trust and loyalty), ritually performed (made real), that in turn shapes the identity of the citizen at the very least as a citizen and preferably, from the State's perspective, as a patriot. (Note that the State can take on the legal role of a person.) I understand this concept and any given instantiation of it to be constructed realities as articulated by sociologists Emil Durkheim and Peter Berger. Actual governments depend on perpetually constructing and maintaining their particular symbolically projected States for their survival.
2. Stephen L. Carter represents what has come to be known as an accommodationist perspective: one that argues for a tension between the State and religion that accommodates religion to a point; he is not entirely clear where this point is located when push comes to shove. See *The Culture of Disbelief* (New York: Anchor Books, 1991). See Ronald Flowers for an overview of various positions in regard to the relationship between Church/Religion and State.

See *That Godless Court? Supreme Court Decisions on Church-State Relations* (Louisville: Westminster John Knox Press, 2006).

3. For example, see Zwingli, "Commentary on True and False Religion," excerpted in *The Protestant Reformation*, ed. Hans J. Hillerbrand (New York: Harper and Row, 1968). See also James S. Preus, *Explaining Religion: Criticism and Theory from Bodin to Freud* (New Haven: Yale University Press, 1987). Moreover, this something called "religion" could, according to the theologians, be judged true or false, strictly on the basis of the orthodoxy of one's beliefs. Unlike the orthodoxy established by the earlier churches, Protestant orthodoxy, in turn, depended upon subordinating practice and observance to sacred text, as according to specific, but often implicit, standards.

4. Some of this material appears in altered and expanded form in a different context in Cooey, *Willing the Good: Jesus Dissent and Desire* (Minneapolis: Augsburg Fortress, 2006).

5. See Talal Asad, *Genealogies of Religion: Discipline and Reasons of Power in Christianity and Islam* (Baltimore: Johns Hopkins Press, 1993) and *Formations of the Secular: Christianity, Islam, Modernity* (Palo Alto: Stanford University Press, 2003).

6. See Clifford Geertz, *The Interpretation of Cultures: Selected Essays* (New York: Basic Books, 1973).

7. See Strenski who argues in Weberian fashion that human rights, and by extension, any doctrine of the rights of "man," develops from Catholic theological development of natural law (*Journal of the American Academy of Religion 2004* 72(3): 631–652.

8. See Navaro-Yashin, *Faces of the State* (Princeton: Princeton University Press, 2002).

9. My conception of discipline is obviously shaped not only by Asad, but also by Michel Foucault. It also reflects the influence of Max Weber. See Weber, *The Protestant Ethic and the Spirit of Capitalism* trans. Talcott Parsons, intro. Anthony Giddens (London: Routledge, 1992) and Foucault's *Introduction to the History of Sexuality, vol.1, an Introduction*, trans. Robert Hurley (New York: Vintage Books, 1988).

10. U.S. Rep. Keith Ellison of Minnesota was sworn in on Thomas Jefferson's copy of the *Quran* on January 4, 2007.

11. The interaction of trust and loyalty centered by a high or highest value is H. Richard Niebuhr's definition of faith. See *Radical Monotheism and Western Culture* (Westminster John Knox: Louisville, 1993).

12. See Foucault, *Discipline and Punish*, trans. Alan Sheridan (New York: Pantheon, 1977) and *Introduction to the History of Sexuality, vol.1, an Introduction*, trans. Robert Hurley (New York: Vintage Books, 1988). Lest there be any doubt about human agency here, please note: I think that we do live in our narratives and traditions like fish in water, that we never exist outside language/culture/ society. I also don't think that this means that we don't have agency, specifically the agency to resist. Rather what agency/resistance we employ emerges out of conflicting narratives and traditions in the midst of changing material

conditions. Within this context or rather the many different contexts generated, we are most definitely agents. The reference to electricity preserves that power flow (including its dependence on resistance) rather than quantifying it and carving it up into "have" and "have-nots."

13. Ibid. *Discipline and Punish.*
14. Bellah, Robert (1991) "Civil Religion in America" in *Beyond Belief: Essays on Religion in a Post-traditionalist World* (Berkeley: University of California Press, 1991) p.168, ff.

Part 2

Theolegal Officials

Little Goat
by Katie Ford

God is not light upon light, no more
than goat is need upon need although there, where it grazes, it is
sun upon coat within which ticks and stray-blown feed
burrow into the pocked skin of such foul scent
covering the underflesh heart that could
eat this farmer's grain or the barren mountain's bark
high in the solitude of sheer animal
peace laid over sheer animal terror.
We ask the animal afflicted by its time,
its impoverished American meadow
that drove it to find birch from which to strip its easy feed
to abide with us. It does not need us.
We think it needs us.
We must forgive God God's story.

Editorial Preface

M any believe God needs political officials to enact God's story by enshrining religious values in public policy. The purpose of this section on theolegal officials is to discuss how religious legislators, judges, and presidents intertwine their religious beliefs with their official actions. Unlike secular and theocratic states, a theolegal nation permits officials to use their diverse religious worldviews, or the religions of their constituents, to make, apply, or administer law because a theolegal democracy does not prevent the use of theology in the public arena. As a result, officials may intentionally or unintentionally draw upon their own religious beliefs, or those of their constituents, thereby becoming theolegal officials.

In Chapter 4 Alan Dershowitz unravels the motivations of the Religious Right to, as he states, highjack the Declaration of Independence. He rejects the trend of those who declare our diverse nation to be a "Christian nation" and those who seek to both lower the wall of separation and infiltrate government with theolegal officials. He compares the historic backlash against a Jewish senator from North Carolina who in 1808 was forced to confess his belief in the New Testament to that of a contemporary Muslim congressman who took his private oath of office on the Quran, leaving some to argue that it exemplified the erosion of "American civilization." He concludes his discussion of theolegal officials with a proposal called "the Ten Command*ments for Politicians"—a comm*end*ment, a guide that draws upon both commandments and amendments. Dershowitz's chapter outlines various abuses of religion by those in the legislative and executive branches.

In Chapter 5 co-editor Edwin Greenlee surveys how judges integrate their beliefs in their decision-making. He analyses how the Judicial Code of Professional Responsibility addresses possible conflicts caused when judges hold strong religious beliefs, yet must remain impartial in cases where those beliefs are challenged. Greenlee uses the tradition of the *red mass* to demonstrate how U.S. Supreme Court justices participate in the Roman Catholic Eucharist as a public spectacle for political solidarity. While a number of judges believe that "religious commitment can coexist with judicial neutrality," he concludes a separationist perspective is most appropriate in the case of judges as public officials. In this way, the legal profession attempts to balance the private nature of an official's theology with the public responsibility of law. This chapter on religious judges demonstrates the natural tendency for legal professionals to integrate their beliefs in their practice while upholding professional neutrality to prevent the United States from becoming a theocracy.

In Chapter 6 Mark Rozell provides a historical snapshot of how theology was used in the political strategies of religious presidents from Carter to Obama. We title the chapter *Religious Presidents* to describe the practice by which commanders-in-chief either overtly or covertly use theology to justify policy decisions, to communicate with voters, and to mobilize resources to maintain their positions of power. Readers should try to discern whether religious presidents appear to believe in a moral code passed down through specific religious teachings that is above the secular laws of our country. Put simply, do religious presidents believe that God's law should determine civil law? In fact, Rozell demonstrates Americans are mostly comfortable with this kind of "God talk" and criticize those who do not use theological language in their policy debates, which leads to the next issue to be addressed. Are liberal presidents theologically constrained to be more public about their faith to appeal to swing voters? Are conservative presidents secularly constrained to be less religious in order to be viewed as constitutionally legitimate?

In Chapter 7 Ted Jelen and Brendan Morris unpack the religious rhetoric of seven U.S. presidents in the context of abortion. Though a highly politicized religious topic, presidents increasingly use secular rationale when discussing abortion, even by political leaders perceived as highly religious. Take for instance how President Clinton mentioned abortion 62 times in public speeches, 23 percent of which was religious rhetoric. George W. Bush, on the other hand, mentioned abortion 77 times with only 9 percent of this rhetoric being explicitly religious. Why is there an increase of secular language in relation to this religiously divisive topic? Could it be that presidents are utilizing more public reasons, aware that theolegal rhetoric is no longer an effective political strategy? Or is it the voters who politicize faith while presidents try to remain neutral? Or maybe even the most religious of presidents feel constrained by a system that punishes the integration of theology and law. Or maybe there has yet to be a uniform way to speak about abortion on theological grounds, as discussed in Chapter 8 on stem cell research.

4

The Religious Right[1]

Alan Dershowitz

In my book *Blasphemy: How the Religious Right is Hijacking our Declaration of Independence,* I demonstrate how many on the Religious Right have engaged in a crusade to convert the United States into a Christian theocracy based on the Bible, more specifically, on the divine authority of Jesus Christ. The following chapter integrates my thesis into a discussion of Nathan C. Walker's theory *theolegal democracy.* I describe how some religious and political officials are trying to promote a theolegal system that would erode the great wall of separation between church and state. This chapter will illustrate the religious motivations of such theolegal officials, proclaim my own Ten Commandments, and challenge the Religious Right's interpretation of the Declaration of Independence.

The Religious Right

This is not the first time in history that religious fundamentalism has sought to declare our heterogeneous country to be a "Christian nation," but all previous efforts in this direction have been rejected. This time a new tactic is being used, and it promises—or threatens—a greater potential for success. In an appeal to the founding fathers, the Religious Right is employing as their primary weapon the Declaration of Independence, which they claim is America's baptismal certificate. They point to the words of the Declaration—its invocation of "Nature's God," "Creator," "Supreme Judge of the World," and "Divine Providence"—as proof that our nation was founded on principles of Christianity, Jesus Christ, and the Holy Bible. They also seek to elevate the Declaration of Independence to equal status with the constitution, which contains no references to God and prohibits any religious test for federal office and any law respecting an establishment of religion. As David Barton, an advocate of a Christianized America, has put it: "Many people erroneously consider the Constitution to be a higher document than the Declaration. However, under our form of government, the Constitution is *not* superior to the Declaration of Independence; a violation of the Declaration is just as serious as a breach of the Constitution" (emphasis in original).[2] Barton further argues that "[t]he Constitution cannot be properly interpreted or applied apart from the natural law principles presented in the Declaration. The two documents must be used together to understand either one individually."[3] This view of the legal status of the Declaration is wrong, both as a matter of history and of law, and it has never been accepted by the courts, but it is regarded as gospel by many on the Religious Right.

Invoking the beliefs of the founders, and especially the Declaration of Independence, is a powerful weapon indeed. As Jon Meacham, the author of *American Gospel*, has written:

> The intensity with which the Religious Right attempts to conscript the Founders into their cause indicates the importance the movement ascribes to historical benediction by association with the origins of the Republic. If [they] convince enough people that America was a Christian nation that has lost its way, the more legitimate their efforts in the political arena seem.[4]

The Washington Post columnist George F. Will has put it more bluntly:

> Not since the medieval church baptized, as it were, Aristotle, as some sort of early – very early – church father has there been an intellectual hijacking as audacious as the attempt to present America's principal founders as devout Christians. Such an attempt is now in high gear among people who argue that the founders were kindred spirits with today's evangelicals, and that they founded a "Christian nation."[5]

Many on the Religious Right are sincere and decent people who deeply believe they are doing God's work. And maybe they are, but they are not doing Jefferson's work, or the work of our other founders who strongly believed in the separation of church and state. The good people who are using the Declaration of Independence to Christianize our nation have a very different conception of governance from that of the founding generation, and it is wrong for these historical revisionists to rewrite our past in an effort to change our future.

The strategy of the current crusade by the Religious Right to Christianize America envisages a two-step process: The first requires a lowering of the wall of separation between church and state to a level that would permit the introduction of generic religion—God, nonsectarian prayer, multiple religious images—into the governmental sphere; once this is accomplished the next step would be to insist that America's true religion is Christianity, since our nation was founded by Christians on Christian principles.

The first step, which sounds benign to many but is seen by the Religious Right as a Trojan horse hiding an army of Christian soldiers, is now becoming mainstream and is likely to be approved, in general terms, by the current Supreme Court. The second step is still the providence of the extreme Religious Right, but that group is growing in size and influence, and its goal—a Christian America, with other religions being tolerated as "second class" and atheism and agnosticism being condemned as immoral—is no longer merely a prayer.

Moreover, experience suggests that once religion, even generic religion, becomes sufficiently entwined in governance, it is only a matter of time before a competition ensues as to which is the true religion of our nation. Jacob Henry, a Jew who was elected to North Carolina's legislature in 1808 but was blocked from taking his seat by a law requiring him to accept the divinity of the New Testament, posed the following rhetorical question: "Will you drive from your shores and from the shelter of your constitution all who do not lay their oblations on the same altar, observe the same ritual, and subscribe to the same dogmas? If so, which among the various sects into which we are divided shall be the favored one?"[6]

As if to demonstrate that intolerance once practiced *against* Jews can also be practiced *by* some Jews against other minorities, a Jewish rightwing talk show host named Dennis Prager led a campaign to disallow the first Muslim elected to Congress (in November 2006) to take an oath of office on the Quran. Prager insisted that congressman Keith Ellison

> should not be allowed to do so – not because of any American hostility to the Koran, but because the act undermines American civilization. Insofar as a member of Congress taking an oath to serve America and uphold its values is concerned, America is interested in only one book, the Bible. If you are incapable of taking an oath on that book, don't serve in Congress.[7]

Prager's bigotry was immediately condemned by Jewish organizations across the ideological spectrum. This is what the Anti-Defamation League of B'nai Brith said:

> Prager is flat out wrong when he asserts that Representative Ellison's use of the Koran would be "damaging to the fabric of American civilization." To the contrary, the U.S. Constitution guarantees that "no religious test shall ever be required" to hold public office in America. Members of Congress,

like all Americans, should be free to observe their own religious practices without government interference or coercion.

Prager's patriotic prattling is misinformed on the facts, too. No member of Congress is officially sworn in with a Bible. Under House rules, the official swearing-in ceremony is done in the House chambers, with the speaker of the House administering the oath of office en masse. No Bible or other holy books are used at all. Members may, if they choose, also have a private ceremony with family and friends. At these unofficial ceremonies, members frequently solemnize the event by taking an oath while holding a personal family Bible. Some members of Congress have refused to swear on any Bible, which is plainly their right.

Prager ridiculously asserts that permitting Representative Ellison to take the oath of office would "be doing more damage to the unity of America and to the value system that has formed this country than the terrorists of 9–11." What he fails to understand is that what truly unifies all Americans is a value system built on religious freedom and pluralism, not dogmatism and coercion.

Prager presents intolerant, ugly views. His comparison of Ellison's desire to "choose his favorite book" to that of the right of a racist elected to public office to use Hitler's *Mein Kampf* is outrageous.

Not to be outdone, former Alabama Chief Justice Roy Moore, who was removed from the bench for refusing to obey a federal court order to remove a monument featuring the Ten Commandments from the Alabama Supreme Court building, said the following:

> Enough evidence exists for Congress to question Ellison's qualifications to be a member of Congress as well as his commitment to the Constitution in view of his apparent determination to embrace the Quran and an Islamic philosophy directly contrary to the principles of the Constitution. But common sense alone dictates that in the midst of a war with Islamic terrorists we should not place someone in a position of great power who shares their doctrine. In 1943, we would never have allowed a member of Congress to take their oath on "Mein Kampf," or someone in the 1950s to swear allegiance to the "Communist Manifesto." Congress has the authority and should act to prohibit Ellison from taking the congressional oath today![8]

To cap it off, a congressman has actually said that he would disallow Ellison from taking his seat because of his request to swear in on the Quran. According to the *New York Times,* Representative Virgil H. Goode Jr. (R-Virginia), in a letter to his constituents, said that voters must "wake up" or else there will "likely be many more Muslims elected to office and demanding the use of the Koran."[9] Of course, Congressman Ellison was allowed to take the oath of office. The question should be whether Congressman Goode should be allowed to take his oath and sit in his elected office. He has, after all, violated his oath of office, in which he promised to "support and defend the Constitution of the United States," which intentionally and emphatically prohibits any and all religious tests.

In the end, Congressman Ellison took his private oath on the Quran. The particular Quran he chose was the one owned by none other than Thomas Jefferson. The Ellison episode demonstrates how the introduction of religion into governmental activities can sow the seeds of religious intolerance. Such intolerance was promoted by former Alabama Chief Justice Roy Moore and Virginia Representative Virgil H. Goode, who serve as examples of what Walker calls theolegal officials. Additional examples illustrate the pervasive nature of the use of theology to make and apply law.

Theolegal Officials

Take for instance, former vice-presidential candidate and Senator Joseph Lieberman who also believes that we are a theolegal nation, citing the Declaration: "Our rights to life, liberty and the pursuit of happiness [are] based on what our Creator, God, gave us, creating each of us in the image of God." (It is the Bible, however, and not the Declaration, that says we are created "in the image of God.")

Former president George H. W. Bush has said that unless a person believes in the God of the Declaration of Independence, he cannot be a true American. This false association between religion and patriotism endangers the very principles of both the Declaration, which mandates equality, and the constitution, which guarantees that "no religious test" shall ever be imposed for officeholding, and presumably for citizenship in the United States. It also threatens the wall of separation erected by the First Amendment.

Judge Andrew Napolitano, the senior judicial analyst for the Fox News Channel, said on *The Big Story with John Gibson*, "in America, as well all know from basic high school social studies, we have a Constitution and a Declaration of Independence that embodies Judeo-Christian moral values."

During his 1996 presidential campaign, Alan Keyes, who was running for the Republican nomination, argued that the authors of the Declaration of Independence intended it to be a "bridge between the Bible and the Constitution–between the basis of our moral faith and the basis of our political life." Keyes agreed with former president George H. W. Bush that unless a person believes in the God of the Declaration of Independence, he cannot be a true American. Keyes also has said that the God of the

Declaration—"Nature's God"—is not "some mechanistic deity of nature."
Rather it is "a very biblical God," a "very personal God."

Keyes started a group called the Declaration Foundation, whose mission
includes the "development of a Declaration curriculum" for use in private and
eventually public schools (which he calls "government schools"). The goal of
this curriculum would be to persuade schoolchildren that the Declaration of
Independence—particularly the references to "creator" and "created"—favor
the teaching of *biblical* creationism, which he characterizes as "not religious"
but "American." He believes that these principles also support prayer in
public schools, while they oppose homosexuality, abortion, and atheism.

Keyes also has complained "that I just want to explain to my son Andrew
what the Declaration says," namely that by referring to a Creator, it supports
biblical creationism. He then goes on to assert: "How dare you stop me," suggesting that anyone in America would try to stop a parent, as distinguished
from a public school teacher, from telling his son about creationism.

Keyes fails to understand the distinction between an official who is
religious, teaching their own children about their beliefs, as compared to a
theolegal official using their beliefs to make laws. A closing example comes
from Senator James Inhofe (R-Oklahoma). In response to whether he would
"vote to confirm an atheist to the Supreme Court," Inhofe answered:

> No, I would not. To me, that totally contradicts everything that this country
> is founded on–including our Constitution, including our original oaths of
> office. Back in the colonial days, the whole purpose that people came here
> and lost their lives was to achieve the freedoms, of which the major freedom
> is freedom to love your Lord.

In other words, this theolegal senator, who took an oath to support the
constitution, has said he would violate the explicit command of Article VI,
Section 2, of the constitution that "no religious test shall ever be required
as a qualification to any office or public trust under the United States."
Moreover, such a refusal to confirm an agnostic or atheist nominee would
have kept the great Justice Oliver Wendell Holmes Jr. off the court, as well as,
perhaps, Justice Felix Frankfurter and Benjamin Cardozo. And who knows
how many other justices, including some currently serving, harbor their
own private doubts about religion? Presidential candidate Mitt Romney
would also impose a religious test for the presidency of the United Sates,
saying on February 19, 2007, that "we need to have a person of faith lead
the country," thus excluding Jefferson and probably Lincoln.

More recently, former Arkansas Governor, Mike Hukabee, who wants to
be president of the United States, argued that our godless constitution—
the first constitution to exclude any reference to a deity—is supposed to

be brought in line with the Bible. He has pointed out that the constitution has been amended, while the Ten Commandments are precisely the same as they were when given by God to the Jewish people more than 3,000 years ago. He's wrong about the Ten Commandments (to say nothing about the constitution). The Ten Commandments have been amended on numerous occasions, especially by Hukabee's personal savior, Jesus.

Let us start with the commandment that mandates a day of rest. It specifically mandates the Seventh Day, namely Saturday, as "a Sabbath unto the Lord." And it gives a specific reason for picking Saturday: "For in Six Days the Lord made Heaven and earth, the sea and all that in them is, and rested on the seventh day; wherefore the Lord blessed the Sabbath day and hallowed it." Along came Christianity and amended that commandment, changing the day of rest from the seventh day to the first day—Sunday. The reason for sanctifying Sunday was also changed. Jesus also amended the prohibition against adultery. When God told the Jewish people not to commit adultery, He was very clear about its definition. It prohibited sex with or by a married woman. Married men, however, were totally free to have sex with as many single women as they chose. Jesus improved on that and made the adultery prohibition gender neutral. And what about the commandment that says: "I the Lord thy God am a jealous God, visiting the iniquity of the fathers upon the children unto the third and fourth generation on them that hate me." When's the last time a minister quoted *that* commandment? As Thomas Jefferson pointed out, it is the most un-American of all commandments since we believe in personal guilt and not guilt being passed from generation to generation. Indeed our constitution specifically prohibits bills of attainder, which are based on the Ten Commandments. Finally, the Ten Commandments mention slavery twice, requiring that slaves be given a day of rest and prohibiting the coveting of a neighbor's slave. You don't see those commandments ever quoted in full in the bumper sticker version that adorns churches and synagogues and that the Hukabees of the world want to see in our schools and courtrooms.

Hukabee cites the constitutional amendments that enfranchised women and abolished slavery. Both were improvements on the Bible, which disenfranchised women and permitted slavery. Bad examples.

Separation is Good for Religion and the State

The fact is the experiment launched by Jefferson and his fellow patriots, separating church from state, has been a resounding success for both churches and for the state—and most important for the citizens. Churches, synagogues, and mosques are thriving throughout America, at a time when many houses of worship, especially churches, are empty throughout Europe. The state remains strong, far stronger than ever anticipated by the founders. Our "godless constitution" has endured longer than any comparable document in history. Our citizens are free to practice any religion or no religion. In the words of an old folk saying, "It ain't broke, so why fix it."

The wall of separation remains standing, despite intense efforts by fundamentalist wall breakers to tear it down. This great wall of America, invisible to the naked eye, yet more powerful than those made of stone, remains in danger because the pressures on its fragile structure are increasing. There are multiple ironies in this danger.

It is no coincidence, in my view, that organized religion is thriving in America and dying in much of Europe. The separation of church and state is good for religion. When church and state merge, natural antagonism that citizens feel toward their government carries over to the church. Moreover, when the state tries to enforce religious practices, enmity is generated. Witness Israel, a country I visit frequently. Because the mechanisms of the state are employed in support of Orthodox Judaism, a sharp division has developed between the Orthodox community and the vast majority of secular Jews. Many secular Jews feel strongly that their freedoms have been impinged, not only by Orthodox Judaism, but by the state as well. Today there is more anti-Orthodox feeling in Israel than in many other parts of the world.

If the wall of separation were to crumble in America, the ultimate losers could well be the churches, the synagogues, and the mosques. To be sure, organized religion would benefit *initially* from the support—financial, political, and ideological—of the state. Many religious leaders who are currently strapped for cash see the wall of separation as a barrier to filling their coffers. But in the long run, organized religions would suffer greatly from state involvement in their affairs. The state, by playing the organist, would call the hymn. This would be a tragedy for both religious and secular Americans. Religion, if it remains independent of the state, can serve as a useful check and balance on excess of government. For example, during the 1920s, eugenics became the rage among scientists, academics, and intellectuals. Thirty states enacted forcible sterilization laws, which resulted in 50,000 people being surgically sterilized. In 1927 the U.S. Supreme Court upheld these laws in a decision by Justice Oliver Wendell Holmes, an atheist, who wrote, "It is better for all the world, if instead of waiting to execute offspring for crime or to let them starve for their imbecility, society can prevent those who are manifestly unfit from continuing their kind." The only dissenting opinion came from a religious Catholic. Churches fought hard against sterilization laws. In this instance, religion was right; government and science were wrong.

In countries where the state controls religion, it is far more difficult for churches to serve as checks upon the excesses of the state. Were the wall of separation to come crumbling down, disbelievers and skeptics would also suffer greatly—at least at the outset. I doubt we would have crusades, inquisitions, or pogroms as in centuries past, but there would be discrimination. Indeed, even today, there is discrimination in practice despite its prohibition under the constitution. In the long run, however, the number of openly skeptical Americans would increase. Church membership would drop.

Would this be good for America? Would this be good for secular humanists? Since none of us is a prophet, it is impossible to know with certainty what an American without a wall of separation would look like. It would almost certainly become a different place from the one we now inhabit, which is still the envy of the world. We are a prudent and cautious people. As such, we should not take the risks of breaking an edifice that has served us so well for so long. The "law" of unintended consequences cautions against taking precipitous actions.

We must have separation between church and state if we really believe in equality in America—and even equality is an experiment if one considers all the countries of the world today and how few espouse and enforce real equality. Look at Eastern Europe, where in many places the shackles of communism are being exchanged for the shackles of religion. Some of the same liberal Romanian students who were demonstrating against communism in the streets are now demonstrating for church-sponsored schools and for laws against abortion. In Poland the government has introduced mandatory Catholic education in public schools, clearly declaring Protestant, Jewish, atheist Poles, and others to be second-class citizens.

America is unique. Aside from the Native American population, we are all immigrants, whether by choice or by force. The recency of our arrival on these shores is only a matter of degree, and as the generations pass, our ethnic origins become less important. In its first century of existence, when it was populated largely by white Anglo-Saxons, the United States was only a small country with great aspirations, much like Canada, Australia, New Zealand, and others that have broken free from Britain. We became the greatest country in the world in our second century, *after* immigration, *after* desegregation, *after* women became enfranchised. We became the great America *because* of our diversity, not *despite* our diversity.

The Ten Commandments

Without separation of church and state, it will be difficult for the United States to continue in our status as leader of the free world. Yet the wall of separation gets challenged at every turn, particularly during elections, when politicians not only wrap themselves in the flag but in the cross as well. During the 1984 presidential campaign, Walter Mondale found it necessary to remind Ronald Regan that in the United States the president, unlike the queen of England, is "not the defender of the faith" but rather the defender of the constitution. At that point I had written a column called "the Ten Commendments for Politicians." A Commendment is something between a commandment and an amendment. They were:

1. Do not claim God as a member of your party or that God is on your side of an issue.
2. Do not publicly proclaim your religious devotion, affiliation, and practices, or attack those of your opponents.
3. Do not denounce those who differ with you about the proper role of religion in public life as antireligious or intolerant of religion.
4. Do not surround your political campaign with religious trappings or symbols.
5. Honor and respect the diversity of this country, recalling that many Americans came to these shores to escape the tyranny of enforced religious uniformity and, more recently, enforced antireligious uniformity.
6. Do not seek the support of religious leaders who impose religious obligations on members of their faith to support or oppose particular candidates.
7. Do not accuse those who reject formal religion of immorality. Recall that some of our nation's greatest leaders did not accept formal or even informal religion.
8. Do not equate morality and religion. Although some great moral teachers were religious, some great moral sinners also acted in the name of religion.
9. When there are political as well as religious dimensions to an issue, focus on the political ones during the campaign.
10. Remember that every belief is in a minority somewhere, and act as if your belief were the least popular.

I wish that instead of the Ten Commandments, the first ten amendments to our constitution would be put up in schools. As demonstrated in the diverse views outlined in this publication, even the most basic issues of separation are not universally accepted in this country. In 1987 Judge W. Brevard Hand of Alabama ruled that each state may establish its own religion, just as it may pick its own bird, flower, song, and motto. Edwin Meese, who was then attorney general, agreed with him. He took out his copy of the constitution and showed it to a friend of mine who was then at the Justice Department and said, "*Show me* where it says that states cannot establish a religion. All it says is that *Congress* may not establish a religion."

And, of course, historically Hand and Meese were absolutely right—if you stop the constitution at about the time of the Civil War. The First Amendment of the constitution was not intended to restrict state establishment of religion, and several states did not establish particular branches of Protestantism as their official state religion. As late as the middle of the nineteenth century, Jews, Turks, infidels, and other non-Christians were precluded from holding office and swearing oaths as witnesses. Catholics, too, did not have full equality during the early period of our nation. Indeed, anti-Catholic bigotry was rampant among our early citizens and political leaders, including Jefferson and Adams. As Walker discusses, it was not until 1961 the U.S. Supreme Court deemed it unconstitutional for states to prevent nonbelievers from holding office or testifying as a witness, and yet several states still have such laws on their books.[10]

When Judge Learned Hand was asked, "What will people do who have no religion or who belonged to a minority religion?" he replied, "A member of a religious minority will simply have to develop a thinker skin if the state establishment offends him." When I saw the statement, I wrote a column in which I gave Hand the "Ayatollah Khomeini Award" for attempting to divide the country along religious lines and described the implications of his view. In Massachusetts, for example, the struggle for official recognition would be between Catholics and Protestants. Where I grew up, in Brooklyn, the religious warfare would be among the Jews. In Utah, Mormonism would prevail; in California, the various cults and fringe religious groups might unite to present a common front. Even if a state settled on Protestantism, which denomination would be the official one? Fortunately the Supreme Court of the United States reversed Judge Hand, characterizing his views as "remarkable," which is a judicial euphemism for "ridiculous." But we are still, even with the U.S. Supreme Court, seeing some very dangerous trends. The current Supreme Court may not be as protective of the wall of separation as were previous courts.

The trend of *broadening* religion in order to make it more acceptable has not gained momentum. The Supreme Court has upheld the constitutionality of placing a crèche scene in a Christmas display, as long as a sufficient number of plastic reindeer and other accoutrements of secularity are included. In Pittsburgh, Pennsylvania, the city sponsored a Christmas tree, a crèche, and a Hanukkah menorah. Significantly, as the court described it, the menorah was placed in "the shadow of the Christmas tree." The court decided that if displays were allowed to include a Christmas tree, they should also allow a Hanukkah menorah. A lot of people in the Jewish community were disarmed by that decision because it gave them standing alongside Christians. But giving special status to religion is only the first step on the short road to tearing down the wall of separation between church and state.

The second step is for the state, once it says religion is to be preferred over nonreligion, to *define* what religion means. You then have to define what is *true* religion and what is *real* religion. I defended Jim Bakker for principled reasons related to that. In imposing his 45-year sentence, U.S. District Judge Robert D. Potter of North Carolina said, "*We* [pointing to himself] who have a *true* religion are offended by those who are charlatans and have a false religion."

It is not the role of a judge in America to distinguish between true and false religions. Judge Potter is a very religious Catholic and belongs to a church whose doctrines often conflict with those of the evangelical movement. The very idea of judges in this country imposing their own religious values on a sentencing process is un-American. And it is intolerable to the continued separation of church and state.

There is another threat to separation that can be characterized as "backdoor establishment." What happens is this: When a majority religion like mainstream Christianity seeks state help in promoting its religious doctrines at Christmas, the courts sometimes say, "Christianity really is the majority religion in this country; therefore, when something happens in the name of Christianity, it's really secular, because so many Americans are Christians. Christmas is a secular holiday. But if a smaller religion were to seek aid from the state, since members are only a minority, then it would clearly be an establishment."

This is *precisely* the opposite of what the framers of our constitution had in mind. The framers were not fearful of small, fringe, minority religions; they were fearful of the *majority* religion.

The late Chief Justice William Rehnquist expressed this view. In 1986, a chaplain in the air force named Dr. S. Simcha Goldman, who was a psychologist, wore a yarmulke to court when testifying in a case. He was disciplined for violating uniform regulations. The Supreme Court did not uphold his claim of religious observance, because to do so would establish religion. Justice Rehnquist, who worried about the establishment of Orthodox Judaism in America, had no problems about the establishment of Christianity. He also participated in the crèche decision, saying crèches were constitutional on public land. But which poses a greater danger of establishment: Christian crèches on public land or a yarmulke on the head of an individual?

Conclusion

These are some of the problems that persist. Fundamentalism, tragically, is pervasive throughout the world today. There is almost *no* part of the world that is not seeing an increase in fundamentalism—in know-nothingism; in "I don't want to hear, I don't want to think, I don't want to know, tell me what to do, give me marching orders, point me in the right direction and I'll go!" Nor is this rejection of reason limited to the uneducated or the ignorant. It is growing even among some sophisticated people grasping at faith to give meaning to their lives. Jefferson abhorred that approach to life and government. He believed that the Declaration of Independence declared our independence from the domination of clericalism over democracy and from the domination of faith over reason. Those who reject that kind of approach in religion, in politics, in personal life, and in law are always going to have a very difficult struggle ahead of them. They count on the possibility that the extremes within the movements have the seeds for self-destruction. But this is a dangerous approach because we are witnessing the emergence of far more intelligent, far more presentable fundamental movements throughout the world.

Every day is a new struggle for the separation of church and state. We must be willing to buck the tide of majority intolerance and to struggle against religious bigotry because we share Jefferson's vision. We know what losing this battle would do to America. We *know* that the greatness of this country depends on its being the most heterogeneous, the most diverse country in the world. We understand the experimental nature of the American dream.

If Thomas Jefferson could observe our nation today, he would, I believe, be pleased as well as surprised. He would be pleased that the wall he deemed so essential still stands, despite so many challenges and threats to make it a theolegal nation. He would be pleased that our complex system of checks and balances—between the branches of government as well as among churches, the media, the academy, the economy, and other nongovernmental institutions—is working. He would be surprised at the increasing power of the federal government, and especially of the executive, and of the relative weakness of the states. He would be surprised, most of all, at how his own views were being hijacked by the Religious Right in an effort to use him as a battering ram against the wall of separation between church and state that was so central to his theory of governance. He would regard this deliberate distortion as a form of civil blasphemy that should be confronted in the marketplace of ideas and soundly rejected.

Notes

1. Excerpts from *Blasphemy: How the Religious Right is hijacking our Declaration of Independence*, introduction, chapter 2, and conclusion (Hoboken, NJ: John Wiley & Sons, Inc., 2007).
2. David Barton, *The Myth of the Separation: What Is the Correct Relationship between Church and State? A Revealing Look at What the Founders and Early Courts Really Said* (Aledo, TX: Wallbuilder Press, 2002), p. 218.

3. Ibid, p. 220.

4. Jon Meacham, *American Gospel: God, the Founding Fathers, and the Making of a Nation* (New York: Random House, 2006), pp. 232–233.

5. George F. Will, "God of Our Fathers: Brooke Allen Argues That the Founding Fathers Did Not Establish a Christian Nation," review of *Moral Minority, Our Skeptical Founding Fathers* by Brooke Allen *New York Times Book Review,* October 22, 2006.

6. Jon Meacham, *American Gospel: God, the Founding Fathers, and the Making of a Nation* (New York: Random House, 2006), p. 109.

7. Dennis Prager, "America, Not Keith Ellison, Decides What Book a Congressman Takes His Oath On," Townhall.com, November 28, 2006, www.townhall.com/columnists/DennisPrager/2006/11/28/america,_not_keith_ellison,_decides_what_book_a_congressman_takes_his_oath_on (accessed December 19, 2006).

8. Roy Moore, "Muslim Ellison Should Not Sit in Congress," WorldNetDaily Exclusive Commentary, December 13, 2006, http://www.wnd.com/news/article.asp?ARTICLE_ID=53345 (accessed December 19, 2006).

9. Rachel L. Swarns, "Congressman Criticizes Election of Muslim," *New York Times,* December 21, 2006.

10. See Introduction for Walker's discussion of *Torcaso v. Watkins,* 367 U.S. 488 (1961) and his reference to laws that go against this ruling as noted in eight states: Arkansas (Constitution, Article 19 Section 1); Maryland (Bill of Rights, Article 36); North Carolina (Constitution Article 6 Section 8); Pennsylvania (Declaration of Rights, Article 1, Section 4); South Carolina (Constitution, Article 4 Section 2); Tennessee (Bill of Rights Article 9); and Texas (Constitution, Article I, Section 4).

5

Religious Judges

Edwin J. Greenlee

Religion is important in the lives of many Americans: members of the judicial branch of government are no exception. This chapter looks at the religious dimension of the lives and decisions of judges. Recognizing the way in which strongly held religious values can influence judicial decision-making on important social issues, like abortion rights, the adoption of children by gay couples, and the death penalty, prominent nominees to high judicial office are often questioned about their religious beliefs and how these beliefs will or will not influence their decision-making. Is it realistic to expect religiously devout judges to leave their beliefs outside the courtroom door? Does the American judicial process produce fair and unbiased results for litigants when judges incorporate their religious values and beliefs in their decision-making process? Does acknowledging the role of religious values in the judicial process help or hinder American democracy?

One very dramatic and colorful ritual celebration of the relationship between judicial and legislative officials and religion is found in the contemporary revival of the "red mass." The "red mass" has medieval origins and was intended to ask God's blessing and the inspiration of the Holy Spirit at the annual opening of parliament. More recently, it has been celebrated in urban centers throughout the United States, most spectacularly in Washington, DC, where prominent Roman Catholic prelates preach and celebrate the Eucharist, and most justices of the U.S. Supreme Court attend, even some of those who are not adherents of Roman Catholicism. One justice, Ruth Bader Ginsburg, attended only one mass, commenting on the highly political nature of the sermon that was preached. The red mass is a symbolic display of the relationship between the judiciary and organized religion. On October 5, 2008, five of the U.S. Supreme Court justices, Chief

Justice John Roberts and Justices Scalia, Kennedy, Thomas, and Breyer, attended the mass. A photograph of the event on the *Washington Times* website featured Chief Justice John Roberts greeting Donald W. Wuerl, Archbishop of Washington, at the door of the Cathedral of St. Matthew the Apostle.

There are mechanisms within the American judicial system, such as the Judicial Code of Professional Responsibility, to deal with potential conflicts that arise when judges holding strong religious beliefs fail to act impartially toward litigants in cases that involve issues at odds with the key religious values that judges may hold. Finally, the statements and reflections of religiously devout judges and justices show how members of the judiciary believe that strongly held religious commitment can coexist with judicial neutrality and be a social good.[1]

This discussion of religiously devout judges is situated within the context of a growing awareness that a strict separation of religious from other values, values which influence decision-making, is not realistic and, in a sense, impinges on the free exercise of religion by members of the judiciary.[2] Since that is the case, the question then is how, in a democracy that is religiously diverse, can we allow members of the government such as judges to take their religious values with them into the courtroom while at the same time requiring them to apply the rule of law fairly and without bias to hot-button social issues.

Like other individuals, judges hold strong beliefs and these beliefs are often informed by their religious experiences and beliefs. The question that must be asked is how judges can hold their deeply held religious beliefs in dynamic tension with the requirement for a judge to be fair and unbiased while dealing with a litigant, particularly when the subject matter of the case is one over which American society is deeply divided, such as the right of a woman to freely choose to have an abortion or the right of gay or lesbian citizens to have custody of their own children.

In a very few instances, judges openly use religion in making their decisions, finding that American law is based upon Judeo-Christian values and, as a consequence, thinking that it is reasonable for religiously observant judges to base their decisions on these values. Annette Mathis notes that in denying gays the right to act as parents, Chief Justice Moore of the Alabama Supreme Court noted in his 2002 opinion that he was basing his judgment partially upon "the law of nature and nature's God as understood by men through reason, but aided by direct revelation found in the Holy Scriptures."[3] Examining Moore's opinion further, Mathis found that Moore "quoted an Old Testament verse calling homosexual conduct 'an abomination.' He concluded that his position was justified because homosexual conduct violates not only common law but also natural and revealed law." This is a clear instance where an important right, the right to the custody of one's own children, was determined by a judge applying his notion of right and wrong directly upon his reading and his own conservative understanding of the Christian tradition. The example of Moore may be viewed as an outlier, but at the time of his decision to deny gay individuals the right to act as parents he was a state supreme court Chief Justice, a rather prominent member of the American judiciary.

While Chief Justice Moore was removed from office in 2003 by Alabama's Court of the Judiciary, he continues to blur his religious beliefs with his political aspirations. In 2010 Moore made a second run for the governorship of Alabama. His platform was congruent with the beliefs he articulated on the bench. If elected governor, under his goals captioned "Morality," Moore promised to:

> Restore prayer and the acknowledgement of God in our schools and public institutions; oppose gambling, prostitution, and pornography while ensuring that traditional marriage between one man and one woman is preserved; and encourage pro-life legislation and stop all state funding and assistance to abortion clinics in Alabama.[4]

Kent Greenawalt has offered a comprehensive examination of the issue of religion and political judgments and sees several potential stances. The first, which he terms the "exclusive position," holds that political decisions in a democracy should not be made on the basis of sectarian views or appeals to external authorities such as the Bible, but rather "should be made on grounds that are shared premises of [democracy . . .] and on forms of justification and ways of determining facts that are accessible to all citizens."[5] Twenty-first century America is not a simple Judeo-Christian nation, but one made up of citizens who adhere to a diversity of religious and spiritual beliefs. (There are Fundamentalist Christians, Evangelical Christians, and Roman Catholics as well as liberal Episcopalians, Reformed and Reconstructionist Jews, Unitarian Universalists, and those with no religious value system whatsoever, in the American population.) The exclusive position would require, in this instance, judges to eschew religious arguments drawn from any particular religious tradition and instead rely upon arguments and determinations that are acceptable to citizens that adhere to a wide array of religious affiliations found in contemporary American society.

The second position that Greenawalt lays out is called the "inclusive position." This position sees decisions being made on the basis of whatever seems most reliable to the individual decision maker. Greenawalt notes, "If a respected religious authority like the Pope, or a divinely inspired text, or one's personal sense of how God relates to human beings, suggests that we should help those who are less fortunate, why should that not count for our position on welfare reform and medical insurance? People do not feel whole if they try to divorce their deepest sources of insight from their political stances." Yet such a stance would inject a strongly sectarian religious component into the judicial decision-making process.

While Greenawalt sees ordinary citizens properly making use of their religious values in making some political decisions, he sees a more limited role for religious arguments in the case of judges. Greenawalt writes that:

> Judges may examine familiar religious sources to show the community's attitudes toward a practice or its deep moral assumptions, and judges occasionally employ traditional religious stories to illustrate a point, but these are not reliance on religious grounds in the sense that I mean. Although judges rarely candidly state the strength of competing arguments, they rely on arguments they believe should have force for all judges. In our culture, this excludes arguments based on particular religious premises.

It appears that the chief justice of the Alabama Supreme Court, in the case of a child custody determination for gay citizens, did not demonstrate this type of restraint and engaged in a more broadly based examination of the issue and its resolution.

Stephen Carter of Yale Law School has also addressed the question of the "religiously devout judge." Carter contrasts the notion of the objective judge with the "morally sensitive judge," a judge who engages in moral reflection and uses her personal moral knowledge in making a judgment. Carter does not find that judges can use totally objective ways of reaching decisions, but rather at times draw upon personal moral reflection and, in the case of religiously devout judges, this moral reflection will include their religious beliefs. This is not a call for judges to use their religious beliefs as the basis for making a judicial decision, but acknowledges the way in which everyone who espouses religious beliefs uses these as a background in their decision-making process. Looking at the models proposed by Greenawalt, Carter sees that the religiously devout judge may legitimately take her religious beliefs into the courtroom and make use of them in the process of deliberation, but *not* when it comes to writing the opinion. The judge will justify her opinion "in accordance with a set of professional norms [that is] said to be a disciplining force on judges who might otherwise let their personal values [whether drawn from religious beliefs or from other sources] run rampant."[6] Carter sees safeguards in the judicial system as preventing religious or other bias from harming litigants. However, Carter's stance can be criticized as giving too much credence to the ability of systemic safeguards to prevent bias from subverting the judicial process.

Legal scholars have also studied the decisions made by judges and looked for patterns of correlation with the religious belief that they espoused. Mark Greenlee argues that while "religious beliefs exert a powerful directing influence upon the sentencing decisions of judges and that judges should not be barred from referring to religious texts such as the Bible, Talmud or Quran as they justify their decisions, so long as they act in accord with the norms of the judicial office they hold such as establishing justice, acting with integrity, remaining impartial, considering the arguments of the parties, basing decisions upon the admitted evidence, exercising discretion within the bounds of fairness, and accounting for the applicable law. Within these limits, judges should be allowed to put their faith into practice on the bench."[7] In this instance, while religious values may have an influence on sentencing decisions, these decisions will be fair in the sense that they are within the limits set by neutral legal principles. Again, safeguards within the legal system will set the parameters for the decisions that religiously devout judges render whether or not they make use of their personal religious value system. But doesn't this amount to using religious reasons to reach a decision which, in theory at least, should be similar to one that would be rendered by a nonreligious judge, following the usual norms of judicial behavior as stated above by Mark Greenlee?

Jake Garn provides an interesting discussion of an attempt to disqualify a federal judge to hear the case of *Idaho v. Freeman* because of his religious affiliation. The judge was a member of the Church of Jesus Christ of Latter Day Saints and held an official church office as a regional representative of the church. The case, filed in 1979, involved a challenge to the attempt of Idaho to rescind its ratification of the Equal Rights Amendment (ERA) and an attempt to extend the deadline for ratification. In this instance, the Mormon Church actively opposed the ratification of the ERA and the extension of the deadline for its ratification. The motion to disqualify the judge was not granted, and the Carter administration declined to appeal that decision even though the Motion to Disqualify that was filed by the U.S. Justice Department alleged bias and an appearance of bias based upon the judge's official organization role, not merely his membership, in the Mormon Church.[8]

Pryor presents a more general overview of how his strongly held Catholic faith informs his work as a judge. He writes that "Religious faith properly informs me, as a judge, in my fidelity to my public duty in at least four ways: in my understanding of my oath of office, in my moral duties to obey lawful authority, and in my responsibility to work both diligently and honestly. Each of these ways is motivational; that is, each concerns the judge's duty to perform his work well. None involved using religious doctrine to decide a case in conflict with the law."[9] Pryor's religious beliefs are not a part of his judicial decision-making, but rather inform his commitment to professionally carrying out his duties as a judge. In this instance, professional standards, ethics, and precedents are used in deciding cases, not religious values.

Discussing the few instances when a religiously devout judge could potentially find his religious duties at odds with his judicial obligations, Pryor also looks to systemic safeguards. What happens when a religiously devout judge has a conflict between legally determined responsibilities and his moral judgment? Using the example of the teaching of the late Pope John Paul II, that members of the legal profession must avoid material cooperation with regard to divorce, Pryor writes that

> although the teaching of the [Catholic] Church about material cooperation makes it unlikely that a federal judge will proximately cooperate with evil or cause scandal, there is a simple remedy when that problem arises. The judge should recuse himself. If the judge cannot perform his legal duty, without violating his moral duty, then the judge must honor both duties by recusal. The judge honors the law by refusing to disobey it, as that would violate his oath, and the judge honors his faith by avoiding cooperation with evil, as that would violate his conscience. The judge cannot be impartial to his moral duty, and Canon 3 [of the Code of Judicial Conduct] requires a judge to "disqualify him or herself in a proceeding in which the judge's impartiality might reasonably be questioned." The law acknowledges that judges, in rare cases, should step aside.

One concern with recusal is the great amount of discretion that resides with the judge making the decision to grant or deny the request. A request for recusal leaves the initial decision as to whether or not a conflict exists with the trial judge. If the parties to an action disagree with the decision, they would have to bear the cost of an appeal. Wendell Griffen, a state appeals court judge and Baptist pastor, argues that there is an important role for religious values in judicial decision-making and that this is a social benefit that would be lost if judges were prevented from engaging in an

> open and uninhibited debate of various sources of moral knowledge. It also dehumanizes religiously devout judges by requiring them to either abandon the role of religious faith in their concept of moral knowledge or falsely mask the operation of that faith in the deliberative process. We ought to

honestly consider the way that religious values can operate within the decision-making process consistent with our views of pluralism and religious tolerance, tempered by our concern for the Establishment Clause to the First Amendment of the Federal Constitution.[10]

Griffen's stance faces the major challenge of fairness in the midst of a religiously pluralistic nation. The role of religion in the area of judicial decision-making is complex. Most of the examples that we encounter posit a judge holding a religious position that is characterized as conservative: a Roman Catholic or Evangelical judge who opposes adoption by gay parents or the right of abortion or is eager to impose the death penalty. America's religious environment is also made up of a variety of religiously devout individuals, some of whom are judges, who could be characterized as progressive. These could be individuals who belong to more liberal religious traditions that are concerned with social justice issues, such as Reform and Reconstructionist Jews, Unitarian Universalists, Quakers, and members of the United Church of Christ, as well as members of a variety of morally conservative religious groups who do not adhere to the positions of their church hierarchy or leadership. Stressing a personal, individual understanding of their religion, liberal Roman Catholics, Evangelical Christians, or Mormons may disagree with the official positions of their churches on key social policy issues. A religiously devout judge from any of these traditions or positions could hold diametrically opposed values to those of a fellow judge who holds her conservative religious values just as ardently.

The notion of total objectivity is not a realistic characterization of what happens with the very human participants in the act of reaching a judicial decision. Also, religious values are an important part of the human experience, and it is detrimental to the individual and to society to exile these from the political sphere. One problem, however, is that the term "religious" is often used synonymously with the term conservative. We must appreciate the wide spectrum of religious values and how these are expressed with regard to judges on particular social issues. Religious values can make religiously devout individuals support marriage equality or oppose it. Both are strongly held, religiously informed positions.

In terms of the judicial process, there are large numbers of institutional controls: precedent; the availability of appeal to a higher court; appropriate rules of procedure and evidence that govern what happens in a courtroom; and rules of professional conduct that also govern a judge's behavior. All of these aim to minimize "bias," be it religious or otherwise, in the judicial process. Thus, the institution of the judiciary itself offers many opportunities to challenge apparent or real bias. The degree to which institutional controls actually prevent bias from distorting a judicial process that is predicated upon fairness to all parties is open to question. In the present system, this is the only major check that is available.

Finally there is the idea that moral thought, often informed by religious experience and belief, is a part of life that cannot be artificially excised when judges enter the courtroom. Better to acknowledge and appreciate it, to encourage its expression by those of a wide variety of religious beliefs, to keep a cautious eye for bias on the part of judges from a variety of sources, and to encourage those who hold a progressive religious value system to participate as fully in the process as do those whose values are more conservative.

In terms of the various stances with respect to religion and state which Walker sets out in his introduction, the separatist view, which is: "skeptical about officials infusing theology into legal rationale and seek to dissociate religion and state, thereby assuring that no God rules," has great appeal in the case of the judiciary. A clear demarcation between our basic system of secular law and religious values offers the best bulwark against the distortions of religious bias in judging. It establishes a bright line test and does not rely upon the judicial system policing itself to prevent bias. However, from the examples that I discussed above, judges hold religious values and at times these play some role in their decision-making. Attempting to enforce a strong separation of religion and state may prove difficult in the case of judicial officials, but it offers the best solution to preventing religious bias from distorting the fairness that America's judicial system requires.

Notes

1. Conkle, Daniel O. "Religiously Devout Judges: Issues of Personal Integrity and Public Benefit." *Marquette Law Review* 81 (1998) pp. 523–531.
2. Beckwith, Francis J. "Taking Theology Seriously: The Status of Religious Beliefs of Judicial Nominees for the Federal Bench." *Notre Dame Journal of Law, Ethics and Public Policy* 20 (2006) pp. 455–470.
3. Mathis, Annette Bulger. "Judges, Thou Shalt Not Use Thine Own Religion in Thy Opinions." *Mississippi College Law Review* 23 (2004) pp. 131–155.
4. Judge Moore for Governor website, http://www.moore2010.com/ (accessed October 24, 2009).
5. Greenawalt, Kent. "Religion and American Political Judgments." *Wake Forest Law Review* 36 (2001) pp. 401–421. See also Greenawalt, Kent. "Religiously Based Judgments and Discourse in Political Life." *St. John's Journal of Legal Commentary* 22 (2007) pp. 445–491.
6. Carter, Stephen L. "The Religiously Devout Judge." *Notre Dame Law Review* 64 (1989) pp. 932–944.

7. Greenlee, Mark B. "Faith on the Bench: The Role of Religious Belief in the Criminal Sentencing Decisions of Judges." *University of Dayton Law Review* 26 (2000) pp. 1–40.

8. Garn, Jake and Lincoln C. Oliphant. "Disqualification of Federal Judges under 28 U.S.C. Section 455(a): Some Observations on and Objections to an Attempt by the United States Department of Justice to Disqualify a Judge on the Basis of His Religion and Church Position." *Harvard Journal of Law and Public Policy* 4 (1981) pp. 1–60.

9. Pryor, William H. "The Religious Faith and Judicial Duty of an American Catholic Judge." *Yale Law and Policy Review* 24 (2006) pp. 347–362.

10. Griffen, Wendell L. "The Case for Religious Values in Judicial Decision-Making." *Marquette Law Review* 81 (1998) pp. 513–532.

6

Religious Presidents

Mark J. Rozell

Although long ignored or at least marginalized as a factor in U.S. political development, since the 1970s with the rise of the evangelical right, analysts have recognized religion as a key variable. In the 1970s, in part as a reaction to the perception of cultural decline and also to the Supreme Court decision of *Roe v. Wade* (1973) that legalized abortion, conservative religious leaders began to mobilize evangelical and born-again Christians into a powerful political movement. By the 1980s the movement known as the "Christian Right" had become a fixture on the national political scene and has remained an important force ever since. The movement may have achieved the height of its influence during the presidency of George W. Bush, and certainly no president ever had been so committed to the views of conservative evangelicals.

Although the rise of the Christian Right has dominated the scholarly discourse on religion and politics in the United States during the past three decades, progressive political leaders increasingly are making successful faith-based electoral and policy appeals. In the post–George W. Bush era, with a Democratic president who similarly is a man of deep religious faith, the terms of the discourse may be changing, as no longer will the Christian Right command what used to seem like a near monopoly of attention in analyses of the intersection of faith and politics in the United States.

This essay traces the evolution of the relationship between prominent national political leaders and faith in the period of the 1970s to the present. Although much of the essay traces the rise and influence of the evangelical right—still the major story in this area of the past three decades—it also describes the countermovement by progressive political leaders and analyzes their prospects for success at employing the politics of faith. Throughout this chapter, it is clear how the concept of a theolegal nation applies to the study of religious-based political movements and religious political leaders in the U.S. Conservative and progressive movements. Republican and Democratic leaders alike resort to religious worldviews to justify policy positions and seek public support.

Carter, Reagan, and the Evangelical Uprising

It was a socially progressive Democrat, Jimmy Carter, who played the initial key role in mobilizing many evangelical Christians into national politics. The former Georgia governor ran for president in 1976 as a proud born-again Christian, and as one who was not hesitant to wear his religiosity out in public. Although many observers expressed discomfort with Carter's open religious commitment, throughout the campaign for the Democratic nomination it became clear that he had strong appeal among some evangelical voters, especially in the South, and he was able to successfully translate that support into some surprising primary victories.

As he shocked the political world with his unlikely victory for the Democratic nomination for president, Carter brought discussion of the faith of political leaders into the mainstream discourse. And his candidacy especially highlighted the potential for a major new force in U.S. politics led by an energized and large evangelical community. *Newsweek* magazine thus declared 1976 "The Year of the Evangelical."[1] Yet not all were comfortable with Carter's public expressions of faith, and more than a few observers treated the topic with bewilderment. Referring to Carter's born-again status, a prominent NBC news anchor, John Chancellor, declared: "Incidentally, we have checked this out. Being 'born again' is not a bizarre experience or the voice of God from the mountaintop. It's a fairly common experience known to millions of Americans—especially if you're a Baptist."[2] Describing a campaign incident at which Carter described his born-again experience, a reporter explained, "an awkward hush fell over the room" as "reporters lowered their eyes to their note pads. Everyone was embarrassed—except the candidate."[3]

Carter ultimately won the general election by a narrow Electoral College margin against Republican President Gerald R. Ford, and a key to Carter's victory was the support he pulled in the South and among the evangelical voters. Yet many southern evangelicals who had been previously apolitical rallied to his candidacy and then eventually rejected Carter because of their disappointment with his social policies. Carter opposed federal financial aid for parochial schools. He also opposed prayer in public schools, and he supported federal taxation of church properties rather than merely taxing church buildings. Most importantly, Carter said he personally opposed abortion, but he did not support a constitutional amendment to ban the procedure. To the conservative evangelicals, Carter's personal morality was not enough. From their standpoint, his policies were wrong.[4]

Partially because of Carter's electoral success, a group of secular conservative leaders saw an opportunity. Such noted "New Right" leaders as Howard Phillips, Richard Viguerie, and Paul Weyrich believed that if they could build a coalition of secular and religious conservative groups, that would make the Republicans the dominant party for years. They reached out to the prominent Virginia televangelist Jerry Falwell, who formed a national political organization called the Moral Majority. They convinced Republican candidate Ronald Reagan to make direct appeals to conservative evangelicals on the belief that, if successfully mobilized, this group could deliver millions of new votes to the *Grand Old Party*—the Republican Party (GOP). Reagan did exactly that and thus the Christian Right became firmly entrenched in the GOP.[5]

The 1980 Republican Party landslide surprised most observers, and Falwell claimed that his Moral Majority had helped to mobilize for the GOP nearly four million new evangelical voters. Falwell became an instant major player in U.S. politics, and the rise of the Christian Right was the big story of the newly resurgent GOP. Although Reagan did not forcefully push the social issues agenda in his two terms as president, the Christian Right had nonetheless achieved legitimacy by having a voice in his administration. And the increasingly Republican leanings of evangelical voters in the 1980s were changing the nature of electoral politics in the United States. Most significantly, the traditionally solid Democratic South had began to transition to a competitive two-party region, with primarily white conservative evangelicals leading the march toward the GOP.[6]

Carter's role in mobilizing voters on the basis of faith-commitment made sense to most observers. A deeply religious man who attended services regularly throughout his life and taught Sunday school classes for many years, Carter spoke comfortably about the role of faith to his public life because that came naturally to him. Reagan's role in mobilizing the Christian Right was more complicated because the fortieth president—divorced, avoided attending religious services as president—did not seem so openly pious or a likely person to mobilize faith-based voters.

Yet whether Reagan was genuinely religious or not did not seem to matter. The former movie actor and brilliant orator had the rare ability to communicate with just about any audience and create a believable sense of togetherness, that he was one of them or that he understood and empathized with them. When Reagan spoke before conservative evangelical audiences, he moved people to see in him a man genuinely committed to their social policy agenda. Indeed, Reagan campaigned in favor of a constitutional amendment to ban abortion and another to allow spoken prayer in public schools.

Reagan today is remembered favorably by conservative evangelicals who appreciate his major role in mobilizing the Christian Right. Whereas other Republican politicians were hesitant to embrace the causes of conservative evangelicals, Reagan spoke without hesitation or embarrassment about his support for the pro-life agenda. Nonetheless, at the time that Reagan was preparing to leave office after two terms as president, there was substantial discontent among conservative evangelicals over the lack of real social policy action from his administration.

Joining the Mainstream

In response to this discontent, Pat Robertson launched a bid for the 1988 Republican nomination for president. Although Vice President George H. W. Bush had shifted from a prochoice position to support Reagan's social conservative views, including a constitutional amendment banning abortion, conservative evangelicals did not trust that Bush was genuinely committed to the pro-life agenda. Robertson's candidacy caused quite a stir when the pastor won more votes than Bush in the Iowa GOP caucuses. But ultimately Robertson lost badly to Bush, securing only 35 pledged delegates to the GOP convention after spending over 36 million dollars on his campaign.

On the Democratic side, another prominent religious leader, Jesse Jackson, sought the Democratic presidential nomination for the second time. Jackson had sought the nomination unsuccessfully in 1984, but in so doing he attracted a considerable following. In 1988 Jackson won several key primaries and the second largest bloc of delegates to the Democratic nominating convention. Jackson sought to build broad-based support, what he termed a "Rainbow Coalition" across racial, ethnic, and religious lines, but he ultimately drew his support predominantly from black Protestants. Similarly, Robertson had sought to build a diverse ecumenical base of support, but he ultimately drew votes from white conservative evangelicals.

Although he did not fare as strongly as Jackson in seeking votes, even in resounding defeat Robertson's campaign had the much larger impact on U.S. politics. The *700 Club* host had mobilized a large number of young, previously apolitical Pentecostal and charismatic Christians into politics. He also converted his historically large contributor list into a national grassroots political organization, the Christian Coalition. Just a year after the Moral Majority had gone bankrupt and disbanded, Robertson began to build what would become the most recognized and influential faith-based political organization in the United States for the next decade. Robertson sought to avoid the widely acknowledged mistakes of the Moral Majority–led phase of the Christian Right, during which leading figures such as Falwell were often more likely to alienate many voters than they were to build mainstream acceptance for their movement.

For the Christian Coalition, Robertson chose as its political director Ralph Reed, a young political operative who could give a fresh look to the Christian Right. Unlike Falwell and some of the other early leaders of the movement, Reed could speak the secular language of politics as well as he could communicate with fellow evangelicals. The Christian Coalition made a major effort to build state, county, and local organizations around the country. Reed recruited state and local leaders whose backgrounds were in business, interest group politics, or civic activity—a major shift from the Moral Majority strategy of recruiting local pastors.

This shift in strategy enabled the Christian Coalition to build a broadly ecumenical organization. The national lobbying office included people from a variety of religious backgrounds, and at one point its legislative director was Jewish. Research suggests that state and local chapters in many parts of the country were similarly diverse.[7] Leaders and supporters of the Christian Coalition may not have agreed on religious doctrine, but they did agree to work together to support pro-life Republican candidates for public office. The organization worked hard at reaching out to social conservatives from a variety of faith traditions, with a special effort to recruit pro-life Catholics. Not all of these efforts were successful, but they did evidence recognition of the importance of coalition-building at the grassroots.

The Christian Right in the 1990s had increasingly become a powerful movement, in large part because its leaders had learned to play politics much smarter than before. Reed, who himself had once compared his political tactics to guerilla warfare and boasted that he ambushed opponents and left them in body bags, recanted the use of such language and wrote to supporters that "phrases like 'religious war' and 'take over' play to a stereotype of evangelicals as intolerant." He urged followers to avoid using threatening-sounding language: "We must adopt strategies of persuasion, not domination."[8] Reed was not alone in this sentiment. Studies of the Christian Right in the 1990s found the rhetorical appeals of leaders to sound more moderate, the issue-appeals more broad-based, and the organizations of the movement had built more broadly ecumenical bases and strong grassroots networks than the first wave of the movement in the 1970s–1980s.[9]

An example of the increased pragmatism of the Christian Right at that time was the recognition by many leaders that abortion rights can be more effectively reduced by focusing on secondary restrictions: parental notification, parental consent, no taxpayer funding, no late-term abortions, mandatory waiting periods and counseling for those seeking abortion, and restrictions on what health-care professionals and educators can tell young women about abortion options. Many of these issue positions are popular with voters outside of the Christian Right. When the Christian Right position on an issue has dovetailed with broader public sentiment, the movement has had some policy successes at the state level.

Christian Right organizations largely succeeded at reaching their core constituency and convincing as many as possible of the need to get involved in politics. As these new activists entered the political world and many participated in training sessions and local political organizations, they became more knowledgeable about how to mobilize and to be effective.[10]

Political organizing led social conservative activists to come into contact more frequently with other, primarily GOP-based, constituencies. Studies of Christian Right activists in the GOP in the 1990s showed that the Christian Coalition had achieved its goals of bringing social conservatives into the mainstream of the party and forging a broad-based coalition of social and secular conservatives. Pro-gun rights and antitax activists did not share the same commitment to social issues as the religious conservatives in the party, but these groups were willing to come together to support each other's favored candidates. In many cases, religious conservative leaders and activists worked for the elections of moderate GOP nominees, with the understanding that such loyalty to the party despite policy differences would be rewarded with support from the moderates for future social conservative candidates and issues.[11]

Despite these successes, frustration abounded in the Christian Right. Following Reagan, the George H.W. Bush administration did very little to advance the causes of the movement. Strong disaffection with Bush on the Right led to the 1992 GOP nomination challenge by commentator Pat Buchanan, who succeeded in attracting some substantial support from conservative evangelicals. Although he won renomination, the challenge from the Right had weakened Bush politically and he ultimately lost his reelection bid to Democratic nominee Bill Clinton. The electoral victories of Clinton in 1992 and 1996 were significant setbacks to the Christian Right.

Although despised by the Christian Right, Bill Clinton professed a strong commitment to his Southern Baptist heritage. As president, he regularly attended religious services, sought counsel from a spiritual adviser, promised a "New Covenant" with the American people, and regularly infused his speeches with religious rhetoric, as noted in Chapter 10. Perhaps surprising, one scholarly study in 2004 found that Clinton invoked Christ in his public utterances more often than did his successor George W. Bush.[12] Yet, it was Clinton's strong support for abortion rights, family planning programs, and other policy positions that made him unacceptable to conservative evangelicals. And Clinton's opponents saw his personal conduct that had led to his impeachment as evidence of a morally depraved man. Despite his personal conduct, Clinton maintained very strong popular support in the country. For many conservative evangelicals, this disconnect showcased just how far moral standards in the United States had declined.

By the late 1990s some religious conservative leaders were openly questioning whether the movement had achieved enough in two decades of active involvement to justify further political activity. The Republican Party had not delivered on its promises on the social issues agenda. Bill Clinton's political successes and high popularity proved that the culture had been "lost." Indeed, some openly speculated whether it was time to give up on politics and to go back to putting their emphasis on building institutions of their own outside of the mainstream culture.[13] The 2000 presidential campaign thus became a key turning point for the Christian Right, as several GOP candidates sought to energize the movement by promising a serious commitment to the social issues agenda.

George W. Bush and the Christian Right

In the 2000s, the Christian Right consolidated its position within the GOP with the election and then reelection of George W. Bush as president. In the 2000 GOP nominating contest, it was strong support from religious conservative voters that gave the edge to Bush over his chief rival Senator John McCain. Like Carter before him, George W. Bush was not shy about presenting his deep religious faith before the voters. While seeking the 2000 GOP presidential nomination, Bush identified Jesus Christ as his most influential political philosopher, a comment that drew derision from many of his critics but connected him strongly to the evangelical core of his party.

As president, Bush's speeches were often infused with born-again rhetoric. For example, he referred to "wonder-working power" in his second State of the Union address, a phrase laden with meaning for born-again Christians. On the first anniversary of the September 11, 2001, terrorist attacks, Bush said: "Our prayer tonight is that God will see us through and keep us worthy . . . Hope still lights our way, and the light shines in the darkness, and the darkness will not overcome it." Many Christians immediately recognized the language as a paraphrase of the Gospel of John's famous metaphor of Christ as the light of the world.[14] When Bush gave a major address on the issue of stem-cell research, he twice referred to prayer and said, "human life is a sacred gift from our creator."[15] These are just a few of many examples of Bush's emphasis on religious rhetoric and Biblical references while president. The key is that in doing so, Bush forged a connection with many Americans who were deeply religious and conservative and who were thus the strongest core of Bush's political support.

Evangelical voters in particular overwhelmingly favored Bush over Democratic presidential nominees in 2000 and 2004, and many observers concluded that the religious "values voters" were the key constituency to Bush's 2004 reelection.[16] Exit polls showed that Bush had won 78 percent of the evangelical vote in his 2004 reelection bid. The exit polls also showed a significant difference in voting between those who regularly attend religious services and those who do not. Regular attenders of religious services voted strongly Republican whereas occasional and non-attenders voted strongly Democratic. Although many attributed Bush's victory largely to his strength among evangelicals, he also won a majority of Catholic voters and significantly increased his margins among Mainline Protestant and even Jewish voters.[17] The Bush reelection also showcased the political power of a growing political alliance between conservative evangelicals and Catholics, two religious groups that for years had not been able to work together effectively despite their common views on some social issues.

The electoral successes of George W. Bush evidenced the wisdom of a strategy of political pragmatism by the Christian Right. When Bush first ran for the GOP nomination in 2000, there were several much more socially conservative candidates in the race. Bush actually had positioned himself as, although deeply religious, also a social moderate in his issue stands. Nonetheless, prominent leaders of the Christian Right backed Bush's candidacy over those of the more conservative candidates because of the belief that he could win the presidency and the more ideologically pure candidates could not. Key support from Pat Robertson and other leading figures played prominently in the GOP nominating contest. And once elected, unlike some past successful GOP candidates for various offices, Bush did not turn his back on his supporters in the Christian Right. He appointed some prominent figures of the movement to top positions in his administration, and appointed social conservatives to federal judgeships, including on the Supreme Court. Bush issued an executive order prohibiting federal funding for international agencies that provide abortions and abortion counseling. And perhaps most important, he created the new federal Office of Faith-Based Initiatives that provided government funding of church-based programs for delivering social services.

Despite these and other gains, Christian Right leaders and activists yet again often complained that the Republican president did not place sufficient emphasis on the social issues agenda. They were especially disappointed after Bush's reelection when the president made social security reform the priority of his domestic agenda and did little to promote issues that had mobilized the "values voters" for his candidacy. Furthermore, as the Bush presidency increasingly seemed mired in a failing war effort in Iraq, conservative evangelicals became impatient with the lack of social issues initiatives. In the 2006 midterm elections, U.S. voters delivered a strong rebuke to Bush and the Republican Party by electing the Democrats as the majority party in both houses of Congress. Exit polls showed that although the GOP had still done well with evangelical voters, that group had slightly shifted its voting toward the Democratic Party, leading some observers to suggest that the evangelical alliance with the Republican Party was beginning to splinter.[18]

Several significant developments suggested the possibility of a future shifting of political loyalties among evangelicals. First, after the 2004 elections certain prominent evangelical leaders began to signal their intention to focus on issues such as environmental protection, poverty, third-world debt, and AIDS, among others. Most of the issues, identified as a new focus for evangelicals, are more commonly identified with the Democratic than the Republican Party. This effort to shift the focus of the agenda away from such core issues as abortion has caused a significant rift in the evangelical community and thus created an opportunity for Democratic politicians to exploit. The evangelical emphasis on environmental issues and the "creation care" movement have attracted the most significant attention in the past several years, as noted in Chapter 12.

Second, the Democratic Party itself started to make a serious effort to reach out to many evangelical voters who have identified with the GOP for years. Democrats much more openly than in the past talk about religion and moral values in the hope of attracting at least some of those voters who for years had only been listening to Republicans. In 2005, the year after the so-called "values vote" election, Democrat Tim Kaine won the Virginia gubernatorial election in part with direct campaign appeals to the faithful. That Kaine prevailed in a somewhat culturally conservative and heavily evangelical state that had backed Bush the year before demonstrated the potential for the Democrats to successfully mobilize voters with religious-based appeals.

Third, there is also some evidence of a generational divide among evangelicals, with the younger voters being more politically independent than their parents. Although the younger evangelicals express a broad interest in issues beyond the social agenda, they do still retain strongly pro-life views and tend to vote Republican, even though they are not as likely as their parents to identify themselves as members of the GOP.

Finally, in recent years there has been substantial political organizing by progressive religious-based groups in an effort to counteract the influence of the Christian Right. Such organizations as the Interfaith Alliance, a coalition of progressive religious leaders and activists, are engaging in their own efforts to identify and mobilize voters sympathetic to progressive political causes. Although groups on the "Religious Left" have not made the kind of major impact that the Christian Right has made, their increased energy showcases the role of religiously motivated political interests across the U.S. political spectrum.

2008 and the Obama Era: The Christian Right in Decline?

In the 2008 presidential campaign, former Baptist minister and governor of Arkansas Mike Huckabee made a strong showing in the GOP nomination contest. His candidacy drew wide attention when he won the Iowa caucuses with the overwhelming support of that state's large share of evangelical voters. Yet once again, Huckabee's candidacy showcased the limits of religious leaders seeking to build broad-based political support at the national level. Like Jackson and Robertson before him, Huckabee never built a support-base outside of his own natural constituency—in this case, white conservative evangelicals.

The eventual GOP nominee, Senator John McCain, was not a favored candidate among the evangelical core of the party. Indeed, in seeking the presidential nomination back in 2000, McCain had openly made known his disdain for certain leaders of the Christian Right, especially Falwell and Robertson. The exit-poll data from the primary contests in 2000 clearly showcased the real power of the Christian Right in the GOP nominating process. In every contested state before McCain dropped out, George W. Bush won the overwhelming majority of voters who identified themselves in the exit polls as belonging to the Christian Right movement. McCain won a majority of all non-Christian Right identifiers in every one of those states. In states with small evangelical populations such as New Hampshire, McCain won big. But in key states with substantial evangelical populations such as South Carolina and Virginia, Bush prevailed. Bush owed his victory to the Christian Right, and McCain would have to wait another day for his turn to try for the presidency again.[19]

In seeking the GOP nomination in 2008, McCain reached out to the Christian Right and sought to claim the support of movement leaders he had earlier lambasted as "evil" and "agents of intolerance."[20] He gave a high-profile address at Falwell's Liberty University in Lynchburg, Virginia, declared publicly for the first time that he was a Baptist, and made a strong push to emphasize social conservative issues. Despite these efforts, McCain did not fully win over the Christian Right until, once nominated, he chose a strongly social conservative running mate, Alaska Governor Sarah Palin. Although this vice presidential nomination helped solidify McCain's support from the Christian Right, Palin's lack of national experience and poor performances in media appearances made her an overall liability to the GOP ticket.

In the Democratic nomination campaign, the controversial sermon of a pastor almost upended the whole dynamic of the race. Jeremiah Wright, longtime pastor and religious mentor to Barack Obama, had made highly inflammatory statements in a sermon that was recorded and widely broadcast. Public outrage at Wright's comments put Obama in the uncomfortable position of addressing his relationship with the pastor and the church in Chicago where he had attended services regularly for many years. In the midst of his closely contested nomination race, Obama denounced Wright's statements, resigned from Trinity United Church of Christ in Chicago, and eventually overcame most of the political damage created by his past association with the pastor.

Although Obama's campaign had suffered a temporary setback from the uproar over Wright, the candidate had some political cover from earlier having credibly established himself as a man of deep religious faith. This perception stood in strong contrast to the situation for the Democratic nominee in the previous national election cycle. During the 2004 presidential campaign, a national opinion poll found that only 7 percent of Americans considered Democratic nominee John Kerry to be a person of strong religious faith.[21] Although not an accurate perception of Kerry, this finding revealed a strong liability to his candidacy. Consider the 2004 Pew Center national survey in which 72 percent of Americans said that they agreed with the statement that "presidents should have strong religious beliefs."[22] A key problem for Kerry was not that he actually lacked faith–commitment, but that he did not communicate in a manner that connected with the faithful.

The Democrats would not have this same liability in 2008. Presidential nominee Barack Obama not only was a candidate of deep religious faith, but also evoked an evangelical style of discourse that connected him deeply to his coreligionists. The effect was not to switch the allegiances of large numbers of so-called "values voters" who had supported Bush and the Republicans in 2004, but to soften the intensity of their opposition and to sway just enough of those voters to improve Obama's electoral prospects.

Exit polls showed that Obama fared better than Kerry among all major religious groupings but not among people who professed no religious identification. Obama won the votes of 54 percent of Catholics, whereas Kerry, who was Catholic, achieved 47 percent. Protestants voted 45 percent for Obama, 40 percent for Kerry. Despite all of the discussion at the elite level about possible changing political allegiances of evangelical Protestant voters, there was not much change in this group. White evangelicals gave only 26 percent support to Obama, but still higher than the 21 percent for Kerry. Jewish voters backed Obama with 78 percent, and Kerry had won 74 percent of their votes. The only categories in which Obama did not fare better than Kerry were "other faiths" and "unaffiliated." Both Obama and Kerry had won about three-fourths of the voters from "other faiths" (a collection of eastern religions, new-age adherents, among other smaller groupings), and Obama lost ground among the unaffiliated (67% to Kerry's 75%). Very telling also was Obama's showing among voters who regularly attended religious services. Among those voters who attended services more often than once per week, Obama won 43 percent (and Kerry had won merely 35% of that group).[23]

Perhaps very important, Obama embraced an open discussion in the campaign about his faith and its impact not only on himself personally, but also on how he viewed a variety of policy issues. The first joint appearance by the two major party presidential nominees—Obama and McCain—took place on August 15, 2008, on a stage shared with conservative evangelical mega-church pastor Rick Warren who had invited the candidates to a forum to talk about faith issues. The event drew enormous media attention and Warren asked the candidates very direct questions about religion, faith-commitment, whether they had committed moral failings in their lives, among also a host of policy issues of deep concern to conservative evangelicals. It is hard to imagine many Democratic candidates in national politics who would be at all comfortable in that environment. Obama not only handled the exchanges comfortably, but also embraced other opportunities to discuss faith and politics, and to the surprise of many, he invited Warren, a most unlikely partner to any Democrat, to give a prayer at the presidential inauguration.

Early in the Obama administration there were some signals of the president's commitment to faith-based approaches to dealing with social and economic issues. On February 5, 2009, he created by executive order a new White House Office of Faith-Based and Neighborhood Partnerships, headed by a young Pentecostal minister. Although different in scope and function from the Bush era Office of Faith-Based Initiatives, the Obama White House office continued his predecessor's philosophy of empowering faith organizations to receive federal support to provide various social services. And even though Obama emphasized that the funds could only be used for secular purposes such as feeding the hungry, rather than for evangelizing, such groups as the American Civil Liberties Union expressed their disapproval that it meant continued government funding for religious-based organizations.

On the same day that he signed this executive order, Obama attended the National Prayer Breakfast at which he discussed issues of faith and the role of the new White House office. There he emphasized that the office would work in a religiously neutral fashion and that his administration would adhere to a proper separation of religion and state. Most widely noted from

Obama's appearance were some of his reflections on how religion too often has been a divisive tool rather than a force for bringing people together. He added, "there is no religion whose central tenet is hate" and "there is no god who condones taking the life of an innocent human being."[24]

Nonetheless, for the conservative evangelicals who have made the Republican Party their political home and who strongly opposed Obama, his efforts at outreach, by including Warren in the inaugural ceremony, and by expressing eloquent words about faith and protecting innocent life, do not overcome disdain for the policies professed by the forty-fourth president. Indeed, one of the first acts by Obama was to issue a memorandum that overturned the controversial Mexico City Policy that had prohibited the use of federal funds for international family planning organizations that provide abortion-related services. The Mexico City Policy, issued by Reagan, reaffirmed by George H. W. Bush, rescinded by Clinton, and then reinstated by George W. Bush, stands for conservative evangelicals as a key marker of a president's overall leanings on "life issues."

Obama's faith background itself is a complicated story that provides some additional context to conservative evangelical discomfort with him. His father was a Muslim who became an atheist, his mother a Christian who became secular, and he was partially raised by a Muslim stepfather. As a young person living both in the United States and South Asia, he attended a variety of services and thus had an exposure to multiple faith perspectives. He was not baptized a Christian until the early 1990s. And despite years of regular attendance at a Christian Church, in the midst of the 2008 presidential campaign a national poll revealed that 12 percent of Americans thought he was a Muslim.[25] That perception mattered politically because, according to a Pew national survey, 25 percent of Americans admit that they would be less likely to vote for someone who is a Muslim.[26] Perhaps a partial motivation for Obama's open expression of his Christian faith during the 2008 campaign was to counter this misperception. Yet, in frequently affirming his Christian faith, Obama did not do so by demeaning any other faith tradition.

In the early stage of the Obama administration, there is much discussion of whether the president himself can help shift the dialogue about the intersection of religion and politics away from the divisiveness that has characterized the era of the Christian Right. Since the 1970s, the leading story about religion and U.S. politics has indeed been the rise and the growing influence of conservative evangelicals, who remain a very powerful, though controversial, force. Progressive religious-based political organizations have not been successful at building an equally strong countermovement. Rather than empowering one side to combat another, Obama's discourse seeks to move the country beyond the divisions of Right and Left and to find ways to unite the faithful of different perspectives to work together. As the experiences of the past three decades suggest, it is a noble but challenging goal for the president to achieve given the serious differences on social issues policy that will continue to divide the United States.

Notes

1. *Newsweek* cover, October 26, 1976.
2. Quoted in John Dart and Jimmy Allen, *Bridging the Gap: Religion and the News Media*. Nashville, TN: First Amendment Center, 2000, p. 60. Available at: http://www.firstamendmentcenter.org/PDF/bridgingthegap.PDF (accessed on February 22, 2009).
3. Jerry F. terHorst, "Carter's Old-Time Religion in a New World," *Los Angeles Times*, April 2, 1976, sec. II, p. 13.
4. See Jeff Walz, "Jimmy Carter and the Politics of Faith," in Mark J. Rozell and Gleaves Whitney, eds., *Religion and the American Presidency* (New York: Palgrave/MacMillan Press, 2007), pp. 157–173.
5. See Kenneth Wald, *Religion and Politics in the United States*, 4th ed. (Lanham, MD: Rowman & Littlefield, 2003), chapter 7.
6. See Lyman A. Kellstedt, James L. Guth, John C. Green, and Corwin E. Smidt, "The Soul of the South," in Charles Bullock III and Mark J. Rozell, eds., *The New Politics of the Old South: An Introduction to Southern Politics* 4th ed. (Lanham, MD: Rowman & Littlefield, 2009), pp. 283–303.
7. Clyde Wilcox, Mark J. Rozell and Roland Gunn, "Religious Constituencies in the New Christian Right," *Social Science Quarterly* (September 1996): 543–558.
8. Joe Taylor, "Christian Coalition Revamping Image," *Richmond Times-Dispatch* (December 7, 1992): B4.
9. Moen, "The Changing Nature of Christian Right Activism," pp. 21–40; Mark J. Rozell, "Growing Up Politically: The New Politics of the New Christian Right," in Smidt and Penning, eds., *Sojourners in the Wilderness,* pp. 235–248; Mark J. Rozell and Clyde Wilcox, *Second Coming: The New Christian Right in Virginia Politics* (Baltimore: The Johns Hopkins University Press, 1996); Clyde Wilcox and Carin Larson, *Onward Christian Soldiers: The Religious Right in American Politics,* 3rd ed. (Boulder, CO: Westview Press, 2006).
10. Jon A. Shields, "The Democratic Virtues of the Christian Right." Doctoral dissertation prepared for the Department of Politics, University of Virginia, Charlottesville, Virginia, 2006.
11. Mark J. Rozell, Clyde Wilcox, and John C. Green, "Religious Constituencies and Support for the Christian Right in the 1990s," *Social Science Quarterly* (December 1998): 815–820.
12. Paul Kengor's statistical analysis cited by James M. Penning, "The Religion of Bill Clinton," in Rozell and Whitney, eds., p. 201.
13. Most prominent was a letter issued on February 16, 1999, by Free Congress Foundation president Paul Weyrich: http://www.nationalcenter.org/Weyrich299.html (accessed October 6, 2009).

14. David L. Greene, "Bush Turns Increasingly to Language of Religion," *Baltimore Sun*, February 10, 2003, p. 11A.
15. Ibid.
16. John C. Green, Mark J. Rozell, and Clyde Wilcox, eds., *The Values Campaign?: The Christian Right and the 2004 Elections* (Washington, DC: Georgetown University Press, 2006).
17. 2004 exit-poll data, cited in Steven Waldman and John C. Green, "It wasn't Just (Or Even Mostly) the Religious Right." Available at www.beliefnet.com/story/155/story_15598_1.html (accessed October 6, 2009).
18. See 2006 exit-poll data and analysis at http://pewforum.org/docs/?DocID=174 (accessed October 6, 2009).
19. See Mark J. Rozell, "The Christian Right in the 2000 GOP Presidential Campaign," in Mary Segers, ed., *Piety, Politics, and Pluralism* (Lanham, MD: Rowman & Littlefield, 2002), pp. 57–74.
20. Rozell, "The Christian Right in the 2000 GOP Presidential Campaign," pp. 66–67.
21. See David Brooks, "A Matter of Faith," *New York Times*, June 22, 2004, p. A19.
22. Pew Forum on Religion and Public Life, "Religion and Public Life: A Faith-Based Partisan Divide," at http://pewforum.org/docs/index.php?DocID=61 (accessed October 6, 2009).
23. 2004 and 2008 national exit polls. Cited at http://pewresearch.org/pubs/1022/exit-poll-analysis-religion (accessed October 6, 2009).
24. Text of Obama speech at http://www.usnews.com/blogs/god-and-country/2009/2/5/president-barack-obamas-speech-at-national-prayer-breakfast.html?s_cid=rss:god-and-country:president-barack-obamas-speech-at-national-prayer-breakfast (accessed October 6, 2009).
25. *Newsweek* poll, July 11, 2008 at http://www.newsweek.com/id/145556 (accessed October 6, 2009.
26. August 1–18, 2007 Pew survey at http://pewresearch.org/pubs/587/religion-campaign-08 (accessed October 6, 2009).

7

Presidential Abortion Rhetoric and Religion

Ted G. Jelen and Brendan Morris

Since the *Roe v Wade* decision of 1973, abortion has been among the most divisive issues in American politics, and has generated unconventional, illegal, and occasionally violent political activity on the part of those who oppose legal abortion. Since the 1990s, abortion has been a partisan issue, dividing Republicans and Democrats.[1]

The purpose of this study is to examine the role of religion in presidential rhetoric concerning abortion. We seek to address the following questions: How frequently do American presidents publicly address the issue of abortion? How often do presidents invoke religious values or arguments in their public discussions of abortion? Are there partisan differences among presidents with respect to either the frequency with which they address the abortion issue, or in their use of religious rhetoric? Does the use of religious language by presidents reflect consensual values among American citizens, or does such rhetoric invoke more particularistic (and potentially divisive) religious beliefs? Finally, how has presidential abortion rhetoric changed over time?

Our motivation for investigating the nature of presidential rhetoric on abortion is to address the extent to which presidents (especially those who take "pro-life" positions on the issue) seek to impose religious values on public policy. Does public attention to the abortion issue by presidents constitute efforts to impose theolegal norms on American politics? Some analysts[2] have suggested that any limitation on abortion rights prior to fetal viability represent violations of the Establishment Clause, and comprise attempts to impose particular religious values into the legal system. Indeed, religious values have repeatedly been shown to be important sources of opposition to legal abortion. Thus, abortion is a religiously charged issue, which raises questions about the role of religious values in the public sphere.

However, it has also been noted that abortion is a "condensational symbol," which invokes values from a number of different cognitive domains, including religion, biology, constitutional law, and feminism.[3] For example, one might oppose abortion on grounds of biology, by arguing that the humanity of the fetus can be established on scientific, rather than theological grounds.[4] A "pro-life" position on abortion is thus not *necessarily* theolegal, unless religious warrants are specifically invoked. Thus, it matters *how* public officials (such as presidents) frame and discuss the abortion issue in order to assess whether, and to what extent, presidential rhetoric on abortion threatens constitutional values such as the separation of church and state.

More generally, presidential rhetoric around this issue is quite important to the practice of democratic discourse. Democracy is a persuasive system. In the final analysis, public officials, interest groups, and proponents of various positions on issues of public policy gain power by persuading ordinary citizens of the acceptability and desirability of the options such political actors offer. Indeed, Richard Neustadt[5] argues that the essence of presidential power is "the power to persuade."

In order for persuasion to occur, there must exist shared premises among those seeking to persuade and the objects of persuasive arguments. If agreement on matters of politics or policy is to occur, members of a community must share common assumptions, which are "publicly accessible."[6]

Does religion provide such publicly accessible assumptions in the United States? Many historical and contemporary analysts have suggested that religion, in fact, provides a common frame of reference within which social and political life can be conducted. Alexis de Tocqueville[7] suggested that "Christian morality" (or "the duties owed from man to man") were the objects of consensus in the United States. More recently, Richard Neuhaus[8] has suggested that shared religious beliefs provide a "sacred canopy" of common meanings and understandings, which has been severed by the pervasive secularism of the later twentieth century. Empirical research has shown that large majorities of Americans share certain general religious beliefs, such as the existence of God or an afterlife.[9]

Conversely, there are religious beliefs in the United States that are not generally shared, and that provide the potential basis for conflict. The validity of such theological values as natural law, biblical inerrancy, and glossalalia create cleavages among (and often within) Christian denominations.[10] Moreover, there appears to be no consensus among Americans (even those highly religious) about such issues as abortion, gay and lesbian rights, and war and peace.

The issue of abortion is an excellent test case to determine the extent to which religion either promotes or inhibits the development of shared premises necessary to democratic political discourse. Kristin Luker,[11] among others, has noted the extent to which activists on both sides of the abortion issue lack common frames of references. Conversely, presidents have incentives to find the "common ground" on which a resolution of the abortion issue might be based. Our purpose here is to consider the extent to which U.S. presidents utilize religious language in their public statements about abortion, and to examine the character of these pronouncements. Moreover, if some U.S. presidents seek to apply theolegal perspectives to matters of public policy, such efforts should be most visible in the area of abortion politics.

Data and Method

This chapter is intended to classify presidential statements on abortion into one of three categories: religious, moral/conscience, or secular. The statements that were collected came from President Nixon through George W. Bush's terms.[12] The statements collected only consisted mostly of times in which the presidents were either running for office, as the president-elect, or serving as president. These statements included verbal communications, such as speeches and press conferences, and written correspondence, such as letters and messages to Congress. The statements included the issue of abortion or abortion-related topics, such as the Supreme Court decision of *Roe v. Wade*, bans on partial-birth abortion, judicial and federal nominees' opinions on abortion, et cetera. Only statements in which the presidents discussed these issues were collected and analyzed.

The presidential statements on abortion were collected through a variety of internet sources (some of Nixon's and Clinton's statements came from published books on their presidencies). While the initial work was conducted through *Google* searches of the individual presidents and abortion-related terms, the overwhelming majority of the statements were collected through the University of California, Santa Barbra's *The American Presidency Project*.[13] This online database archives presidential papers, speeches, and other documents related to the Executive Office. Using the database's search function, the term abortion was used as the only search parameter. Approximately 340 documents were collected. Each document represented a specific speech or written correspondence and was analyzed as a single unit.

Treating each collected document as a single unit of analysis, each document was coded for the manner in which each president discussed the issue of abortion. Using the categories of religious, moral/conscience, and secular, the statements were reviewed for any connotations of the three categories. The categories were given preference in the order given above, so if a document consisted of religious undertones in regards to abortion with one statement, but moral undertones as well, the unit was classified as "religious." Even though some documents consisted of several references to abortion issues, the document was analyzed as a whole and classified into one of the categories only.

The classification process consisted of coding for specific terms and concepts with respect to the manner in which each president discussed abortion. For religious statements, overt terms such as God, the Creator, Jesus Christ, the Ten Commandments, and Judeo-Christian beliefs were highlighted. Other terms with religious undertones such as spiritual, sanctity, sacred, soul, and prayer/worship were also highlighted as being religious. Statements in which the presidents legitimatized or gave authority over the issue of abortion to certain religious beliefs or groups were also classified as being religious statements. This included naming the Pope, certain churches, and identifying Christian or religious beliefs. While not every statement consisted of the presidents explicitly using religion to make their arguments, statements in which a president brought up religion were coded as religious statements. Thus, our coding category of "religious" is as broad as we could plausibly make it.

For the moral/conscience classification, any normative judgments about abortion that did not involve specifically religious references, such as the "tragedy" of abortion or "culture of life,"[14] caused the statements to be classified under this category. Other terms such as morality, ethical, and personal beliefs where religion was not mentioned, or statements of conscience, classified statements as moral/conscience as well. The last category of secular consisted of any statements that did not fit into the two other categories. For example, arguments that invoked biology, or constitutional principles such as the separation of powers, were coded as secular.

Findings

The gross quantitative contours of presidential rhetoric on abortion are depicted in Table 7.1, which contains the number of secular, moral/secular, and religious statements made by each U.S. president since Nixon, who was in office when the *Roe* case was decided.

Table 7.1 contains several interesting findings. First, the frequency of presidential statements on abortion increased dramatically during the Reagan administration. Presidents Nixon, Ford, and Carter did not speak frequently about abortion. The Reagan administration marks a turning point in the frequency of presidential pronouncements on abortion, and

Table 7.1   Presidential rhetoric on abortion

Presidents	Religious	Moral	Secular	N
Nixon	2	1	0	3
(%)	66.67	33.33	0.00	
Ford	1	2	3	6
(%)	16.67	33.33	50.00	
Carter	2	10	10	22
(%)	9.09	45.45	45.45	
Reagan	27	18	12	57
(%)	47.37	31.58	21.05	
G. H. W. Bush	16	11	8	35
(%)	45.71	31.43	22.86	
Clinton	21	30	40	91
(%)	23.08	32.97	43.96	
G. W. Bush	22	79	8	109
(%)	20.18	72.48	7.34	
N	91	151	81	323
(%)	28.17	46.75	25.08	

suggests the increased importance of the Christian Right during the late 1970s and early 1980s.[15] This increase corresponds to the emergence of abortion as a *partisan* issue in the late 1980s.[16] Indeed, if the number of presidential statements on abortion is doubled for President Bush I (owing to the fact that George H. W. Bush served only one term, unlike Reagan, Clinton, or President Bush II), the number of presidential statements on abortion increases monotonically from the Reagan administration to that of President Bush II.

Second, the percentage of presidential abortion statements with explicitly religious themes decreases monotonically between Reagan and Bush II. While slightly fewer than half of Reagan's statements invoked specifically religious language, about one statement in five from George W. Bush utilized religious language. Perhaps interestingly, the proportion of moral/conscience statements is relatively constant in the period that includes the Reagan, Bush I, and Clinton administrations. By contrast, nearly three-quarters of the abortion statements offered by George W. Bush fall into the moral/conscience category.

Third, while about a fifth of statements from President Reagan and President George H. W. Bush fall into the "secular" category, almost half of Clinton's abortion statements are secular in nature. By contrast, fewer than one statement in ten from President Bush II can be considered secular. This finding provides further evidence that the abortion issue was the focus of partisan polarization during the period following the 1989 case of *Webster v. Missouri Reproductive Services.*[17]

Thus, any hypotheses that presidential rhetoric on abortion is highly theolegal in nature, or that there is a greater tendency for Republican presidents to employ religious language when discussing abortion, must be carefully qualified. Obviously, in making any assessment, the distinction between "religious" and "moral/conscience" statements is important. Clearly, the Reagan administration constituted a turning point in presidential abortion rhetoric, with abortion being addressed with increasing frequency since the Reagan presidency. Explicitly religious statements have declined since Reagan, and the trend has been monotonic across Republican and Democratic administrations.

The interpretation of these results would be different if the distinction between religious and moral/conscience statements is not granted. If the two categories are collapsed, about three-quarters of presidential statements from Reagan and Bush I (74.45% and 77.14%, respectively) can be considered "nonsecular." The comparable figure for Clinton (the only Democratic president in the period under discussion) is 56.05 percent, while virtually all of the statements made by George W. Bush (92.66%) are of a nonsecular nature.

Thus, the question of whether presidential abortion rhetoric (especially from GOP presidents) can be considered theolegal may depend on whether theolegal language includes presidential statements that involve questions of morality or conscience. It is possible to gain further insight into the nature of public presidential pronouncements concerning abortion by shifting to a more qualitative mode of analysis, and examining the content of religious and secular statements. In general, presidents of either party who employ religious rhetoric invoke more general, consensual aspects of American religion, such as belief in God, religious autonomy, or the sanctity of life, than more specific doctrinal aspects of religious belief.

We begin with a sampling of moral/conscience statements on abortion, since, as noted, a large majority of presidential pronouncements on abortion are not specifically religious.

In one of the earlier presidential statements, Gerald Ford bemoaned the rigidity that resulted from making abortion a constitutional issue:

> In my opinion, the Supreme Court decision did go too far. It, in effect, permitted what can be categorized as abortion on demand. On the other hand, the proposals that are made by some for a constitutional amendment, I think, are far too restrictive.
>
> My own view, and this is a view that I hold very deeply, is that the question of where we should go or how we should handle it is a deep moral issue. And I don't believe that you should have ironclad decisions by a Supreme Court or an ironclad constitutional amendment on the other side. It is my feeling when these deep moral issues are involved, that you shouldn't be

rigid in what is sought to be done by either the courts on the one hand, or the Constitution on the other.[18]

This statement is considered a member of the "moral/conscience" category, even though the bulk of the statement deals with issues of constitutional law.

Similarly, Jimmy Carter emphasized the need for programs that would prevent unwanted pregnancies, thus limiting the number of situations in which abortion might seem an attractive option, while mentioning the moral considerations involved in abortion decisions:

> I am against abortion. I think abortion is wrong and I'm doing everything I can as President to hold down the need for abortion. I don't think any woman and her partner ever have intercourse in order to create a child that's going to be destroyed by abortion. It's quite often a mistake or because of ignorance. And to think the best thing to do is prevent the conception of the child ahead of time, and this is something that I think needs to be done with comprehensive programs.[19]

As noted above, Ronald Reagan addressed the abortion issue far more frequently than his predecessors.[20] In several of his many nonreligious statements on the issue, Reagan turned the lack of consensus on the ontological status of the fetus into an argument against legal abortion:

> More than a decade ago, a Supreme Court decision literally wiped off the books of 50 States statutes protecting the rights of unborn children. Abortion on demand now takes the lives of up to one and a half million unborn children a year. Human life legislation ending this tragedy will some day pass the Congress, and you and I must never rest until it does. Unless and until it can be proven that the unborn child is not a living entity, then its right to life, liberty, and the pursuit of happiness must be protected.[21]

Nonreligious themes were also emphasized by presidents George H. W. Bush and Bill Clinton. President Bush I emphasized alternatives to abortion, and noted the politically controversial nature of the issue:

> And there's a national tragedy: More than a half a million abortions in this country every year. We know there's got to be a better way, human alternatives like adoptions and abstinence. Seven times I have ignored the polls and acted on what I believe is fundamental principle and vetoed, as Virgil very generously pointed out, abortion legislation. And I promise you again today, no matter the political price, and they tell me in this year that it's enormous, I am going to do what I think is right. I am going to stand on my conscience and let my conscience be my guide when it comes to matters of life.[22]

President Clinton noted the controversial nature of the "personhood" of the fetus, and emphasized the tragic nature of the choice to have an abortion. The following statements are examples of the "secular" category: "Our vision should be of an America where abortion is safe and legal, but rare."[23]

Everyone knows life begins biologically at conception. No one knows when biology turns into humanity. Most abortions that don't involve the life or health of the mother are chosen by scared young women and girls who don't know what else to do. It's hard to apply the criminal law to acts that a substantial portion of the citizenry doesn't believe should be labeled crimes, (as with Prohibition). I thought then [in the 1973 *Roe v. Wade* decision] and still believe that the Court reached the right conclusion.[24]

Conversely, in several of his numerous secular statements on abortion, George W. Bush noted the consensual nature of many public attitudes on abortion, and sought to identify his opponent in 2004, John Kerry, with an extreme and unpopular position. Moreover, President Bush II used the image of a "culture of life" (borrowed from Pope John Paul II) to emphasize attitudes that are the subject of general agreement in the United States.

We stand for a culture of life in which every person matters and every person counts. We've been making progress on building the culture of life here in America. Members of both political parties believe that moms and dads should be involved in important decisions of their minor daughters. Members of both parties came together to pass the Unborn Victims of Violence Act, to punish the violent crimes against mothers and their unborn children. Members of both parties voted to end the brutal practice of partial-birth abortion. Republicans and Democrats agree on these issues. Yet on these positions that so many Americans share, my opponent is on the other side.[25]

As shown in Table 7.1, all post-*Roe* presidents, except Ford, have invoked some sort of religious language in their public statements about abortion. However, most of these references have been of a general, consensual nature, and have not typically invoked specific matters of doctrine or scrip-ture. As we will show below, Ronald Reagan constitutes an important, but limited, exception to this pattern.

Richard Nixon, who was president when the *Roe* decision was announced, noted his personal religious opposition to abortion:

From personal and religious beliefs I consider abortions an unacceptable form of population control. Further, unrestricted abortion policies, or abortion on demand, I cannot square with my personal belief in the sanctity of human life–including the life of the yet unborn. For surely the unborn have rights also, recognized in law, recognized even in principles expounded by the United Nations.

Ours is a nation with a Judeo-Christian heritage. It is also a nation with serious social problems—problems of malnutrition, of broken homes, of poverty and of delinquency. But none of these problems justifies such a solution.[26]

In his sole public religious reference to abortion, Jimmy Carter invoked the general Christian symbol of Jesus Christ. Carter, of course, was known for his evangelical Christian beliefs, which makes both the infrequency of his religious pronouncements on abortion and the general nature of the single reference noteworthy: "I am convinced that every abortion is an unplanned tragedy, brought on by a combination of human errors, . . . I have never believed that Jesus Christ would approve . . . abortions."[27]

As noted previously, the frequency of public presidential statements on abortion increased drastically under Ronald Reagan. While most of Reagan's abortion statements were secular in nature, he did make substantial use of religious language as well. Moreover, Reagan was much more likely to invoke specific scriptural language, although such references did not invoke passages that have been argued to invoke the abortion issue directly.[28] The following samples are illustrative of Reagan's approach:

Victoria [an adopted infant] has received assistance from a Christian couple, and from Sav-A-Life, a new Dallas group run by Jim McKee, a concerned citizen who thinks it's important to provide constructive alternatives to abortion. There's hope for America. She remains powerful and a powerful force for good, and it's thanks to the conviction and commitment of people like those who are helping Victoria. They're living the meaning of the two great commandments: "Thou shalt love the Lord thy God with all thy heart, and with all thy soul, and with all thy might" and "thou shalt love thy neighbour as thyself."[29]

Now, Therefore, I, Ronald Reagan, President of the United States of America, do hereby proclaim Sunday, January 22, 1984, as National Sanctity of Human Life Day. I call upon the citizens of this blessed land to gather on that day in homes and places of worship to give thanks for the gift of life, and to reaffirm our commitment to the dignity of every human being and the sanctity of each human life.[30]

I believe no challenge is more important to the character of America than restoring the right to life to all human beings. Without that right, no other rights have meaning. "Suffer the little children to come unto me, and forbid them not, for such is the kingdom of God."[31]

Respect for the sanctity of human life has not died in America. Far from it. With every passing year it shines ever more brightly in the hearts of more and more of our citizens as they come to see the issue with greater clarity in all of its dimensions. As we carry this message to our courts, our legislatures, and our fellow citizens, let us never be discouraged. Let us put our trust in God, the Lord and Giver of Life, the Creator Who endowed us with our inalienable rights. May we soon rejoice in the day when reverence for human life is enshrined as surely in our laws as in our hearts.[32]

At the heart of our Judeo-Christian ethic is a reverence for life. From the Ten Commandments to the Sermon on the Mount, the mission of faith is to cherish and magnify life—and through it God's holy name. Yet since the Supreme Court's decision in Roe v. Wade, there have been 20 million abortions in America. And as the Bloomington baby case showed, this callousness for life can spill over into other areas, leading to decisions on who is good enough to live and who is not.[33]

Reagan's successors returned to the more general use of religiosity when discussing abortion. George H. W. Bush emphasized the importance of prayer in seeking guidance on the issue, and assistance for those seeking alternatives to abortion:

One of the key issues connected with the sanctity of life, abortion, has been a divisive issue in our Nation for many years. The prevalence of abortion in America today is a tragedy not only in terms of human lives lost, but also in terms of the values we hold dear as a Nation. We pray for a recognition that the principle of life's sanctity should guide public policy on this question and others, just as moral principles should guide our individual lives. We pray also for wisdom and guidance as those with public responsibilities consider this question. We ask all levels of government and all sectors of society to promote policies to encourage alternatives such as adoption, and to extend policies that make adopting easier for families who want children and can provide a loving, supportive home for them, particularly for children with special needs. We hope for the day when devoted families who want to adopt will no longer be disappointed. On this day, we also thank God for the advances in medicine that have improved the care of unborn children in the womb and premature babies. These scientific advances reinforce the belief that unborn children are persons, entitled to medical care and legal protection.[34]

Bill Clinton, by contrast, acknowledged the religious dimension of the abortion issue, but emphasized the personal nature of religious belief:

I have always believed that the decision to have an abortion should be between a woman, her conscience, her doctor, and her God. I strongly believe that legal abortions—those abortions that the Supreme Court ruled in *Roe v. Wade* must be protected—should be safe and rare. I have long opposed late-term abortions except, as the law requires, where they are necessary to protect the life of the mother or where there is a threat to her health. In fact, as Governor of Arkansas, I signed into law a bill that barred third trimester abortions except where they were necessary to protect the life or health of the woman, consistent with the Supreme Court's rulings.[35]

More recently, George W. Bush repeatedly took note of the connection between God and an important national symbol: The Declaration of Independence. Bush also invoked the Judeo-Christian notion of a soul, while emphasizing the soul's mysterious nature:

> It is important for all Americans to remember that our Declaration of Independence states that every person has the right to life, liberty, and the pursuit of happiness. It also states that these rights come from our Creator and that governments are formed to secure these rights for all their citizens. And we believe every human life has value, and we pray for the day when every child is welcome in life and protected into law.
>
> Babies can now survive outside the mother's womb at younger and younger ages. And the fingers and toes and beating hearts that we can see on an unborn child's ultrasound come with something that we cannot see, a soul.[36]

Conclusion

Abortion is, of course, a morally charged issue, and a source of religious and (since the 1990s) partisan division. However, the notion that presidents invoke theocratic or theolegal language in their public pronouncements on abortion seems generally disconfirmed by the evidence presented here. Most statements about abortion do not invoke specifically religious themes, but place the abortion issue into the context of more general "morality," or personal (or collective) "conscience." Moreover, those statements in which religious values are mentioned invoke general, consensual values, such as belief in God, the efficacy of prayer, or the sanctity of human life. Moreover, religious rhetoric has been used by presidents to support both sides of the abortion issue. Thus, only the most generous coding of "religious" themes would support the notion that presidents seek to impose religious values on public policy with respect to abortion. Most presidential abortion rhetoric, whether explicitly religious or invoking considerations of morality, is of generally shared, nonsectarian values.

One prominent exception to these generalizations is Ronald Reagan. As noted, the Reagan administration witnessed a rather dramatic increase in public presidential discussion on abortion, and in the use of relatively specific religious rhetoric in such pronouncements. To an extent not observed in previous or subsequent presidents, Reagan invoked specific biblical passages, as well as the image of the "Judeo-Christian tradition." Perhaps not coincidentally, the Reagan administration witnessed the rise of the Christian Right as a rhetorical and electoral force in American politics, and immediately preceded the emergence of abortion as an explicitly partisan issue. Yet, even here, Reagan's use of scripture was quite general, and did not invoke passages that abortion opponents have argued specifically relate to the abortion issue.[37]

Thus, presidential rhetoric surrounding abortion has had a visible, yet limited, religious component. Presidents who use religious language in public discussions of abortion are most likely to use very general, consensual religious imagery, and seem relatively reluctant to make more explicitly theological arguments or assertions. At the level of the highest office in the United States, presidents appear constrained, either by personal preferences or political considerations, from making explicitly religious or sectarian arguments about abortion.

Notes

1. Adams, Greg D. 1997. "Abortion: Evidence of Issue Evolution," *American Journal of Political Science* 41: 718–737; Abramowitz, Alan. 1995. "It's Abortion, Stupid: Policy Voting in the 1992 Presidential Election," *Journal of Politics* 57: 176–186; Cook, Elizabeth Adell, Ted G. Jelen, and Clyde Wilcox. 1992. *Between Two Absolutes: Public Opinion and the Politics of Abortion* Boulder, CO: Westview; Jelen, Ted G., and Clyde Wilcox. 2003. "Causes and Consequences of Public Attitudes Toward Abortion: A Review and Research Agenda," *Political Research Quarterly* 56: 489–500.

2. Wenz, Peter. 1992. *Abortion Rights as Religious Freedom* Philadelphia: Temple University Press.

3. Staggenborg, Suzanne. 1994. *The Pro-Choice Movement: Organization and Activism in the Abortion Conflict* New York: Oxford University Press.

4. Grindstaff, Laura. 1994. "Abortion and the Popular Press: Mapping Media Discourse from *Roe* to *Webster*," In Ted G. Jelen and Marthe A. Chandler (eds.). *Abortion Politics in the United States and Canada: Studies in Public Opinion* Westport, CT: Praeger, pp. 57–88; Jelen, Ted G. 1992. "The Clergy and Abortion," *Review of Religious Research* 34: 132–151.

5. Neustadt, Richard E. 1991. *Presidential Power and the Modern Presidency* New York: Free Press.

6. Greenawalt, Kent. 1988. *Religious Convictions and Political Choice* New York: Oxford University Press; Perry, Michael J. 1991. *Love and Power: The Role of Religion and Morality in American Politics* New York: Oxford University Press; Jelen, Ted G. 1998. "In Defense of Religious Minimalism," In Mary C. Segers and Ted G. Jelen, *A Wall of Separation? Debating the Public Role of Religion* Lanham, MD: Rowman-Littlefield, pp. 3–51.

7. Tocqueville, Alexis de. 1945. *Democracy in America* ed. P. Bradley. 2 vols. New York: Vintage Books.

8. Neuhaus, Richard John. 1984. *The Naked Public Square* Grand Rapids, MI: Eerdemans.
9. Wald, Kenneth D., and Allison Calhoun-Brown. 2007. *Religion and Politics in the United States* (5th edition) Lanham, MD: Rowman-Littlefield.
10. Jelen, Ted G. 1993. *The Political World of the Clergy* Westport, CT: Praeger.
11. Luker, Kristin. 1984. *Abortion and the Politics of Motherhood.* Berkeley, CA: University of California Press.
12. We have excluded statements from President Obama because at the time of this writing it is still early in the Obama administration.
13. The American Presidency Project's website can be found at: http://www.presidency.ucsb.edu/index.php.
14. Obviously, the categorization of statements as "religious" or "moral/conscience" involves some judgment. As noted, we have attempted to be conservative in our coding decisions, coding statements that are difficult to classify as religious. A reviewer of an earlier draft of this paper questioned our coding of "culture of life" as nonreligious, since the quote comes from Pope John Paul II. We would argue that such a statement is not explicitly religious because it invokes a more general value (the importance of human life) and we suspect that most mass publics would not recognize the statement as having Catholic origins. A complete list of statements, with coding decisions, is available from the first author.
15. Wilcox, Clyde, and Carin Larson. 2006. *Onward, Christian Soldiers: The Religious Right in American Politics* (3rd edition) Boulder, CO: Westview.
16. Jelen, Ted G., and Clyde Wilcox. 2003. "Causes and Consequences of Public Attitudes Toward Abortion: A Review and Research Agenda," *Political Research Quarterly* 56: 489–500.
17. Cook, Elizabeth Adell, Ted G. Jelen, and Clyde Wilcox. 1992. *Between Two Absolutes: Public Opinion and the Politics of Abortion* Boulder, CO: Westview; Adams, Greg D. 1997. "Abortion: Evidence of Issue Evolution," *American Journal of Political Science* 41: 718–737.
18. Remarks and a question-and-answer session in Buffalo Grove, Illinois, March 12, 1976.
19. Los Angeles, California. Remarks during a televised question-and-answer session with area residents, May 17, 1977.
20. Of course, part of the differences between the Reagan administration and its predecessors can be attributed to the fact that Reagan, unlike Nixon, Ford, or Carter, served two full terms.
21. Remarks at the Annual Convention of the National Association of Evangelicals in Orlando, Florida, March 8, 1983.
22. Remarks to the Knights of Columbus Supreme Council Convention in New York City, August 5, 1992.
23. Remarks on signing memorandums on medical research and reproductive health and an exchange with reporters, January 22, 1993.
24. Bill Clinton. 2005. *My Life* New York: Random House, p. 229.
25. Remarks in Marquette, Michigan, July 13, 2004.
26. Bruce, Mazlish. 1972. *In Search of Nixon: A Psychohistorical Inquiry* New York and London: Basic Books, Inc., p. 32.

27. *Google.*
28. Cook, Elizabeth Adell, Ted G. Jelen, and Clyde Wilcox. 1992. *Between Two Absolutes: Public Opinion and the Politics of Abortion* Boulder, CO: Westview.
29. Remarks at the Annual Convention of the National Religious Broadcasters, January 31, 1983.
30. Proclamation 5147—National Sanctity of Human Life Day, 1984, January 13, 1984.
31. Remarks at the Annual Convention of the National Religious Broadcasters, January 30, 1984.
32. Proclamation 5430—National Sanctity of Human Life Day, 1986, January 15, 1986.
33. Remarks at the Annual Convention of the National Religious Broadcasters Association, February 1, 1988.
34. Proclamation 6090—National Sanctity of Human Life Day, 1990, January 19, 1990.
35. Letter to Representative John Conyers, Jr., on Abortion Legislation, February 28, 1996.
36. Telephone Remarks to the March for Life, January 22, 2007.
37. For a discussion of biblical passages used in contemporary abortion discourse, see Cook, et al., 1992.

Part 3

Theolegal Democracy

Rarely
by Katie Ford

Rarely do I remember another month, August.
Rarely another day do I remember.

I threw tarps over a life
and never could they reach—

Still hastily I gathered
tarps more rare by the hour

in the city of nothing to spare
I draped true but thin shores

for shipwreck
as the radio said:

Rarely does as rarely has
grown tired of not doing.

Take your rarities
Take your household gods.

If you have no gods:
make them.

Editorial Preface

In the aftermath of Hurricane Katrina, many disenchanted citizens turned to religion when government failed them. In other times in history, many used religion to strengthen government policies so that their country would not fail them. The following chapters on stem cell research, evolution, and marriage highlight the fact that some social policies have significant theological dimensions. The question posed to these contributors is simply: what role does religion play in a theolegal democracy that seeks to prevent itself from becoming a purely secular nation or theocracy?

One of the most highly contested political questions of our time is not only religious but also scientific—whether or not taxpayers should fund stem cell research. In Chapter 8, Robert George, a former member of President George W. Bush's Council on Bioethics, deliberately removes explicit religious rationale from the discourse on stem cell research. Rather, he begins his chapter by making clear his religious standpoint as a Catholic while affirming the God-given attribute of reason to sufficiently and publicly discern the nature of embryos. George demonstrates that laws need not be justified by theology, but should be derived from science, morality, and universal principles, which transcend any one religious tradition. He uses secular rationale to persuade those on the left to reconsider the issue from a nonreligious perspective. As a result, George demonstrates that theology need not be the predominant rationale for determining law; rather public officials should draw upon reason, ethics, and conscience.

In Chapter 9, biologist Michael Zimmerman demonstrates that religion and science need not be in conflict with one another. He does so by examining the legal and political landscape of the evolution/creation controversy. We invite readers to pay particular attention to how Judge John E. Jones III, appointed by George W. Bush, found a local Pennsylvania school board to be "religiously motivated" to teach intelligent design (i.e., creationism) in the public schools. This landmark case, *Kitzmiller v. Dover Area School District,* is a powerful example of how local political officials used theology to determine policy. Yet Judge Jones prevented this theolegal practice by not only ruling against the religious motivations of the school board but also by deeming intelligent design to be inherently theological, not scientific.

This case ties nicely to Greenlee's previous chapter on religious judges, in that Judge Jones was a known Lutheran and Republican who chose not to use the Bible as legal rationale. This case demonstrates how the God of the Judge need not rule, nor the God of the moral majority. For instance, days before Judge Jones' ruling, the citizens of Dover elected nine new school board members, eight of whose campaigns were aligned with Judge Jones' eventual verdict. Television evangelist Pat Robinson responded, "I'd like to say to the good citizens of Dover, if there is a disaster in your area don't turn to God because you just rejected him from your city."

Liberals are quick to point fingers at religious conservatives who pervasively use theology in public discourse—but the truth is, religious liberals also contribute to a theolegal nation. For example, it is commonly recognized that biblical references have been the primary source for legally defining conjugal marriage, a marriage between one man and one woman. As Stacey Sobel and Edwin Greenlee illustrate in Chapter 10, coalitions of liberal Christian and Jewish clergy question the legal discourse on marriage, which narrowly represents a conservative Judeo-Christian worldview. In response, liberal religious coalitions have formed around alternate readings of scripture and thereby use alternative theology to promote marriage equality. Sobel and Greenlee go on to say, "In the struggle for marriage equality, Reconstructionist and Reform Jews, Unitarian Universalists, Episcopalians, Quakers, members of the United Church of Christ, Methodists, Presbyterians, Independent Catholics, American Baptists and Western Buddhists, among other religious groups, have shaped the question of marriage equality as a positive dimension of their religious belief."

There is an emerging philosophy that separates religious marriage and civil marriage. In Chapter 11 Christine Carlson discusses the term *theolegal marriage*. She proposes a separationist system where the sacrament of marriage would no longer be tied to civil marriage. Carlson argues it is in the best interest of conservative religious institutions to grant a divorce between religion and the state. No longer would conservatives fear the state threatening their freedom of belief by forcing them to marry same-sex couples. Rather, all clergy will have the autonomy to define religious marriages, whereas the state will have the authority to legally define civil marriages. As a result, separationists would deflate the political power of the religious majority, while secular arguments based on reason, not faith, would become the primary rationale to legally define civil marriages. Carlson rightfully claims this will benefit both religious liberals and conservatives.

8

Stem Cell Research[1]

Robert P. George

Appeals to religious authority have their place. That place is plainly not in philosophical debates, including philosophical debates about public policy. Do such appeals have a legitimate place in political advocacy? I think they do.

A vibrant democracy depends in part on the freedoms that allow reasonable number of people of goodwill on all sides of contested issues to make their case in the public square. That leaves as much room for arguments based on religious traditions as for those based on secular or secularist belief systems. Nor would appeals to religious authority be ruled out on constitutional grounds; the U.S. Constitution does not forbid a citizen or lawmaker to draw on religious teachings in policy debates. And though religion should not be seen as purely instrumental, religious principles often have a special and valuable power to motivate people to act for the common good. In American history, the deeply religiously motivated movements for abolition and desegregation are prime examples.

At the same time, I have some sympathy with John Rawls's proposition that appeals to religious authority in political advocacy are legitimate only where they are offered to buttress, and motivate people to act on, positions that are defensible even apart from such appeals. Like Rawls, I believe that public policy should be based on "public reasons," even though I believe that Rawls's own particular conception of what qualifies as a public reason is unreasonably narrow.[2] I understand public reasons to exclude any claim based on the allegedly "secret knowledge" of a gnostic elite or the putative truths revealed only to a select few. But this leaves room for any claims, however controversial, that are put forward for acceptance on the basis of rational argumentation, as truths accessible to reasonable persons as such.

Of course, anyone who believes God has revealed that some polity's public policy must be settled in a certain way has, by his own lights, a conclusive reason for supporting that option irrespective of whether there are any grounds for it apart from revelation. My scruples, or Rawls's, would—and should—simply cut no ice for a person in this position. Ultimately, then, I suppose that I have these scruples because I believe that God simply does not (at least not anymore) reveal that some policy should be adopted irrespective of whether there are independent grounds for it. My differences with those who have no such scruples therefore implicate certain theological judgments.

Such people may believe that God sometimes has either no reason for the public policies He commands or no reasons available to human understanding. But I join many, perhaps most, believers in holding that God is a God of *justice*, who cares what the public policy of society is on morally significant questions—for example, embryo-destructive research, abortion, marriage and sexuality, capital punishment, civil liberties and human rights, economic justice, et cetera—and does so at least in part *for reasons accessible to us as rational beings.* God's reasons in these matters are specified, I believe, by the human good, and we can ascertain the human good's requirements—principles of justice—by reason. Indeed, I think that the identification of these reasons by philosophical inquiry and analysis, supplemented sometimes by knowledge derived from the natural and/or social sciences, is *critical* to an accurate understanding of the content of revelation in, say, the Bible or Jewish or Christian tradition.

In short, I—along with most informed Catholics and many Protestants and observant Jews—understand reason not only as a truth-attaining power, but as a power through which God directs us as individuals and communities in the way of just and upright living. In this chapter, I will argue that human embryo-destructive research is unjust. But I do not consider it unjust because it is a sin (i.e., an offense against God). Rather, I consider it a sin *precisely because it involves the unjust taking of innocent human life.* That is my reason for opposing it; and that is God's reason, as I can best understand it, for opposing it and requiring that human communities protect human embryos against it. I believe that this reason can be identified and acted on even independently of God's specially revealing it.

Indeed, I believe that the precise content of what God reveals on the subject ("in thy mother's womb I formed thee...") cannot be known without the application of human intelligence, by way of philosophical and scientific inquiry. Both philosophical analysis and knowledge obtainable only by scientific inquiry were essential to settling, and continue to be essential to understanding, the precise content of the authoritative teaching of the Magisterium of the Catholic Church declaring direct abortion and embryo-destruction to be intrinsically immoral and violations of human rights.

After all, it is difficult to see how theological principles *could* settle the relevant but fundamentally scientific question of whether the embryo is a whole human being, an individual member of the species *Homo sapiens*. (Taking things a step further, suppose that this *were* an explicit tenet of revelation. Would scientific knowledge or analysis not still be needed to determine whether a particular entity is in fact an embryo rather than, say, a hydatidiform mole?) Even the apparently relevant data of, for example, Judeo-Christian revelation—for example, that some beings are made in God's image and likeness and therefore have special moral status—require unpacking by philosophical analysis. What does it mean to be made in God's image and likeness, and which entities—teratomas, hydatidiform moles, blastocysts, teenagers—are so made?

As we might expect, then, on the question of embryo ethics, different Christian denominations have interpreted and applied the shared principles of Christian revelation in different ways. Some communities, including the Church of Jesus Christ of Latter-Day Saints, the Lutheran Evangelical Church, and the Presbyterian Evangelical Church, have not officially pronounced on the permissibility of embryo-destructive research. Other Christian communities, like the Episcopal Church, have declared it permissible. Others still, including the United Methodist Church, consider embryo-destruction permissible only under defined conditions. Finally, communities like the Orthodox Church in America, the Lutheran Church-Missouri Synod, the Assemblies of God, and the Southern Baptist Convention join the Catholic Church in opposing embryo-destruction as the unjust taking of innocent human life.

But again, contrary to a common misunderstanding, the Catholic Church does not try to draw *scientific* inferences about the humanity or distinctness of the human embryo from *theological* propositions about ensoulment. It works the other way around. The theological conclusion that an embryo is "ensouled" would have to be drawn on the basis of (among other things) scientific findings about the self-integration, distinctness, unity, determinateness, et cetera of the developing embryo. In fact, the Catholic Church has not declared a teaching on the ensoulment of the early embryo, even though it affirms the rational necessity of respecting the dignity of the human being at all developmental stages, including the embryonic stage.

Thus, as I argue here for the impermissibility of human embryo-killing, I will say nothing else about religion or theology. This is not a tactical decision; rather, it reflects my view about how to think about the dispute over killing human embryos. One need not engage questions of whether human beings have immortal spiritual souls in considering whether human embryos are human beings. Nor must one appeal to any theology of ensoulment to show that there is a rational basis for treating all human beings—including those at the embryonic stage—as creatures possessing intrinsic worth and dignity.[3]

Rather, we can and should resolve our national debate over embryo-destructive research on the basis of the best scientific evidence as to when the life of a new human being begins, and the most careful philosophical reasoning as to what is owed to a human being as such, irrespective of not only race, ethnicity, and sex but also age, size, stage of development, and condition of dependency.

If we were to contemplate killing mentally handicapped infants to obtain transplantable organs, no one would characterize the controversy that would erupt as a debate about organ transplantation. The dispute would be about the ethics of killing handicapped children to harvest their vital organs. We could not resolve the issue by considering how many gravely ill people we could save by extracting a heart, two kidneys, a liver, et cetera from each mentally handicapped child. Instead, we would have to answer this question: is it right to relegate a certain class of human beings—the handicapped—to the status of objects that can be killed and dissected to benefit others?

By the same token, strictly speaking, ours is not a debate about stem cell research. No one would object to the use of pluripotent stem cells in biomedical research or therapy if they could be obtained from non-embryonic sources, or if they could be acquired by using embryos lost in miscarriages.[4] The point of controversy is the ethics of deliberately destroying human embryos to produce stem cells. The threshold question is whether it is right to kill members of a certain class of humans—those in the embryonic stage of development—to benefit others.

Supporters of embryo-destructive research insist, however, that human embryos are not human beings—or if they are human beings, that they are not yet "persons." It is therefore morally acceptable, they say, to "disaggregate" them for the sake of research aimed at finding cures or treatments for juvenile diabetes and other horrible afflictions. At the heart of the debate over embryo-destructive research, then, are two questions: is a human embryo a human being, and, if so, what is owed to an embryonic human as a matter of justice?

The adult human being that is now you or me is the same being who, at an earlier stage, was an adolescent and, before that, a child, an infant, a fetus, and an embryo. Even in the embryonic stage, you and I were undeniably whole living members of the species *Homo sapiens*. We were then, as we are now, distinct and complete—though, in the beginning, developmentally immature—human organisms. We were not mere parts of other organisms.

A human embryo is not something different *in kind* from a human being, like a rock, or a potato, or a rhinoceros. A human embryo is a human individual in the earliest stage of his or her natural development. Unless severely damaged or deprived of a suitable environment, an embryonic human being will, by directing his or her own integral organic functioning, develop himself or herself to each new stage of developmental maturity along the gapless continuum of a human life. The embryonic, fetal, infant, child, and adolescent stages are just that: *stages* in the development of a determinate and enduring entity—a human being—who comes into existence as a single-celled organism (zygote) and grows, if all goes well, into adulthood many years later.[5]

By contrast, the gametes whose union brings into existence the embryo are not whole or distinct organisms. Each is functionally (and genetically) identifiable as *part* of the male or female (potential) parent. Moreover, each gamete has only half the genetic material needed to guide the development of an immature human being toward full maturity. They are destined either to combine with an oocyte or spermatozoon and generate a new and distinct organism, or simply to die. When fertilization occurs, they do not survive; rather, their genetic material enters into the composition of a new organism.

But none of this is true of the human embryo, from the zygote and blastula stages onward. The combining of the chromosomes of the spermatozoon and of the oocyte generates what human embryology identifies as a new, distinct, and enduring organism. Whether produced by fertilization, somatic cell nuclear transfer (SCNT), or some other cloning technique, the human embryo possesses all of the genetic material and other qualities needed to inform and organize its growth. The direction of its growth is not extrinsically determined, but is in accord with the information *within* it. Nor does it merely possess organizational information for maturation; it actively uses that information in an internally directed process of development. (The first one or two divisions, in the first 36 hours, occur largely under the direction of the messenger RNA acquired from the oocyte. Still, the embryo's genes are expressed as early as the two-celled stage and are required for subsequent development to occur normally.) The human embryo, then, is a whole and distinct human organism—*an embryonic human.*

If the embryo is not a complete organism, what can it be? Unlike the spermatozoa and the oocytes, it is not merely a part of a larger organism, namely, the mother or the father. Nor is it a disordered growth or gamete tumor, such as a complete hydatidiform mole or teratoma.

Someone might say that the early embryo is an intermediate form, something that regularly emerges into a whole human organism but is not one yet. But what could cause the emergence of the whole human organism, and cause it with regularity? As I have already observed, from the zygote stage forward the development of this organism is *directed from within*, or by the organism itself. So, after the embryo comes into being, no event or series of events occur that we could construe as the production of a new organism—that is, nothing extrinsic to the developing organism itself acts on it to produce a new character or a new direction in development.

A supporter of embryo-destructive research might concede that a human embryo is a human being in a biological sense, yet deny that we owe human beings in the early stages of their development full moral respect, such that we may not kill them to benefit more fully developed human beings who are suffering from afflictions.

But to say that embryonic human beings do not deserve full respect, one must suppose that not every human being deserves full respect. And to do that, one must hold that those human beings who warrant full respect deserve it not by virtue of *the kind of entity they are*, but, rather, because of some acquired characteristic that some human beings (or human beings at some stages) have and others do not, and that some human beings have in greater degree than others do.

This position is untenable. One need not be *actually* or immediately conscious, reasoning, deliberating, making choices, et cetera in order to be a human being who deserves full moral respect, for plainly we should accord people who are asleep or in reversible comas such respect. But if one *denied* that human beings are valuable by virtue of what they are, and required an additional attribute, it would have to be a capacity of some sort, and, obviously, a capacity for certain mental functions.

Of course, human beings in the embryonic fetal and early infant stages lack immediately exercisable capacities for mental functions characteristically carried out by most human beings at later stages of maturity. Still, they possess these very capacities *in principe vel radice*, that is, in radical or "root" form.

Precisely by virtue of the kind of entity they are, they are from the beginning actively developing themselves to the stages at which these capacities will (if all goes well) be immediately exercisable. Although, like infants, they have not yet developed themselves to the stage at which they can perform intellectual operations, it is clear that they are *rational animal organisms*. That is the *kind* of entity they are. (For an entity to have a rational nature is for it to be a certain type of substance; *having a rational nature*, unlike, say, being tall, or Croatian, or gifted in mathematics, is not an accidental attribute. Each individual of the human species has a rational nature, even if disease or defect blocks its full development and expression in some individuals. If the disease or defect could somehow be corrected, it would perfect the individual as the kind of substance he is; it would not transform him into an entity of a different nature.)

Here, it is important to distinguish two senses of the "capacity" for mental functions: an immediately exercisable capacity, and a basic natural capacity, which develops over time. We have good reason to believe that the second sense, and not the first, provides the basis for regarding human beings as ends in themselves, and not as means only—as subjects possessing dignity and human rights, and not as mere objects.

First, the developing human being does not reach a level of maturity at which he or she performs a type of mental act that other animals do not perform—even animals such as dogs and cats—until at least several months after birth. A six-week-old baby lacks the *immediately exercisable* capacity to form abstract concepts, engage in deliberation, and perform many other characteristically human mental functions. If we owed full moral respect only to those who possess immediately exercisable capacities for characteristically human mental functions, it would follow that six-week-old infants do not deserve full moral respect—a conclusion that my Princeton colleague Peter Singer acknowledges and accepts. Therefore, if we may legitimately destroy human embryos to advance biomedical science, then logically, subject to parental approval, the body parts of human infants should also be fair game for scientific experimentation.

Second, the difference between these two types of capacity is merely a difference between stages along a continuum. (That is why I spoke of "two senses of the capacity"; strictly speaking, they are not distinct types of capacity.) The immediately exercisable capacity for mental functions is only the development of an *underlying* potentiality that the human being possesses simply by virtue of the kind of entity it is. The capacities for reasoning, deliberating, and making choices are gradually brought toward maturation, through gestation, childhood, adolescence, and so on. But the difference between a being that deserves full moral respect and a being that does not (and can therefore legitimately be killed to benefit others) cannot consist only in the fact that while both have some feature, one has *more* of it than the other. A mere *quantitative* difference cannot by itself provide a justification for treating entities in radically different ways.[6]

Third, the acquired qualities proposed as criteria for personhood, such as self-consciousness or rationality, come in an infinite number of degrees. If human beings are worthy of full moral respect only because of such qualities, and those qualities come in varying degrees, humans should possess rights in varying degrees. The proposition that all human beings are created equal would be relegated to the status of a myth: since some people are more rational than others (i.e., have developed that capacity to a greater extent than others have), some people would be greater in dignity than others, and the rights of the superiors would trump those of the inferiors. This conclusion would follow regardless of the acquired quality we chose as qualifying some human beings (or human beings at some developmental stages) for full respect.

So it cannot be the case that some human beings, and not others, are intrinsically valuable by virtue of a certain degree of development. Rather, *all* human beings are intrinsically valuable (in the way that enables us to ascribe to them equality and basic rights) because of the *kind* of being they are.

Since human beings are intrinsically valuable and deserve full moral respect by virtue of *what* they are, it follows that they are intrinsically and equally valuable *from the point at which they come into being.* Even in the embryonic stage of our lives, each of us was a human being and, as such, worthy of concern and protection. Embryonic human beings, whether brought into existence by union of gametes, SCNT, or other cloning technologies, should be accorded the respect given to human beings in other developmental stages.[7]

I wish to turn now to some arguments that advocates of embryo-destructive research have advanced to cast doubt on the proposition that human embryos deserve to be accorded full moral status.

In defending research involving the destruction of human embryos, Ronald Bailey, a science writer for *Reason* magazine, developed an analogy between embryos and somatic cells in light of the possibility of human cloning.[8] Bailey claims that every cell in the human body has as much potential for development as any human embryo. Embryos therefore have no greater dignity or higher moral status than ordinary somatic cells. Bailey observes that each cell in the human body possesses the entire DNA code; each has become specialized (as muscle, skin, etc.) because most of that code has been turned *off.* In cloning, those previously deactivated portions of the code are reactivated. So, Bailey says, quoting Australian bioethicist Julian Savulescu, "if all our cells could be persons, then we cannot appeal to the fact that an embryo could be a person to justify the special treatment we give it." Since plainly we are not prepared to regard all of our cells as human beings, we should not regard embryos as human beings.

Bailey's analogy between somatic cells and human embryos collapses, however, under scrutiny. The somatic cell is something from which (together with extrinsic causes) a new organism can be *generated* by the process of SCNT, or cloning; it is certainly not, however, a distinct organism. A human embryo, by contrast, already is a distinct, self-developing, complete human organism.

Bailey suggests that the somatic cell and the embryo are on the same level because both have the "potential" to develop into a mature human being. The kind of "potentiality" possessed by somatic cells that might be used in cloning differs profoundly, however, from the potentiality of the embryo. A somatic cell has a potential only in the sense that something can be done to it (or done with it) so that its constituents (its DNA molecules) enter into a distinct whole human organism, which is a human being, a person. In the case of the embryo, by contrast, he or she already is actively—indeed dynamically—developing himself or herself to the further stages of maturity of the distinct organism—the human being—he or she already is.

True, the whole genetic code is present in each somatic cell; and this code can guide the growth of a new entire organism. But this point does nothing to show that a somatic cell's potentiality is the same as a human embryo's. When scientists remove the nucleus of an ovum, insert the nucleus of a somatic cell into the remainder of the ovum, and give it an electric stimulus, they are doing more than merely placing the somatic cell in an environment hospitable to its continuing maturation and development. They are generating a wholly distinct, self-integrating, entirely new entity—an embryo, in other words. The embryo brought into being by this process is radically different from the constituents that entered into its generation.

Recently, Agata Sagan and Peter Singer have argued against the position of the last paragraph that the enucleated ovum, or the ovular cytoplasm, is indeed only environment (and so the fusion of a stem cell with it does not produce a new entity). For, they contend, if the nucleus of a stem cell were transferred to a different egg with different cytoplasm, this would not result (in their judgment) in a different embryo. They conclude, then—comparing embryos to stem cells rather than to somatic cells (a la Bailey)—that "it would seem that if the human embryo has moral standing and is entitled to protection in virtue of what it can become, then the same must be true of human embryonic stem cells."

The question is whether the cytoplasm is merely a suitable environment enabling an already existing organism (the somatic cell or stem cell) to develop capacities already within it (the claim of Bailey, Sagan, and Singer) or, on the contrary, an agent that causes a substantial change resulting in the coming to be of a new organism, the embryo (our view). However, an embryo generated by the interaction of A and B *could be* numerically identical with the embryo that might have been generated by the combination of C and B, and yet both A and C be agents producing new organisms rather than mere environments. Prior to the splitting of a flat worm, for example, there is a single flat worm, but any of various mechanical forces might produce two flat worms, and thus be the cause of the coming to be of a new substance. The splitting is more than just an environment. And the change consists not just in the internal development of what was latent all along, but rather, the production of a new organism.

In the transformation of a stem cell into a whole organism when it is fused with ovular cytoplasm, it is even more obvious that the cytoplasm is more than a suitable environment, and that the change is a coming to be of a new organism—for two reasons. First, the stem cell was not a whole organism before this fusion; before its fusion it functioned together with the other parts of a larger organism for the survival and flourishing of *that* organism, not of itself. After the fusion, there is a new whole organism, no longer a part. Second, the environment does not enter into an organism and modify its internal parts, resulting in an entity with a new developmental trajectory (evidence thus of a new entity); but the ovular cytoplasm does do just that in regard to the somatic or stem cell (or its nucleus) placed within it. The cytoplasm, or factors in the cytoplasm, *reprogram* the nucleus of the cell (whether somatic or stem) fused with it. Factors of the cytoplasm *change the epigenetic state* of what was hitherto a somatic cell or stem cell (or their nucleus). These factors modify the genes in various ways—for example, adding methyl groups to key molecules in the somatic or stem cell's DNA—so that it becomes de-differentiated, which is to say, it ceases to be a somatic cell or a stem cell (a part of a larger organism), and a new whole organism is produced (an embryo). Mere environments do not enter within a thing and rearrange its inner constituents; but the cytoplasm does, and the result is an organism with a completely different (because it is now a whole, not a part) developmental trajectory.

Somatic cells, in the context of cloning, then, are analogous not to embryos, but to the gametes whose union results in the generation of an embryo in the case of ordinary sexual reproduction.

You and I were never either a sperm cell or an ovum. Nor would a person who was brought into being by cloning have once been a somatic cell. To destroy an ovum or a skin cell whose constituents might have been used to generate a new and distinct human organism is not to destroy a new and distinct human organism—for no such organism exists or ever existed. But to destroy a human embryo is precisely to destroy a new, distinct, and complete human organism—an embryonic human being.[9]

Michael Gazzaniga, a psychologist and neuroscientist at the University of California, Santa Barbara, has proposed a different argument. While agreeing that a human embryo is an entity possessing a human genome, he has suggested that a "person" comes into being only with the development of a brain. Prior to that point we have a human organism, but one lacking the dignity and rights of a person.[10] We may therefore legitimately treat human beings in the earliest stages of development as we would treat organs available for transplantation (assuming, as with transplantable organs, that proper consent for their use is given, etc.).

In presenting his case, Gazzaniga observes that modern medicine treats the death of the brain as the death of the person—authorizing the harvesting of organs from the remains of the person, even if some physical systems are still functioning. If a human being is no longer a person with rights once the brain has died, then surely a human being is not yet a person prior to the development of the brain.

This argument suffers, however, from a damning defect. Under prevailing law and medical practice, the rationale for brain death is not that a brain-dead body is a living human organism but no longer a person. Rather, brain death is accepted because the irreversible collapse of the brain is believed to destroy the capacity for self-directed integral organic functioning in human beings who have matured to the stage at which the brain performs a key role in integrating the organism. In other words, at brain death a unitary organism is believed no longer to exist. By contrast, although an embryo has not yet developed a brain, it is clearly exercising self-directed integral organic functioning, and so it *is* a unitary organism. Its capacity to develop a brain is inherent and progressing, just as the capacity of an infant to develop its brain sufficiently for it actually to *think* is also intrinsic and unfolding.

Unlike a corpse—the remains of what was once a human organism but is now dead, even if particular systems may be artificially sustained—a human organism in the embryonic stage of development is a complete, unified, self-integrating human individual. It is not dead but very much alive, even though its self-integration and organic functioning are not brain-directed at this stage. Its future lies ahead of it, unless it is cut off or not permitted to develop its inherent capacities. Therefore, defenders of embryonic human life insist that the embryo is not a "potential life," but is rather a life *with potential*. It is a potential *adult*, in the same way that fetuses, infants, children, and adolescents are potential adults. It has the potential for agency, just as fetuses, infants, and small children do. Just like human beings in the fetal, infant, child, and adolescent stages, human beings in the embryonic stage are already, and not merely potentially, human beings.[11]

In an essay in the *New England Journal of Medicine*, Harvard political theorist Michael Sandel claimed that human embryos are different *in kind* from human beings at later developmental stages. This argument truly takes us to the heart of the matter: is a human embryo a human being? At its core is this analogy: Although every oak tree was once an acorn, it does not follow that acorns are oak trees, or that I should treat the loss of an acorn eaten by a squirrel in my front yard as the same kind of loss as the death of an oak tree felled by a storm. Despite their developmental continuity, acorns and oak trees are different kinds of things. He maintains that just as acorns are not oak trees, embryos are not human beings.

Sandel's argument begins to go awry with his choice of analogates. The acorn is analogous to the embryo, and the oak tree (he says) is analogous to the *human being.* But in view of the developmental continuity that science fully establishes and Sandel concedes, the proper analogate of the oak tree is the *mature* human being, in other words, the adult. Sandel's analogy has its apparent force because we feel a sense of loss when a mature oak is felled— assuming it is a magnificent or beautiful oak. But while it is true that we do not feel the same sense of loss at the destruction of an acorn, it is also true that we do not feel the same sense of loss at the destruction of an oak *sapling*. But clearly the oak tree does not differ in kind from the oak sapling.

This example shows that we value oak trees not because of the kind of entity they are, but because of their magnificence. The magnificence of an oak tree reflects either accidental properties or instrumental worth; a mature tree provides our house with shade and is aesthetically pleasing to behold. Neither acorns nor saplings are magnificent, so we do not experience a sense of loss when they are destroyed. If oak trees were valuable by virtue of the *kind* of entity they are, then it would follow that it is just as unfortunate to lose an acorn as an oak tree.

The basis for our valuing human beings is profoundly different from the basis for valuing oak trees. As Sandel concedes, we value human beings precisely because of the *kind* of entities they are. Indeed, that is why we consider all human beings to be equal in basic dignity and human rights. We most certainly do not believe that especially magnificent human beings—such as Michael Jordan or Albert Einstein—are of greater *fundamental* worth and dignity than human beings who are physically frail or mentally impaired. We would not tolerate the killing of a handicapped child or a person suffering from, say, brain cancer in order to harvest transplantable organs to save Jordan or Einstein.

And we do not stand for the killing of infants, *which on Sandel's analogy would be precisely analogous to the oak saplings whose destruction we do not necessarily regret.* Managers of oak forests freely kill saplings, just as they might destroy acorns, to ensure the health of the more mature trees. No one gives it a second thought. This is precisely because we do not value members of the oak species—as we value human beings—because of the *kind* of entity they are. If we did value oaks in this way, then we would have no less reason to regret the destruction of saplings, and possibly even acorns, than that of mature oak trees. Conversely, if we valued human beings in a way analogous to the way we value oak trees, then we would have no grounds to object to killing human infants or even mature human beings who are "defective."

Sandel's defense of human embryo-killing on the basis of an analogy between embryos and acorns collapses the moment one brings into focus the profound difference between the basis on which we value oak trees, and that on which we ascribe value to human beings. We value oaks for their accidental properties and their instrumental worth. But we value human beings because of the intrinsic worth and dignity they possess by virtue of the kind of entity they are.

I now consider a final objection. Some have claimed that the phenomenon of monozygotic twinning shows that the embryo in the first several days of its gestation is not a human individual. The suggestion is that as long as twinning can occur, what exists is not yet a unitary human being, but only a mass of cells—each cell being totipotent and allegedly independent of the others.

It is true that if a cell or group of cells is detached from the whole at an early stage of embryonic development, the detached part can become an organism with the potential to develop to maturity as distinct from the embryo from which it was detached. But this does nothing to show that before detachment the cells within the human embryo constituted only an incidental mass.[12]

Consider again the case of dividing a flatworm. Parts of a flatworm have the potential to become a whole flatworm when isolated from the present whole of which they are a part. Yet no one would suggest that prior to the division of a flatworm, the original flatworm was not a unitary individual. Likewise, at the early stages of human embryonic development, before specialization by the cells has progressed very far, cells or groups of cells can become whole organisms if they are divided and exist in an appropriate environment after the division. But that fact does not in the least indicate that prior to the twinning event, the embryo is other than a unitary, self-integrating, actively developing human organism. It certainly does not show that the embryo is a mere "clump of cells."

Based on detailed studies of other mammals, it is highly likely that in the first two weeks, the cells of the developing embryonic human being already manifest a degree of specialization and differentiation. From the beginning, even at the two-celled stage, the cells of mouse embryos differ in their developmental fates; they will ultimately contribute to distinct tissues within the embryo.[13] By the four-celled stage, there are clear molecular[14] and developmental[15] differences between cells of the developing mouse. At no time is the embryo a mere "clump of cells," that is, a collection of homogeneous cells that do not function together as an organismic whole.

Now some people have claimed that the human embryo does not become a human being until implantation, because (they assume) the embryo cannot establish a basic body plan until it receives external maternal signals at implantation. Only then is it a self-directing human organism. According to this view, these signaling factors somehow transform what was hitherto a mere bundle of cells into a unitary human organism.

However, embryologists argue about whether any such maternal signaling actually occurs. As Hans-Werner Denker observed, it was once assumed that in mammals, in contrast to amphibians and birds, polarity in the early embryo depends upon some external signal, since no clear indications of bilateral symmetry had been found in oocytes, zygotes, or early blastocysts.[16] But this view has been revised in the light of emerging evidence: "[I]ndications have been found that in mammals the axis of bilateral symmetry is indeed determined (although at first in a labile way) by sperm penetration, as in amphibians. Bilateral symmetry can already be detected in the early blastocyst and is not dependent on implantation."

Denker refers specifically to the work of Magdelena Zernicka-Goetz and her colleagues at Cambridge University, and that of R. L. Gardner at Oxford University, which show that polarity exists even at the two-celled stage. In contrast, Davor Solter and Takashi Hiiragi of the Max Planck Institute for Immunobiology in Freiburg argue that in the early embryo (prior to compaction and differentiation into inner cell mass and trophoblast), external factors determine the fate of each cell, rather than an internal polarity. In other words, the issue is not definitively settled. However, whichever of the two is true, it is less than candid for anyone to assert the older view without acknowledging that credible scientists from leading universities have published research contradicting it in major peer-reviewed scientific journals.

Moreover—and here is the most important point—even if it *is* the case that polarity does not emerge until a maternal signal is received at implantation, that would *not* provide any evidence that such a signal transformed a bundle of cells into a unitary, multicellular human organism. Just as the lungs begin to breathe at birth only in response to certain external stimuli, so it would make sense (if the older view is true) that differentiation into the rudiments of the distinct body parts (basic bilateral polarity) would begin only in response to some external stimuli. And this is exactly how embryology texts interpreted such signals, even prior to the publications of Zernicka-Goetz and Gardner and their teams.

There is much evidence that the human embryo is from the first day onward a unitary organism, and never a mere bundle of cells. Development in the embryo is complex and coordinated, including compaction, cavitation, and other activities in which the embryo is preparing itself for implantation.

And here is the clearest evidence that the embryo in the first two weeks is not a mere mass of cells but a unitary organism: if each cell within the embryo before twinning were independent, there would be no reason why each would not develop on its own. Instead, these allegedly independent, noncommunicating cells regularly function together to develop into a single, more mature member of the human species. This fact shows that the cells are interacting from the very beginning (even within the zona pellucida, before implantation), restraining them from individually developing as whole organisms and directing each of them to function as a relevant part of a single, whole organism continuous with the zygote. The evidence indicates that the human embryo, from the zygote stage forward, is a unitary human organism.

Supporters of embryo-destructive research have advanced other arguments against the proposition that human embryos are embryonic human beings bearing basic dignity and full moral worth. I have focused in this essay on the strongest arguments against my position and laid aside the weaker ones, such as those proposing to infer something of moral relevance from the fact that human embryos are tiny and not yet sentient; or from the fact that a high percentage of human embryos are naturally lost early in pregnancy; or from the claim that people typically either do not grieve for the loss of embryos in early miscarriages, or grieve but not as intensely as they do for children who die later in gestation or as infants.

If there is a valid argument to show that human embryos are something other than human beings in the embryonic stage of development, or that embryonic human beings lack the basic dignity and moral worth of human beings in later developmental stages, it is one of the arguments I address here. I have given my reasons for believing that none of these arguments can withstand critical scrutiny.

The debate about the value of embryonic human life is sure to continue. But if that debate is informed by serious attention to the facts of embryogenesis and early human development, and of the profound, inherent, and equal dignity of human beings, then we, as a nation, will ultimately reject the deliberate killing of embryonic humans, regardless of the promised benefits.

This does not necessarily mean we must sacrifice such benefits. Scientists have already made tremendous progress toward the goal of producing fully pluripotent stem cells by non–embryo-destructive methods. If such methods are pursued with vigor, the future might see the promise of stem cell science fulfilled, with no stain on anyone's conscience.

Notes

1. Substantial portions of this essay are drawn from two of George's previous essays. "God's Reasons: The Role of Religious Authority in Debates on Public Policy," remarks at the 1998 American Political Science Association Convention, and "Embryo Ethics," *Daedalus* 137 (1) (Winter 2008): 23–35. © 2008 by the American Academy of Arts and Sciences.
2. For a fuller development of my critique of Rawls's position, see Robert P. George, "Public Reason and Political Conflict: Abortion and Homosexuality," *Yale Law Journal* 106 (1997): 2475–2504.

3. On the Catholic Church's development of doctrine on abortion, see John Connery, S.J., *Abortion: The Development of the Roman Catholic Perspective* (Chicago: Loyola University Press, 1997). For a clear statement of Catholic teaching and its ground, see the document *Donum Vitae*, issued by the Congregation for the Doctrine of the Faith on February 22, 1987, http://www.vatican.va/romancuria/congregations/cfaith/documents/rc_con_cfaith_doc_19870222_respect-for-humanlife_en.html: "[T]he conclusions of science regarding the human embryo provide a valuable indication for discerning by the use of reason a personal presence at the moment of this first appearance of a human life: how could a human individual not be a human person?" (Section 5, I, 1, para. 3).

4. It appears that we will soon be able to obtain embryonic stem cells, or their equivalent, by means that do not require the destruction of human embryos. Important successes in producing pluripotent stem cell lines by reprogramming (or "de-differentiating") human somatic cells have been reported in highly publicized papers by James A. Thomson's research group, "Induced Pluripotent Stem Cell Lines Derived from Human Somatic Cells," *Sciencexpress*, www.sciencexpress.org/22 November2007/ 10.1126science.1151526, and Shinya Yamanaka's research group, "Induction of Pluripotent Stem Cells from Adult Fibroblasts by Defined Factors," *Cell* (published online, November 20, 2007). Citing these successes, Ian Wilmut of Edinburgh University, who is credited with producing Dolly the sheep by cloning, has decided not to pursue a license granted by British authorities to attempt to produce cloned human embryos for use in biomedical research. According to Wilmut, embryo-destructive means of producing the desired stem cells will be unnecessary: "The odds are that by the time we make nuclear transfer [cloning] work in humans, direct reprogramming will work too. I am anticipating that before too long we will be able to use the Yamanaka approach to achieve the same, without making human embryos." Wilmut is quoted in Roger Highfield, "Dolly Creator Ian Wilmut Shuns Cloning," *Telegraph.co.uk*, November 16, 2007. For a survey of possible non–embryo-destructive methods of obtain pluripotent stem cells, see The President's Council on Bioethics, "White Paper: Alternative Sources of Pluripotent Stem Cells," May 2005, available at www.bioethics.gov.

5. A human embryo (like a human being in the fetal, infant, child, or adolescent stage) is not a "prehuman" organism with the mere potential to become a human being. No human embryology textbook known to me presents, accepts, or remotely contemplates such a view. Instead, leading embryology textbooks assert that a human embryo *is*—already and not merely potentially—a new individual member of the species *Homo sapiens*. His or her potential, assuming a sufficient measure of good health and a suitable environment, is to develop by an internally directed process of growth through the further stages of maturity on the continuum that is his or her life. Nor is there any such thing as a "preembryo." That concept was invented, as Lee Silver pointed out in his book *Remaking Eden* (New York: Avon Books, 1997), 39, for political, and not scientific, reasons. Keith Moore and T. V. N. Persaud, in *The Developing Human: Clinically Oriented Embryology*, perhaps the most widely used embryology text, makes the following unambiguous statement about the beginning of a new and distinct human individual: "Human development begins at fertilization when a male gamete or

sperm (spermatozoon) unites with a female gamete or oocyte (ovum) to form a single cell—a zygote. This highly specialized, totipotent cell marked *the beginning of each of us as a unique individual.*" Keith Moore and T. V. N. Persaud, *The Developing Human: Clinically Oriented Embryology* (Philadelphia: Saunders/ Elsevier, 2008), 15 (emphasis added).

6. Michael Gazzaniga has suggested that the embryo is to the human being what Home Depot is to a house, that is, a collection of unintegrated components. According to Gazzaniga, "it is a truism that the blastocyst has the potential to be a human being. Yet at that stage of development it is simply a clump of cells . . . . An analogy might be what one sees when walking into a Home Depot. There are the parts and potential for at least 30 homes. But if there is a fire at Home Depot, the headline isn't 30 homes burn down. It's Home Depot burns down." Quoted as "Metaphor of the Week" in *Science* 295 (5560) (March 2002): 1637. Gazzaniga gives away the game, however, in conceding, as he must, that the term "blastocyst" refers to a *stage of development* in the life of a determinate, enduring, integrated, and, indeed, self-integrating entity. If we must draw an analogy to a Home Depot, then it is the gametes (or the materials used in cloning to generate an embryo), and not the embryo, that constitute the "parts and potential."

7. For a development of the argument that human beings are valuable in virtue of the kind of entity that they are, see Patrick Lee and Robert P. George, "The Wrong of Abortion," in Andrew I. Cohen and Christopher Wellman, eds., *Contemporary Debates in Applied Ethics* (New York: Blackwell Publishers, 2005), 13–26.

8. For an argument that somatic cells are morally equivalent to embryos in view of the possibility of cloning, see Ronald Bailey, "Are Stem Cells Babies?" available at http://www.reason.com/rb/rb071101.html.

9. Lee and I replied to Bailey in a series of exchanges on *National Review Online* here: (1) (Our critique) http://www.nationalreview.com/comment/comment-george072001.shtml; (2) (Bailey's response) http://www.nationalreview. com/comment/comment-bailey072501.shtml; (3) (Our response) http:// www.nationalreview.com/comment/comment-george073001.shtml. We have responded to similar arguments recently advanced by Lee Silver in his book *Challenging Nature* here: (1) (Our critique) http://article.nationalreview.com/ ?q=otniywm2ZjJiywvlN2IyMzFjowywwmdzmmtc4MzU2mgu=; (2) (Silver's response) http://article.nationalreview.com/?q= Mjg2Y2Rkndm1Mzlkmgmy MjI3NjhkYmE0ztrjotgyzde=; (3) (Our response) http://article.nationalre-view.com/?q=MjNmZmYyN2NhNjFkywrhNmExmda2Yzhimdy5YzMyyti=; (4) (Silver's second response, followed by our second response) http://article. nationalreview.com/?q=zdk5zte4MjBimdfmZjc0M2EyNjE0mdc2ZjA4YmRm N2U=. See also Agata Sagan and Peter Singer, "The Moral Status of Stem Cells," *Metaphilosophy* 38 (2007), 264–284.

10. For Gazzaniga's argument that a human person comes into being only with the development of a brain, see President's Council on Bioethics, Session 5 meeting, January 18, 2002, transcript available at http://bioethics.gov/transcripts/ jan02/jan18session5.html.

11. Patrick Lee and I respond to the claim that human clones are not human beings and to Sandel's claim that human embryos differ in kind from human beings

at other stages in Robert P. George and Patrick Lee, "Acorns and Embryos," *New Atlantis* 7 (2005): 90–100. We reply to arguments that identify the human "person" as the brain or brain activity, and the human "being" as the bodily animal, in Robert P. George and Patrick Lee, "Dualistic Delusions," *First Things* February, 2005. Accessed at http://www.firstthings.com/article/2007/01/ dualistic-delusions--17.

12. William Hurlbut of Stanford University has pointed out that "[m]onozygotic twinning (a mere 0.4 percent of births) does not appear to be either an intrinsic drive or a random process within embryogenesis. Rather, it is a disruption of normal development by a mechanical or biochemical disturbance of fragile cell relationships that provokes a compensatory repair, but with the restitution of integrity within two distinct trajectories of embryological development." He goes on to explain that "the fact that these early cells retain the ability to form a second embryo is testimony to the resiliency of self-regulation and compensation within early life, not the lack of individuation of the first embryo from which the second can be considered to have 'budded' off. Evidence for this may be seen in the increased incidence of monozygotic twinning associated with IVF by Blastocyst Transfer. When IVF embryos are transferred to the uterus for implantation at the blastocyst stage, there is a two- to tenfold increase in the rate of monozygotic twinning, apparently due to disruption of normal organismal integrity." *Human Cloning and Human Dignity: An Ethical Inquiry*, Report of the President's Council on Bioethics, Washington, DC, July 2002, personal statement of William Hurlbut. Lee and I argue that the human embryo is a unitary human being even before implantation in Patrick Lee and Robert P. George, "The First Fourteen Days of Human Life," *New Atlantis* 13 (Summer 2006): 61–67.

13. For details of mouse embryogenesis as a guide to mammalian embryogenesis generally, see B. Plusa et al., "The First Cleavage of the Mouse Zygote Predicts the Blastocyst Axis," *Nature* 434 (7031) (March 2005): 391–395; R. L. Gardner and T. J. Davies, "The Basis and Significance of Pre-Patterning in Mammals," *Philosophical Transactions of the Royal Society B: Biological Sciences* 358 (2003): 1338–1339; J. Rossant and P. P. Tam, "Emerging Asymmetry and Embryonic Patterning in Early Mouse Development," *Developmental Cell* 7 (2004): 155–164.

14. M. E. Torres-Padilla et al., "Histone Arginine Methylation Regulates Pluripotency in the Early Mouse Embryo," *Nature* 445 (7124) (January 2007): 214–218; J. A. Stanton, A. B. Macgregor, D. P. Green, "Gene Expression in the Mouse Preimplantation Embryo," *Reproduction* 125 (2003): 457–468.

15. K. Piotrowska-Nitsche et al., "Four-Cell Stage Mouse Blastomeres Have Different Developmental Properties," *Development* 132 (3) (February 2005): 479–490.

16. On the debate regarding polarity in the early embryo, see Hans-Werner Denker, "Early Human Development: New Data Raise Important Embryological and Ethical Questions Relevant for Stem Cell Research," *Naturwissenschaften* 91 (1) (2004): 21 ff. See also Gretchen Vogel, "Embryologists Polarized Over Early Cell Fate Determination," *Science* 308 (5723) (May 2005): 782–783.

9

Evolution v. Creation

Michael Zimmerman

It is no secret that Charles Darwin was hesitant to publish his ideas on evolution and speciation because he feared the response he might receive from both scientists and religious leaders. When his ideas were forced into the open upon the receipt of an article from Alfred Russel Wallace in 1858 outlining the basics of natural selection, the core of what Darwin had been working on for decades, he quickly moved forward with the publication of *On the Origin of Species* the following year.[1]

The response was mixed with many scientists and religious leaders praising the work for its logic and good sense, while others attacked it as being unnecessary and poorly reasoned. Although, on the whole, the attack on Darwin and his ideas from religious leaders was not particularly severe; some regularly attempted to argue that his analysis was in direct contradiction to a religious worldview. Perhaps the first review of *On the Origin of Species,* published four days prior to the official release of the book, made this case clearly. As was the custom of the time, an anonymously published review, likely written by John Leifchild,[2] concludes as follows:

> The work deserves attention and will, we have no doubt, meet with it. Scientific naturalists will take up the author upon his own peculiar ground; and there will we imagine be a severe struggle for at least theoretical existence. Theologians will say—and they have a right to be heard—Why construct another elaborate theory to exclude Deity from renewed acts of creation? Why not at once admit that new species were introduced by the Creative energy of the Omnipotent? Why not accept direct interference, rather than evolutions of law, and needlessly indirect or remote action? Having introduced the author and his work, we must leave them to the mercies of the Divinity Hall, the College, the Lecture Room and the Museum.

In relatively short order, however, the vast majority of scientists and religious leaders came to understand the importance of Darwin's theory of evolution and there was little, if any, serious controversy on this front. Indeed, on April 26, 1882, Darwin was given the rare honor of being buried in Westminster Abbey in an extremely well-attended ceremony.

The reception Darwin's ideas received in the United States was similar to the British response, with scientists and clergy being quite supportive. For example, one of America's best known and most respected scientists, Asa Gray, a devout Christian and professor of natural history at Harvard University, was an early supporter and was responsible for bringing out an American edition of *On the Origin of Species* in January of 1860.

Evolutionary theory also found its way into textbooks relatively quickly. By the beginning of the twentieth century, most texts openly discussed the principles of evolution. The best selling biology textbook in the United States, *A Civic Biology* by George William Hunter, had an extensive section on evolution in its first edition in 1914.[3]

None of this is to imply, however, that the concept of evolution was not controversial or that there were no voices asking that evolution not be taught. Typical of this perspective is the Victorian woman who, in a perhaps apocryphal tale told by Stephen Jay Gould, upon hearing of evolutionary theory said, "Let us hope that what Mr. Darwin says is not true; but if it is true, let us hope that it will not become generally known."[4] Her comments, whether accurately reported or not, became typical of the first major wave of antievolution activity in the United States.

That first wave largely arose, somewhat ironically, when fundamentalist Christians banded together with social progressives in an attempt to legislate their religious agenda. As Edward Larson points out, the experience promoting the Eighteenth Amendment to the U.S. Constitution outlawing the public sale of alcohol was a critical factor that helped shape the antievolution movement. "Passage of the Eighteenth Amendment in 1919 left these evangelical prohibitionists free to agitate for other reforms. It also left them with the experience of successfully invoking law to reform social and moral behavior—successful, that is, until the Twenty-first Amendment repealed prohibition in 1933."[5]

The crest of that first antievolution wave was very broad and clearly demonstrates the belief that many thought it appropriate to use the legal system to promote a sectarian religious view. Lawrence Levine notes that, "The thirty-seven anti-evolution bills that were introduced into twenty state legislatures between 1921 and 1929 were products of the American faith that legislative action can bring into being pure morals, right thinking, and patriotic action."[6] The best known of these laws was the Butler Act (Tennessee HB 185), passed in Tennessee in 1925. John Scopes was tried in Dayton, Tennessee, during the summer of 1925 for violating this act.

The goal of the Butler Act was very simple: it outlawed the teaching of any theory that "denies the Story of the Devine Creation of man as taught in the Bible." The operative portion of the law reads, in full:

> That it shall be unlawful for any teacher in any of the Universities, Normals and all other public schools of the State which are supported in whole or in part by the public school funds of the State to teach any theory that denies the Story of the Devine Creation of man as taught in the Bible, and to teach instead that man has descended from a lower order of animals.

Three things should be noted about this law. First, the teaching of evolutionary theory itself was not prohibited. Rather, it was only when a discussion of humans occurred that the law was violated. Second, the Bible was explicitly brought into the picture as the arbiter of what was and what was not appropriate in public schools. Third, the law demonstrated no interest in ensuring that students heard different views on the subject. Instead, the law prohibited students from learning about the scientific theory of human origins.

Once the law was adopted, the American Civil Liberties Union (ACLU) began to advertise for someone to test the legality of the statute. City leaders in Dayton, believing that the attention from such a trial might be a wonderful thing to help bolster the falling economic fortunes of the town, encouraged John Scopes to serve in that capacity. From that perspective, coupled with the fact that Scopes was not the biology teacher and he only ran a review session for the final exam, the trial was a manufactured event. The goal of the ACLU was not to prove Scopes's innocence but to have the law thrown out on constitutional grounds, most likely on appeal. In this, they failed. After a circus of a trial, Scopes was convicted of violating the statute and was fined $100. When the defense team appealed the decision to the Tennessee Supreme Court, their constitutional argument was taken off the table because the court ruled that the fine was improperly assessed. According to Tennessee law, any fine over $50 had to be levied by the jury rather than the judge, and in the present case Judge John T. Raulston told the jury that he would set the fine at $100 unless they had an alternative opinion. The Tennessee Supreme Court thus overturned the verdict on this technicality. They actually went further, saying, "The Court is informed that the plaintiff in error is no longer in the service of the State. We see nothing to be gained by prolonging the life of this bizarre case. On the contrary, we think the peace and dignity of the State, which all criminal prosecutions are brought to redress, will be better conserved by the entry of a *nolle prosequi* herein. Such a course is suggested to the Attorney-General."[7] (*Nolle prosequi* is a Latin legal phrase meaning "do not pursue," and thus the court was encouraging the state to let the matter drop.) All attempts by the ACLU to raise constitutional issues and substantive complaints about the law were thus short circuited since no further appeal was possible because Scopes was no longer guilty of anything.

As mentioned above, the Scopes Trial was quite a circus with media representatives coming to view the event from around the world. Media coverage was not favorable for either Dayton or Tennessee, with many reports and political cartoons ridiculing both locals and the law. H. L. Mencken's acerbic reports for the Baltimore Sun set the early tone. These accounts, coupled with significant literary license taken by playwrights Jerome Lawrence and Robert Edwin Lee in *Inherit the Wind*, first on Broadway and then in the screen version, gives the impression that the outcome of the Scopes Trial was a resounding defeat for the antievolution movement. The reality of the situation, however, is not quite that simple.[8]

In the three years immediately following the conclusion of the Scopes Trial, numerous antievolution measures were introduced in state legislatures throughout the American south. Additionally, antievolution measures were taken up at the state and local level by a host of school boards. After failing to have an antievolution law passed in Arkansas, proponents managed to have an initiative placed on the November 1928 ballot.[9] The language was very similar to the Butler Act, and it was approved overwhelmingly, with approximately two-thirds of voters in favor.

Even more problematic for the teaching of high-quality science, however, was the fact that publishers made a conscious choice to steer clear of the controversy and amended their texts accordingly. In general, sections on evolution were removed from books. When the topic was discussed, most frequently the word "evolution" was no longer used, having been replaced by the more generic, and less scientifically appropriate, "change." Hunter's *A Civic Biology*, the book Scopes was using when he violated the Butler Act, and, incidentally, the book mandated for use in public school biology classes by the State of Tennessee, had its long sections on evolution completely removed in a revision that came out soon after the trial. Similarly, from 1925 through approximately the early 1960s, evolution was often omitted from biology classes around the country. In essence then, the goal of the Butler Act, to limit the teaching of evolution in public school classes because it conflicted with one religious view, was largely achieved for almost three decades.

Although the Butler Act was not enforced, neither was it repealed until 1967, 42 years after it was originally enacted.

The Arkansas act that was passed via ballot initiative in 1928 also remained viable for many decades. It wasn't until the U.S. Supreme Court ruled in 1968 in *Epperson v. Arkansas* that the law was found to be unconstitutional. That ruling accomplished two things. First, the ruling was solidly based on the establishment clause in the First Amendment. Second, it began a new round of activity designed to bring religious precepts into the science classroom. The Epperson decision was absolutely clear in asserting that content cannot be banned from the science classroom solely on religious grounds.

> The law must be stricken because of its conflict with the constitutional prohibition of state laws respecting an establishment of religion or prohibiting the free exercise thereof. The overriding fact is that Arkansas' law selects from the body of knowledge a particular segment which it proscribes for the sole reason that it is deemed to conflict with a particular religious doctrine; that is, with a particular interpretation of the Book of Genesis by a particular religious group. The antecedents of today's decision are many and unmistakable. They are rooted in the foundation soil of our Nation. They are fundamental to freedom.[10]

Because of that clarity, those who objected to the teaching of evolution on religious grounds realized that they were not going to be able to prevent the topic from being presented in public schools across the country. Rather than giving up, they turned to a new strategy. They took the basic Biblical principles they cared about most, a young earth, divine creation of all species, a worldwide flood, et cetera, couched them in pseudo-scientific terminology, and called the amalgam "creation science." They then began to assert that academic freedom dictated that "creation science," in their view a meaningful scientific discipline, must be taught whenever and wherever evolution is offered. Not to do so, they asserted, would be both unfair from an intellectual perspective and an infringement of the rights of those who accept divine creation as a central tenet of their religious faith. The main proponent of this strategy was attorney Wendell Bird, who outlined his thoughts in a *Yale Law Journal* article in 1978.[11] The crux of his argument was absolutely straightforward: "Incorporation of scientific creationism to neutralize public school instruction in the origin of the universe and life would not have the primary effect of advancing some religions." After graduating from law school, Bird joined the staff of the Institute for Creation Research, where he shaped his law journal article into a resolution to be introduced to local school boards. In that resolution he also focused heavily on the issue of fairness, using the term "balanced treatment" as a means to bring his religious views into science classrooms and laboratories. The resolution found its way to state legislatures across the country where it was introduced as legislation on 23 occasions in 1980 and 1981. Arkansas was one of those states and the bill cleared the Senate 22 to 2 after 15 minutes of debate and then passed in the House of Representatives by 69 to 18 without any substantive debate in the chamber. Governor Frank White signed the bill (Act 590 of 1981)[12] into law just two days later, a mere two weeks after the bill was originally introduced. Around the same time a similar bill, resulting from Bird's original resolution, was winding its way through the Louisiana legislature. Ultimately, it too was passed and was signed into law by Governor David C. Treen and became known as the Louisiana Balanced Treatment Act.

Immediately upon passage of Act 590 in Arkansas, the ACLU filed suit seeking to overturn the law on constitutional grounds. A trial was held from December 7, 1981, to December 17, 1981, in U.S. District Court before Judge William R. Overton. In a decision that was absolutely devastating to "creation science," Judge Overton ruled that Act 590 was unconstitutional on First Amendment grounds.[13] Judge Overton relied heavily on the ruling issued by the U.S. Supreme Court in 1981 in the case of *Lemon v. Kurtzman*.[14] In that case, the court set up a three-prong test, known thereafter as the Lemon test, to be used to determine whether the establishment clause of the First Amendment was being violated. The three prongs were as follows: the government's action must have a secular legislative purpose; the government's action must not have the primary effect of either advancing or inhibiting religion; and the government's action must not result in an excessive government entanglement with religion.

Judge Overton found that Act 590 failed each prong of the Lemon test, and in so doing he articulated very clearly for evolution and against "creation science." Consider just the following three brief excerpts from his opinion:

> It was simply and purely an effort to introduce the Biblical version of creation into the public school curricula. The only inference which can be drawn from these circumstances is that the Act was passed with the specific purpose by the General Assembly of advancing religion.
>
> The conclusion that creation science has no scientific merit or educational value as science has legal significance in light of the Court's previous conclusion that creation science has, as one major effect, the advancement of religion.
>
> Assuming for the purposes of argument, however, that evolution is a religion or religious tenet, the remedy is to stop the teaching of evolution, not establish another religion in opposition to it. Yet it is clearly established

in the case law, and perhaps also in common sense, that evolution is not a religion and that teaching evolution does not violate the Establishment Clause.

This conservative Arkansas judge ruled in a manner that kept the state from mandating that one particular brand of religion be inserted in public school science classrooms under the auspices of balanced treatment. He also made it clear that dressing religion up to look scientific does not make it scientific. Judge Overton's decision was also important because it was leaned on heavily by the U.S. Supreme Court when the constitutional challenges to the Louisiana Balanced Treatment raised by the ACLU reached it. The court, in an equally forceful decision,[15] also used the Lemon test to declare the Louisiana statute unconstitutional. As of these rulings, it was definitively illegal to ban the teaching of evolution and to mandate the teaching of religious doctrines in the name of science. While that should have put an end to the attempt to merge religion and science, creationist strategies evolved yet again and a new challenge for science presented itself. "Creation science" morphed into "intelligent design" and the battle was engaged anew.

The push for intelligent design is largely the product of the very well-funded Discovery Institute and, in almost every way, this attack on science is more far reaching and dangerous than that which creation science advocates initially had in mind. The Discovery Institute produced a planning document entitled "The Wedge,"[16] and that document makes it clear that the goal of intelligent design is "nothing less than the overthrow of materialism and its cultural legacies . . . . Design theory promises to reverse the stifling dominance of the materialist worldview, and to replace it with a science consonant with Christian and theistic convictions." This new view of science is particularly troubling in light of the fact that a significant amount of the Discovery Institute's funding has come from Howard F. Ahmanson Jr. As Steve Benen points out, Ahmanson has had "a long-time relationship with Christian Reconstructionism, an extreme faction of the Religious Right that seeks to replace American democracy with a harsh fundamentalist theocracy."[17]

As intelligent design is defined and promoted, it brings the supernatural into the realm of science. In other words, the existence and actions of a supernatural agent becomes a scientific explanation for natural phenomenon in the world. Since the hallmark of scientific investigation for the past 400 years or so has been the concept of falsifiability, promoting intelligent design requires a complete redefinition of science. And that redefinition brings religion front and center. The main proponents of intelligent design, Michael Behe and Scott Minnich, have testified under oath that they and many intelligent design advocates believe that the designer is the Christian God.[18]

The concept of intelligent design found its way into the courts after the Dover (PA) Area School District passed a resolution[19] in 2004 requiring that students in biology classes be read a disclaimer about evolution and be told about an alternative text they might want to explore. This alternative text, *Of Pandas and People*,[20] is nothing more than a cynical revision of an earlier version[21] with "intelligent design" replacing "creation," and "intelligent agency" replacing "intelligent creator."[22] Thus, intelligent design is defined in *Of Pandas and People* as follows: "Intelligent design means that the various forms of life began abruptly through the agency of an intelligent agency, with their distinctive features already intact—fish with fins and scales, birds with feathers, beaks and wings, etc." The book goes on to ask, "What kind of intelligent agent was it [the designer]" and to answer: "On its own science cannot answer this question. It must leave it to religion and philosophy."

Yet again, the ACLU joined the fray and brought suit against the Dover Area School District claiming that the District's policy was an obvious violation of the establishment clause of the First Amendment. The case was heard before Judge John E. Jones, a conservative judge appointed to the federal bench by President George W. Bush in 2002. Like his predecessors in other creationism cases, Judge Jones applied the Lemon test and found the District's policy to fail. Accordingly, he ruled that the policy could not be implemented. His decision is comprehensive and pulls no punches, making it very clear that it is inappropriate to force a religious perspective on public school students. Judge Jones went even further, anticipating a personal attack by those who would not be pleased by his decision:

> Those who disagree with our holding will likely mark it as the product of an activist judge. If so, they will have erred as this is manifestly not an activist Court. Rather, this case came to us as the result of the activism of an ill-informed faction on a school board, aided by a national public interest law firm eager to find a constitutional test case on ID [intelligent design], who in combination drove the Board to adopt an imprudent and ultimately unconstitutional policy. The breathtaking inanity of the Board's decision is evident when considered against the factual backdrop which has now been fully revealed through this trial. The students, parents, and teachers of the Dover Area School District deserved better than to be dragged into this legal maelstrom, with its resulting utter waste of monetary and personal resources.

Literally minutes after Judge Jones's decision was released, his prediction came to pass. The Discovery Institute issued a press release attacking him for being an activist judge: "The Dover decision is an attempt by an activist federal judge to stop the spread of a scientific idea and even to prevent criticism of Darwinian evolution through government-imposed censorship rather than open debate, and it won't work."[23]

From the 1920s through the present, religious fundamentalists have been attempting to force their particular brand of religion into the nation's public school science classrooms and laboratories. The American judicial system, at all levels, has repeatedly fought back this assault, often through the efforts of conservative, religious judges. Both Judge Overton in Arkansas and Judge Jones in Pennsylvania made particular reference to the "contrived dualism" being promoted by those clamoring for equal time for views other than evolution. They had the good sense to recognize that, despite the arguments by those who want their religious views promoted, religion and science need not be in conflict with one another. Despite loud claims to the contrary by religious fundamentalists, the controversy should not be seen as one between religion and science but as a struggle between different religious worldviews.

Thousands upon thousands of religious leaders have joined together in an organization called The Clergy Letter Project[24] to make just this point. These clergy members are countering the notion that one narrow Christian viewpoint should be privileged as the normative religious view in the country, instead, recognizing that our complex society needs to have respect for all religions as well as for those individuals who do not hold religious views. These religious leaders are calling for a paradigm shift in the relationship between religion and science. As The Christian Clergy Letter says, "Religious truth is of a different order from scientific truth. Its purpose is not to convey scientific information but to transform hearts . . . We ask that science remain science and that religion remain religion, two very different, but complementary, forms of truth." Happily, the U.S. courts seem to agree.

Notes

1. Darwin, Charles. 1859. *On the Origin of Species by Means of Natural Selection; or the Preservation of Favoured Races in the Struggle for Life.* John Murray: London.
2. *The Athenaeum*, Review of *On the Origin of Species*, November 19, 1859, 1673: 659–660.
3. Hunter, George William. 1914. *A Civic Biology: Presented in Problems.* American Book Company: New York.
4. Gould, Stephen Jay. 1999. Darwin's More Stately Mansion. *Science* 284: 2087.
5. Larson, Edward J. 1985. *Trial and Error: The American Controversy Over Creation and Evolution.* Oxford University Press: New York.

6. Levine, Lawrence W. 1965. *Defender of the Faith: William Jennings Bryan: The Last Decade, 1915–1925.* Oxford University Press, New York.

7. *Scopes v. State,* Appeal to Tennessee Supreme Court, January 17, 1927. Accessed at http://www.law.umkc.edu/faculty/projects/ftrials/scopes/statcase.htm on March 8, 2009.

8. Larson, Edward J. 2009. "Myth 20. That the Scopes Trial Ended in Defeat for Antievolutionism" in Numbers, Ronald L. (ed.). *Galileo Goes to Jail and Other Myths About Science and Religion.* Harvard University Press: Cambridge, MA.

9. The full text of Initiative No. 1 reads as follows: "Initiated Act No. 1, Ark. Acts 1929; Ark. Stat. Ann. 80–1627, 80–1628 (1960 Repl. Vol.). The text of the law is as follows: "80–1627.—Doctrine of ascent or descent of man from lower order of animals prohibited.—It shall be unlawful for any teacher or other instructor in any University, College, Normal, Public School, or other institution of the State, which is supported in whole or in part from public funds derived by State and local taxation to teach the theory or doctrine that mankind ascended or descended from a lower order of animals and also it shall be unlawful for any teacher, textbook commission, or other authority exercising the power to select textbooks for above mentioned educational institutions to adopt or use in any such institution a textbook that teaches the doctrine or theory that mankind descended or ascended from a lower order of animals." "80–1628.—Teaching doctrine or adopting textbook mentioning doctrine—Penalties—Positions to be vacated.—Any teacher or other instructor or textbook commissioner who is found guilty of violation of this act by teaching the theory or doctrine mentioned in section 1 hereof, or by using, or adopting any such textbooks in any such educational institution shall be guilty of a misdemeanor and upon conviction shall be fined not exceeding five hundred dollars; and upon conviction shall vacate the position thus held in any educational institutions of the character above mentioned or any commission of which he may be a member."

10. *Epperson v. Arkansas,* U.S. Supreme Court, November 12, 1968. Accessed at http://www.talkorigins.org/faqs/epperson-v-arkansas.html on March 8, 2009.

11. Bird, Wendell R. 1978. Freedom of Religion and Science Instruction in Public Schools, *Yale Law Journal* 83: 515–570.

12. Arkansas Act 590 of 1981. Accessed at http://www.antievolution.org/projects/mclean/new_site/legal/act_590.htm on March 8, 2009.

13. *McClean v. Arkansas Board of Education,* Federal District Court, January 5, 1982. Accessed at http://www.talkorigins.org/faqs/mclean-v-arkansas.html on March 8, 2009.

14. *Lemon v. Kurtzman,* U.S. Supreme Court, June 28, 1971. Accessed at http://caselaw.lp.findlaw.com/scripts/getcase.pl?navby=CASE&court=US&vol=403&page=602 on March 8, 2009.

15. *Edwards v. Aguillard,* U.S. Supreme Court, June 19, 1987. Accessed at http://www.talkorigins.org/faqs/edwards-v-aguillard.html on March 8, 2009.

16. *Center for the Renewal of Science & Culture. 1998.* The Wedge. Discovery Institute: Seattle.

17. Benen, Steve. 2000. From Genesis To Dominion: Fat-Cat Theocrat Funds Creationism Crusade. *Church & State* July/August. Accessed at http://www.au.org/media/church-and-state/archives/2000/07/from-genesis-to.html.

18. *Kitzmiller, et al. v. Dover Area School District*, United States District Court, December 20, 2005. Accessed at http://www.pamd.uscourts.gov/kitzmiller/kitzmiller_342.pdf on March 8, 2009.

19. The resolution adopted by the Dover Area School Board required that the following statement be read to biology students: "The Pennsylvania Academic Standards require students to learn about Darwin's Theory of Evolution and eventually to take a standardized test of which evolution is a part. Because Darwin's Theory is a theory, it continues to be tested as new evidence is discovered. The Theory is not a fact. Gaps in the Theory exist for which there is no evidence. A theory is defined as a well-tested explanation that unifies a broad range of observations. Intelligent Design is an explanation of the origin of life that differs from Darwin's view. The reference book, *Of Pandas and People*, is available for students who might be interested in gaining an understanding of what Intelligent Design actually involves. With respect to any theory, students are encouraged to keep an open mind. The school leaves the discussion of the Origins of Life to individual students and their families. As a Standards-driven district, class instruction focuses upon preparing students to achieve proficiency on Standards-based assessments."

20. Davis, P. W., and Kenyon, D. H. 1989. *Of Pandas and People: The Central Question of Biological Origins*. Foundation for Thought and Ethics: Dallas.

21. Davis, P. W., and Kenyon, D. H. 1986. *Biology and Creation*, unpublished draft.

22. Forrest, Barbara, and Gross, Paul R. 2004. *Creationism's Trojan Horse: The Wedge of Intelligent Design*. Oxford University Press: New York.

23. Discovery Institute. 2005. Press release entitled "Dover Intelligent Design Decision Criticized as a Futile Attempt to Censor Science Education," December 20, 2005. Accessed at http://www.discovery.org/a/3107 on March 8, 2009.

24. The Clergy Letter Project, www.theclergyletterproject.org, has collected signatures of thousands of U.S. clergy members who support the teaching of evolution in public school classrooms. Additionally, The Clergy Letter Project sponsors an annual Evolution Weekend event (on the weekend closest to the anniversary of the birth of Charles Darwin, February 12, 1809) in which hundreds of congregations around the world participate by doing something to elevate the quality of the discussion about the relationship between religion and science.

10

Marriage Equality

Stacey L. Sobel and Edwin J. Greenlee

Religious groups are increasingly involved in legislative and ballot initiative measures related to the rights of lesbian, gay, bisexual, and transgender (LGBT) individuals and families. A number of constitutional concerns are raised when these efforts endeavor to limit or recognize the rights of LGBT people. They include equal protection and due process guarantees in the Fifth and Fourteenth Amendments of the U.S. Constitution, as well as equal protection and due process guarantees that are included in most state constitutions.

The attempts to limit or remove rights from this group of people raise additional questions when the efforts are based upon religious tenets or beliefs. There will always be a tension between constitutional guarantees of the free exercise of religion and the imposition of religious ideas of the majority on state and federal laws, particularly when those issues are related to constitutionally protected rights and fundamental liberties. While religious values, both conservative and progressive, have a role in a theolegal democracy, basic constitutional guarantees for LGBT people should not be removed if they come in conflict with religious values. The U.S. Supreme Court has held that they will not allow morality to govern their decisions in socially controversial matters including LGBT cases. In *Lawrence v. Texas*, the Supreme Court explained:

> that the Court in *Bowers* was making the broader point that for centuries there have been powerful voices to condemn homosexual conduct as immoral. The condemnation has been shaped by religious beliefs, conceptions of right and acceptable behavior, and respect for the traditional family. For many persons these are not trivial concerns but profound and deep convictions accepted as ethical and moral principles to which they aspire and which thus determine

the course of their lives. These considerations do not answer the question before us, however. The issue is whether the majority may use the power of the State to enforce these views on the whole society . . . "Our obligation is to define the liberty of all, not to mandate our own moral code."[1]

The Supreme Court's analysis shows that religious beliefs cannot trump the rights granted to individuals through the constitution.

The issue of LGBT rights began showing distinct pluralistic tendencies when LGBT individuals started seeking legal protections in the 1970s. As a result of these efforts, legislation limiting the rights of LGBT people was introduced in state legislatures throughout the country. These legislative activities increasingly attempted to limit relationship recognition rights for same-sex couples and their families. Evangelical, Catholic, Mormon, or other conservative religions or affiliated groups were and are often at the forefront of these pieces of legislation. While each state and national attempt has involved a variety of religions or organizations, the arguments against relationship recognition are very similar: allowing recognition of same-sex couples will destroy traditional marriage and undermine families,[2] force religious organizations to perform marriages for same-sex couples, and lead to polygamy, among other things.[3]

Many of these organizations have stated that they speak for the faith community on these matters. This is not true. Many religions, denominations, and individual faith leaders perform religious marriages or other religious ceremonies recognizing same-sex couples regardless of their state's civil marriage laws. Members of a number of religious groups, including Lutherans, Methodists, Episcopalians, Presbyterians, American Baptists, Independent Catholics, Reform and Reconstructionist Jews, Unitarian Universalists, Quakers, United Church of Christ members, and Western Buddhists support relationship recognition for same-sex couples. In addition, individual members of conservative religious groups, such as Roman Catholics, Evangelical Christians, and Mormons, may reject the official stance of their churches and, as individuals, support the movement for marriage equality.

The link between marriage and faith is strong, but the rights involved in legal relationship recognition are related to civil marriage, not religious marriage. The history of marriage in this country has always included civil marriage. In the Massachusetts Bay Colony, the Puritans believed that marriage was a civil contract and it was "executed" by a magistrate, not a minister.[4] Yet, those who oppose equal marriage rights for same-sex couples appear to be unable to divorce religion from the more than one thousand federal and hundreds of state civil rights granted to married people.

Religious voices have always been engaged in the evolution of family law in our country. The difficulty for legislators, however, arises when the application of legal precedent and constitutional law conflicts with some religious views on emerging legal issues, especially when these views are well funded and organized. Since conservative religious voices have tended to have greater monetary and organizational support, their views often have a disproportionate impact on the legislative process.

In the area of marriage equality, conservative religious groups have taken the lead in actively opposing legislation that would bring about marriage equality and supporting legislation that would define marriage in a way that reflects their own religious beliefs: as between one man and one woman. In the 2008 California fight to pass Proposition 8, the conservative religious coalition was primarily made up of Roman Catholics, Mormons, Evangelical Christians, and conservative black and Latino pastors.[5] While there are individual congregants among these groups who do not support the political activism of their leaders, these groups amassed money, media coverage, and volunteers to get their religious views enshrined in the state constitution after the California Supreme Court ruled that the state constitution required marriage equality.

Other, more moderate religious groups, such as Methodists, Lutherans, and Episcopalians, view the struggle for marriage equality as a justice issue. They do not see marriage equality as objectionable on religious grounds, but something that their religious beliefs actively require them to support. For example, Unitarian Universalists, in their first principle, "covenant to affirm and promote the inherent worth and dignity of every human being."[6] For Unitarian Universalists, achieving marriage equality would be one very concrete way of expressing this principle. For other progressive religious groups, the principles of justice and fairness encourage them to struggle against all forms of discrimination, and unequal treatment by the state of same-sex relationships is viewed as a form of legal discrimination.

Progressive religious groups have become increasingly active in the struggle for marriage equality. This has led to a pluralist approach to the issue where multiple faith perspectives are now being raised on LGBT legislation. One example is the Religious Coalition for the Freedom to Marry, a coalition of religious groups that supported the struggle in Massachusetts to bring about marriage equality. Even though progressive religious groups often do not get the mass media coverage that conservative religious groups and leaders receive when they make pronouncements about controversial social issues such as marriage equality, they are increasingly impacting legislators on this issue. Conservative religious groups, such as the Roman Catholic Church, also employ paid lobbyists who act to ensure that a conservative social legislative agenda is enacted into law. All of this political activity is supported financially and by means of large numbers of activist religious volunteers. Progressive religious groups, to date, usually have not matched the financial might, the media connections, or the number of dedicated activist volunteers that are required to be successful in the political sphere, but some legislators are relying on these alternate religious perspectives to support marriage equality or oppose anti-LGBT legislation.

Too often the media presents a one-dimensional view of how religiously committed citizens view controversial social issues like marriage equality: it is seen as something that is opposed, usually on doctrinal, traditional, or scriptural grounds. Despite the growth in progressive religious participation in issues like marriage equality, the media continues to portray the debate as a one-dimensional one that ignores the vast array of beliefs that exist not only between different religious groups but even among members of religious groups that officially oppose marriage equality.[7]

The Rise of Relationship Legislation

After years of a limited number of organizations stating that they provided the religious perspective on relationship issues, religious entities with more progressive views began to raise their voices in support of legal recognition of LGBT couples. In most states, this occurred at times when anti-LGBT rhetoric and legislation threatened to deprive citizens of rights, particularly through state constitutional amendments that attempted to limit or prohibit marriages for same-sex couples and legal recognition of any relationships other than marriage for heterosexuals.

The pragmatic efforts to prevent same-sex couples from receiving recognized marriages began after a series of Hawai'i state court decisions holding that denying marriage to a lesbian couple was sex discrimination.[8] Hawai'i Future Today and the Alliance for Traditional Marriage were created in response to these decisions by the Roman Catholic Church, the Mormon Church, and fundamentalist Protestants. These faith-related group efforts to limit relationship recognition for same-sex couples set the standard for faith organizing in other states. As a result of the Hawai'i court actions, Congress passed the Defense of Marriage Act (DOMA) that defines marriage as "... only a legal union between one man and one woman as husband and wife, and the word 'spouse' refers only to a person of the opposite sex who is a husband or a wife." DOMA further states that:

> [n]o State, territory, or possession of the United States, or Indian tribe, shall be required to give effect to any public act, record, or judicial proceeding of any other State, territory, possession, or tribe respecting a relationship between persons of the same-sex that is treated as a marriage under the laws

of such other State, territory, possession, or tribe, or a right or claim arising from such relationship.[9]

Shortly after the federal law was passed, state legislatures throughout the country passed "mini-DOMA" laws prohibiting marriage equality on the state level. Even more states passed mini-DOMAs and in some cases, "super-DOMA" laws, preventing any legal recognition of unmarried couples after Vermont began civil unions at the behest of its Supreme Court in 1999.[10] Currently, 41 states have DOMA laws.

Another round of backlash legislation began after the Massachusetts Supreme Court ruled that same-sex couples must be granted the same rights and responsibilities of marriage as heterosexual couples.[11] Some members of the U.S. Senate and House of Representatives have introduced "Federal Marriage Amendments" to prohibit relationship recognition for same-sex couples in the U.S. Constitution. While the attempts to amend the U.S. Constitution in the last few years have failed, many states have successfully amended their state constitutions to prohibit marriage equality, and some states have gone even further by also prohibiting relationship recognition of any kind for unmarried couples. Thirty states now have constitutional provisions prohibiting marriage equality or more. In each of these states, religious voices were actively involved in the efforts to limit relationship recognition rights.

As these efforts to strip LGBT people of basic relationship rights have continued, gradually more states are recognizing same-sex relationships in a variety of forms. Massachusetts, Connecticut, Vermont, Iowa, New Hampshire, New York, and the District of Columbia grant full marriage equality, five states have civil unions or some other legal status granting all of the rights and responsibilities of marriage, and five additional states have more limited recognition rights for same-sex couples.

Legal Rights for LGBT Couples in Pennsylvania

Pennsylvania was one of the first states to pass a mini-DOMA law in 1996. This legislation was passed as an amendment to another piece of legislation and moved swiftly through the legislature with more than 90 percent of state legislators voting in favor of the legislation. The state DOMA passed so quickly that little organizing or lobbying was needed for passage and the role of religious voices was relatively limited.

No public efforts to limit relationship recognition in the state arose again until 2004 after Massachusetts' *Goodridge* decision. *Goodridge*, as well as marriages conducted in San Francisco and other places in the country, caused concern among Pennsylvania state legislators. Even though Pennsylvania already had a DOMA law, legislators feared it would not be enough to stop the push for relationship recognition for LGBT couples. Some legislators, in conjunction with faith-related organizations, began to look at legislative fixes to prevent same-sex couples from marrying and other types of relationship recognition in the Commonwealth.

Consequently, more than 50 separate anti-LGBT amendments to an adoption bill were introduced, attempting to prohibit not only relationship recognition for same-sex and heterosexual unmarried couples, but also banning adoption by all unmarried individuals, ending common law marriage, prohibiting domestic partner benefits to state employees and anyone doing business with the state, among other things. This package of legislation reached far beyond marriage equality and caused activists to form a new alliance: the Value All Families Coalition (VAFC).

By sweeping so broadly, these amendments engendered their own defeat. For the first time in the state's history, the LGBT community worked with its non-gay allies to halt legislation that primarily targeted LGBT rights. The VAFC was created and coordinated by the Center for Lesbian and Gay Civil Rights (CFCR and now known as Equality Pennsylvania) and the ACLU of Pennsylvania. This newly formed coalition was comprised of LGBT organizations, children's advocates, labor unions, religious organizations, and other allied groups. The coalition worked to successfully halt the amendments through significant press coverage opposing the legislation and an unprecedented amount of constituent phone calls, letters, and emails asking legislators not to support the legislation. The prime sponsor of this legislation voluntarily withdrew the bills with the warning that there would be further efforts to prevent same-sex couples from marrying in the next legislative session.

In the end of 2005, legislators in both the Pennsylvania House and Senate began seeking support for an amendment to the state constitution, prohibiting legal recognition of unmarried couples. These efforts were strongly supported by the Pennsylvania Family Institute and the Pennsylvania Catholic Conference. The Roman Catholic Church, through the Pennsylvania Catholic Conference, maintains a strong lobbying presence in Harrisburg,[12] the capitol of the Commonwealth, and utilized its resources for the constitutional amendment.

As it became clear that the only voices organizing the support of the constitutional amendment were religious or religiously affiliated groups, opponents to the legislation recognized the need to provide alternative religious voices to the discourse. In the spring of 2006, the CFCR along with the VAFC's faith-related organizations began organizing the Faith Coalition for Pennsylvania Families. The Faith Coalition was coordinated by the CFCR with significant leadership from individual faith leaders that belonged to the coalition. The coalition quickly grew to include more than 100 faith leaders and organizations from across the Commonwealth. While the Faith Coalition was organizing, the constitutional amendment was winding its way through the Pennsylvania House of Representatives.

The constitutional amendment passed the House in June 2006 and was sent to the Senate. In response to this development, the Faith Coalition organized a press conference to announce its formation and to urge legislators to oppose the constitutional amendment. The press conference included faith leaders from Presbyterian, Episcopal, Quaker, American Baptist, Independent Catholic, United Church of Christ, Reform Judaism, Metropolitan Community Church congregations, and the Lancaster Theological Seminary.

The Faith Coalition created a brochure explaining its opposition to the constitutional amendment, stating in pertinent part,

> William Penn started a "holy experiment" in Pennsylvania—a beacon of religious liberty where all people would be welcome to worship according to their conscience, not according to the dictates of their rulers. Penn, a Quaker, experienced religious persecution for his beliefs in England, where Quakers and others suffered the refusal of the state to recognize their marriages, and faced imprisonment and death. Pennsylvania's religious tolerance served as a haven for communities persecuted for their beliefs and became a model for the United States. Today, Penn's legacy of religious liberty is under attack in Pennsylvania, as lawmakers debate adding an amendment to the Commonwealth's constitution that would define marriage according to the doctrines of some religious sects, while denying other religious denominations the freedom to live according to their deeply-held beliefs. Civil marriage is a contract between two adults who agree to commit to one another for life. Clergy from a variety of religious traditions from across Pennsylvania have formed the Faith Coalition for Pennsylvania Families to fight this amendment.

The coalition members then visited every state senator requesting them to not amend the constitution. Coalition members were asked to visit particular legislators because their congregations or congregants were located in a legislator's district. Other coalition members visited legislators of the same faith background to discuss their opposition to the legislation based upon their faith perspective.

Many legislators were shocked to see an organized faith response opposing the legislation. Typically, the Pennsylvania Catholic Conference is the most organized and active faith lobbying voice in the Capitol. When many of the Faith Coalition members, dressed in their religious vestments, visited legislators, the legislators incorrectly assumed that the coalition members supported the constitutional amendment. By the end of June, all state senators and their staff were familiar with the Faith Coalition and its opposition to the legislation. The constitutional amendment was amended in the Senate by limiting its language to prohibiting marriage for same-sex individuals and removing the language related to other relationship recognition. The Faith Coalition played an invaluable role in educating the legislators. Many of the senators voted for this version hoping that the legislature would run out of time to pass the same version in both chambers and, consequently, killed the measure.

For individual clergy leaders, taking a stance against the Pennsylvania Marriage Amendment was an expression of deeply held religious beliefs. Riess W. Potterveld, President of the Lancaster Theological Seminary (United Church of Christ), has written that:

> Over the past three decades, one of the conclusions reached is that our communities include couples of the same-sex or gender orientation who quite naturally discover each other, develop strong and enduring relationships, in some cases establish families with children, and become important social units within our communities . . . But regardless of whether or not they are even seeking societal or legal recognition, they do see Senate Bill 1250 [the Pennsylvania Marriage Protection Amendment] as a further attempt by some legislators to delegitimize the status of their relationships and to restrict their rights and privileges as citizens. Many of their stories contain an enormous amount of pain inflicted by society and by individual persons that directly and indirectly refuse to accept their legitimacy and offer not affirming words but bile; words that exclude, recriminate, discriminate, offer injustice and denial of rights . . . The commitment of a growing number of clergy is to find ways to support these couples and families, to encourage their faithfulness and growth. Actions taken have included the performance of holy unions or holy covenanting ceremonies that to some extent parallel the marriage ceremony of heterosexual couples legally recognized by the state. These are opportunities to offer part of what the state has denied—a time of sacred blessing, an opportunity for families and friends to gather to share in a deep ritual through which commitments are articulated and bonds deepened. What we want for all people in relationships is support, dignity, an opportunity to shape a common life.[13]

Supporting marriage equality in Pennsylvania, thus, was an expression, by a clergyperson, of deeply held religious values. Bishop Tim Cravens, of the Independent Catholic Christian Church in Media, Pennsylvania, finds that the denial of marriage equality to all citizens is an act of alienation and social isolation that is contrary to his religious views. He writes that:

> The Independent Catholic Christian Church believes that Jesus Christ came to abolish the alienation and isolation separating people from God and one another. One source of this alienation is the rigid classification of people based on sex, sexual orientation, or parentage. We believe that ALL are invited by Christ to participate fully in the life of the church, regardless of sex or sexual orientation. We see this beautifully articulated in Galatians 3:28—"There is no longer Judean nor Greek, there is no longer slave nor free, there is no longer male and female; for all of you are one in Christ Jesus." Our interpretation of this is that all Christians are to be treated equally as regards the sacraments—which means that all marriages between two baptized persons entering into lifelong covenant are sacramental. There can be nothing disordered about lifelong, committed covenanted love—and to declare as "disordered" a marriage because the partners are not of the "right" sex or ethnic heritage is to repudiate one of the central messages of reconciliation in the Gospel. The Independent Catholic Christian Church is a creedally orthodox, scripturally based, and in many ways fairly traditional church. For our legislators to enshrine into law the doctrines of other churches and deny ours is to establish the Roman Catholic, Southern Baptist, and Mormon denominations, among others, as quasi-official state religions and to deny our church the right to the free exercise of ours. As people of faith who are very serious about our walk with Christ and our prayer lives, we deserve to have our voices heard equally with those of the Religious Right, who do not have a monopoly on the serious practice of religion. Every religious community should have the right to determine its own policies regarding who may and may not be married—I once met a rabbi who, in responding to my question about whether she would marry same-sex couples, replied without missing a beat "As long as they're both Jewish"—but the state should offer civil marriage to all adult couples willing to commit their lives to one another, regardless of their religious affiliation or lack thereof.[14]

Bishop Cravens sees that transforming the religious beliefs of particular groups of citizens into law, as would occur if the Pennsylvania Marriage Amendment was enacted, is establishing the beliefs of one religiously conservative group of believers at the expense of the beliefs of other, more socially progressive religious groups.

The efforts to pass a constitutional amendment in the state were dormant until early 2008. At that time, action began in the state Senate. Once again, the Pennsylvania Catholic Conference was extremely active. In Pennsylvania, the Roman Catholic Church financially supported the large conservative religious coalition, Pennsylvania for Marriage,[15] which is pushing for passage of the Marriage Protection Amendment. The newspaper *Catholic Accent* reports that "The coalition received a big boost as the national and state councils of the Knights of Columbus . . . donated a check in the amount of $300,000 on Sept. 18 (2007) to Cardinal Justin F. Rigali, Archbishop of Philadelphia, who in turn presented the check to Pennsylvania for Marriage."[16] Pennsylvanians for Marriage organized an extensive grassroots effort in support of the legislation and encouraged involvement through websites, churches, and billboards on the Pennsylvania Turnpike. The same sort of financial support by the Roman Catholic Church was seen in the 2008 California campaign for Proposition 8. In that instance the Roman Catholic Church's opposition to marriage equality was demonstrated when the Knights of Columbus contributed $1 million to support the passage of the proposition.[17] The Mormons provided even greater financial support to Proposition 8 in California by contributing $5 million to the effort.[18]

During the six-month period that the constitutional amendment was active in the legislature, many legislators received phone calls from constituents on Monday mornings as a result of extensive church outreach. These efforts were primarily conducted in Catholic Churches and included pleas in church bulletins and services for congregants to contact their legislators and ask for them to support the constitutional amendment.

Meanwhile, progressive faith organizations raised their voices in opposition to the legislation. Their activities included a Unitarian Universalist lobby day at the Capitol and hundreds of people of faith attending a Capitol rally opposing the legislation. The legislation was once again defeated.

In the end, most Pennsylvania legislators would have preferred that the constitutional amendment issue not even be raised in the legislature. But for the religious voices in opposition to relationship recognition, it is highly unlikely that the issue would have even been raised.

Conclusion

The U.S. Constitution grants extensive First Amendment rights and religious protections. As a result, faith-related organizations have exercised these rights to impact legislation on both the federal and state levels on a wide variety of issues. Religious voices have been particularly involved in social issues and most recently have fostered the movement of legislation prohibiting or limiting legal relationship recognition for same-sex couples. Ironically, these conservative religious efforts to restrict the rights of LGBT people have caused more socially progressive clergy and religious organizations to organize themselves in opposition to anti-LGBT legislation.

Religious perspectives will always play a role in social issues of the day. It is critical, however, for legislators to remember that while people of faith have their rights to give their faith perspective on an issue, governments should be making decisions on the basis of state and federal law.

America is a theolegal nation in the sense that religious groups have, and will continue to have, a strong impact on the outcome of legislation around contentious social issues. While many progressives may look to the ideal of a strict separation of church and state in the area of legislation, this does not describe what actually occurs.

The participation of religiously committed individuals and groups in the legislative process is not inherently undemocratic. However, the recent dominance of conservative voices and groups, the inordinate media coverage that these groups receive, and the financial and volunteer support that conservative religious groups muster to enact legislation that is congruent with their religious views needs to be balanced by a similar commitment from progressive religious groups and individuals. In order to effectively pursue a pluralist approach to these issues, progressive religious groups need more visibility. They need to talk to the media, lobby their legislators, volunteer in campaigns, and provide the needed financial support. In addition, they can add their voices and their skills to those of secular groups who support civil rights and social justice issues.

The involvement of progressive religious groups with legislation and legal change in America has a long history. In the nineteenth century many progressive religious groups supported the abolition of slavery. In the twentieth century they supported the civil rights struggle and the struggle for gender equality. In the early twenty-first century we see the beginning of a movement among progressive religious groups and individuals to support marriage equality and other legal reforms that will bring about equal treatment under the law for LGBT citizens. Progressive religious groups are again contemplating how their values are being reflected in the world that we create day-by-day through our actions in the political sphere, and discerning whether a more active involvement with progressive political causes would be congruent with their deeply held values.

Notes

1. 539 U.S. 558, 571 (1992), quoting *Planned Parenthood of Southeastern Pa. v. Casey,* 505 U.S. 833, 850, 112 S.Ct. 2791, 120 L.Ed.2d 674 (1992).
2. Some people argue that marriage has always been the same, marriage rights have never been extended to same-sex couples and they should not be granted now. This limited view denies the reality of "traditional marriage" throughout history, including polygamy as related in Judeo/Christian religious teachings. It also ignores the diminished legal status of married women in many states

in this country well into the twentieth century and the fact that women were considered the property of their husbands for most of recorded history. Marriage laws also prohibited two people of different races from marrying until the twentieth century in many states in this country.

3. Schuman offers an exhaustive examination of many of the reasons that religious groups opposed same-sex marriage.

4. David Hackett Fischer, *Albion's Seed: Four British Folkways in America* (New York: Oxford University Press, 1989), 78–79.

5. Jesse McKinley and Kirk Johnson, Mormons Tipped Scale in Ban on Gay Marriage, *New York Times*, November 15, 2008, p. A1.

6. John A. Buehrens and Forrest Church, *A Chosen Faith: An Introduction to Unitarian Universalism* (Boston: Beacon Books, 1989), xxiv.

7. Saul M. Olyan and Martha C. Nussbaum, eds., *Sexual Orientation and Human Rights in American Religious Discourse* (New York: Oxford University Press, 1998) present a detailed look at the dynamics within a number of religious groups with respect to marriage equality and to other issues relating to sexual orientation including Roman Catholic, Jewish, Mainline Protestant, and African American churches and synagogues.

8. *Baehr v. Lewin*, 852 P.2d 44 (Haw. 1993). (Best Cite?)

9. 1 U.S.C. § 7. 28 U.S.C. § 1738C (1996).

10. *Baker v. Vermont*, 744 A.2d 170 (Vt. 1999).

11. *Goodridge v. Dep't of Pub. Health*, 798 N.E.2d 941 (Mass. 2003).

12. A 2007–2008 report on the Pennsylvania Department of State website, for example, lists 36 individuals registered as lobbyists as well as two lobbying firms engaged by the conference.

13. Personal email communication, February 16, 2009.

14. Personal email communication, February 18, 2009.

15. Pennsylvania for Marriage is a coalition made up of the Pennsylvania Family Institute, the Pennsylvania Catholic Conference, and the Pennsylvania Pastors Network. See Activists Renewing Push for Same-Sex Marriage Amendment in Pennsylvania, *Pittsburgh Tribune-Review* Monday, December 3, 2007.

16. Group wins grant to promote Marriage Protection Amendment, *Catholic Witness* Thursday, October 11, 2007, p. 16.

17. Knights of Columbus contributes $1 million to Proposition 8 Campaign, Catholic New Agency, August 20, 2008, at www.catholicnewsagency.com.

18. Jesse McKinley and Kirk Johnson, Mormons Tipped Scale in Ban on Gay Marriage, *New York Times*, November 18, 2008, p. A1.

11

Theolegal Marriage

Christine Carlson

I was baptized twice. The first time was in a hospital delivery room. Born a month premature with fluid-filled lungs, and not expected to live, a well-intentioned Catholic nurse immediately performed the ritual so that if I died, I would gain entrance to heaven. Several weeks later, released to my parents' care, my formal baptism occurred in the sanctuary of the picture-perfect white clapboard Catholic Church tucked in the hills of Lenni, Pennsylvania. I was anointed with holy water dipped from a seemingly ancient marble font as the priest blessed me in the name of the Father, Son, and Holy Spirit. I can imagine the joy of my godmother as she held me, my tiny frame draped in a lace-trimmed christening gown, knowing I had survived and was now officially in God's care. To commemorate this event, the Catholic Church awarded me a baptismal certificate that gave me significant religious benefits, most notably, absolution from original sin, entrance into the Catholic community, and the opportunity to attain eternal life in heaven.

At the same time, the Commonwealth of Pennsylvania issued me a birth certificate thereby giving me significant public benefits, including the rights and privileges that U.S. citizenship provides. Thus, as a result of my birth, I retain two documents. Each provided me with distinct and separate religious and public benefits. The first a Catholic baptismal certificate signed by a religious professional, and the latter, a birth certificate, signed by a public official.

As an adult, I married. Part of me regrets that the ceremony was not held in that picturesque church-on-a-hill, but since I had abandoned Catholicism, it was not permitted. But had I remained true to the faith of my birth, what a wedding it would have been—walking down the familiar aisle wrapped in the security of my late mother's satin wedding gown, sunlight streaming through stained-glass windows. The priest, a long-time family friend, would have blessed the union with abundant religious benefits, including permission to have sexual relations with the intent of going forth and multiplying, as well as the support of our Catholic community as my spouse and I endeavored to honor each other until death. Instead, the ceremony was held beneath the glaring skylights of a contemporary Unitarian Universalist church, performed by a minister who offered me the security that my ceremony would be sacred.

Pennsylvania also endorsed our union by granting us many public benefits. With our newly formed, state-endorsed partnership, we received the 1,049 federal rights and privileges given to married couples. We could own property as tenants in the entirety, and would be recognized officially as a distinct entity in all circumstances, by all people and organizations.

As a result of that marriage, I received one document—a marriage license. It is an official license issued by the state, yet it is signed by a member of the clergy. Unlike the baptismal and birth certificates that clearly delineate the separate religious and public benefits I received at my birth, my marriage license seeks to give me both. It is, in effect, a theolegal marriage license—a government-issued document conferred by a religious professional performing the "sacrament" of marriage as a civil act.

And so I wonder: why do those wishing to marry in a church obtain a license from the state? Why does the state recognize religious marriages? And why do clergy, whose solemnization of the religious marriage results in a couple's ability to receive public benefits, serve as public officials?

Our current dual system of marriage is a theolegal system, and it is so ingrained in our society that we can't see the forest for the trees. We do not see that where the institution of marriage is concerned, church and state are married. And in order for the relationship to prosper in the best interests of both religion and the public, divorce proceedings should be initiated.

The Wedding

The characteristics of marriage as practiced in the United States originated much earlier than the time of our country's founding, with the dawn of Christianity. Early Christians consented to marry one another. In the Gospels of the New Testament, Jesus is quoted as saying that "two shall become one."[1] St. Paul set limits on sexual behavior and prohibited polygamy and homosexuality in his missives to the Corinthians and the Romans.[2] In the first century, St. John Chrysostom pronounced that, "The wife is a second authority. She should not demand equality, for she is subject to the head." During the same period, St. Augustine wrote that marriage is "the ordained means of procreation."[3] Thus, Christian marriage came to encompass specific characteristics: it was to be a consensual, permanent, monogamous, heterosexual, patriarchal, child-bearing union with the purpose of protecting society and serving God. This view of marriage differed markedly from the concurrent practice of the Romans and those in other parts of the world. Nancy Cott writes, "The belief systems of Asia, Africa and Australia, of the Moslems around the Mediterranean, and the natives of North and South America all countenanced polygamy and other complex marriage practices."[4] And Martha Nussbaum also notes that, "in all pre-Christian Mediterranean traditions and civilizations, same-sex romantic relationships were highly regarded."[5]

Early Christians made their wedding vows to one another, often in private, and their families and society accepted these marriages as valid. As Catholicism grew, it controlled both the civil and religious realm of Western Europe. In the sixteenth century, new laws were enacted to ensure church control of the legitimacy of Catholic marriages: couples wishing to marry were required to publish banns of marriage—post notice of their intent to marry—in the church three times prior to the wedding. Members of the community were obligated to notify a priest if there was reason to deny permission to marry. Couples were also required to have their vows solemnized by a priest with at least two witnesses.[6] Throughout the Enlightenment and Reformation, Catholic and then Anglican Church law influenced the development of English Common Law.

Given their origin, it is no surprise then that the founding fathers of the United States adopted the marriage characteristics and practices of this system. But they also saw marriage as a valuable tool for promoting good citizenship in a new kind of government, thus ensuring the enduring success of a new nation. As Cott notes:

> The United States was a political experiment, an attempt to establish a republic based on popular sovereignty in a large and diverse nation. The character of the citizens mattered far more than in a monarchy. Concern for honor drove monarchy; fear made despotism work. In a republic, the people were sovereign, and its motivating principle was political virtue. The government would depend on the people's virtue for its success.[7]

The state's interest in supporting marriage was to create domestic stability in the nation through the creation of established households. Our nation was formed without the establishment of a national religion, but its laws concerning marriage were directly derived from religious practices.

This system of marriage as first developed, and traditions still practiced, supports the premise that the United States is a theolegal nation.

The U.S. federal government has since created a legal and social framework that supports this theological interpretation of marriage, and the individual states defined specific rules to oversee it. In addition to the traditional Christian marital characteristics of consent, permanence, monogamy, heterosexuality, patriarchy, and procreation, marriage was also defined by the underlying cultural assumptions of the time, especially those involving the belief that those created in God's image were white, and "we the people" applied only to Caucasian men. For example, African American slaves were not granted marital rights: the enforcement of such would have interfered with white slaveholders' interests. While early colonial states had laws against whites marrying nonwhites, most southern states did not officially outlaw these marriages until after the Civil War because the thought of such unions was contrary to Southern antebellum cultural norms. As our country expanded westward, Christian marriage characteristics were imposed on an often matrilineal and polygamous Native American population in an effort to create stability in what were considered uncivilized territories.[8] Twentieth-century legislation continued to support marriage as culturally desirable: when the New Deal created the social security and welfare support systems, social security provided a higher level of benefits to married women while welfare provided a much lower level of benefits to unmarried women. The married woman earned superior benefits by virtue of their having been married.

By the late 1800s, states began requiring marriage licenses. The states' decision to become involved in determining marital status derived from the need to protect the legal rights of married persons and to settle property disputes and estates. Perhaps it would have been appropriate at that time to officially separate the individual functions of religious and public marriages. We seem to have missed a perfect opportunity to separate sacramental rites from civil rights.

Irreconcilable Differences

Congress and the Supreme Court have since overturned many of the traditional Christian and cultural marriage characteristics: with the abolishment of slavery, African-Americans were permitted to marry; interracial marriage with whites[9] became legal and no longer a cultural anomaly; women's rights ended legal patriarchy; legalization of birth control and abortion gave married and unmarried couples choices regarding procreation; no-fault divorce set permanence aside.

Three of the traditional characteristics remain: consent, monogamy, and heterosexuality. First, in a nation that promotes the right to liberty and the pursuit of happiness, marriage is and should be, consensual.

Second, marriage is, and should be, monogamous. This was a difficult concept for me: after all, shouldn't a religion's sanction of polygamy be protected by the First Amendment? The Supreme Court determined that polygamy was not protected under the First Amendment's free exercise clause.[10] Chief Justice Waite based his findings on the writings of Francis Lieber, who believed that "polygamy was the essence of patriarchy, and patriarchy in turn was associated with despotism, not republican democracy."[11] In this way polygamy extends beyond the religious realm: social consequences conflict with both the state's desire to create stability and the individual's right to liberty. Since marriage is an agreement between two equals, there is no true equality in a polygamous relationship. In actuality, women in polygamous relationships are subjugated and forced to abandon their liberty, and the resulting exceptionally large families often become the recipients of government financial support, thereby burdening society. The rationale used by the court proves how strong society and the law valued the concept of monogamy as a Christian and cultural tradition.

Third, heterosexuality as a marriage requirement is now the focus of public debate at both state and federal levels. When some states began to consider legalizing same-sex marriage, it hit a nerve in the collective psyche of the majority, thus spurring Congress to pass, and President Clinton to sign, the Defense of Marriage Act in 1996. The act defines marriage as "only a legal union between one man and one woman as husband and wife," and gives states the opportunity to disavow same-sex marriages legalized in other states. A majority of states have since passed similar laws or amended their constitutions to limit marriage to heterosexual couples. The passage of these laws serves as recent examples of the government striving to uphold this religious characteristic of marriage. The state constitutions of Iowa and California, two states where heterosexual marriage has been successfully challenged in the courts, have concluded that marriage is a civil right for all individuals. As confirmed by the Iowa Supreme Court in its April 2009 ruling of *Varnum, et al. v. Brien*, the use of intermediate scrutiny reveals that the state's objectives with regard to marriage are not substantially furthered by the exclusion of same-sex couples from civil marriages.[12] In 2008, over 7 million voters in California (52%) followed the national trend to define marriage between a man and a woman by passing the California Marriage Protection act, known as "Proposition 8." This *tyranny of the majority* was overturned when U.S. District Judge Vaughn Walker ruled it unconstitutional on the basis that it violated due process and equal protection.[13] The final outcome of this case is yet to be determined.

In his ruling, Judge Walker found that domestic partnerships are inferior to marriages, implying that separate civil unions for homosexuals and legalized marriages for heterosexuals is unconstitutional. But what if all couples had the right to domestic partnerships or civil unions as an alternative to marriage? France began allowing civil unions in 1999. Since then, the majority of couples participating in civil unions are heterosexual. This allows them the public benefits of marriage without the religious influence.[14] Regardless of one's stance for or against heterosexuality as a marriage requirement, the theolegal scope of religion's influence on marriage goes well beyond this single issue.

Because it is enmeshed in Christian religious tradition, does our system of theolegal marriage violate the First Amendment? The religious clauses read: *Congress shall make no law respecting the establishment of religion, or prohibiting the free exercise thereof.* While the Supreme Court has ruled on cases challenging some of the traditional characteristics of marriage, and may soon hear arguments with respect to the heterosexuality requirement, it has not ever looked at the institution in a holistic way. If it were to do so in the future, some previous establishment and free exercise clause rulings give an indication what the court might consider.

In *Lemon v. Kurtzman*,[15] the Supreme Court ruled that public funds could not be used to reimburse private schools, most of which are religious, for expenses. In deciding this case, the court established a three-prong test that became known as the Lemon Test: the government's action must have a secular legislative purpose; the government's action must not have the primary effect of either advancing or inhibiting religion; and the government's action must not result in an excessive government entanglement with religion.

When the state prevents clergy from solemnizing marriages that meet the criteria of religious doctrine (without interfering with life, liberty, and the pursuit of happiness), it inhibits religion. A civil marriage has a secular purpose and does not advance or inhibit religion, and furthermore the clergy are not asked to serve as de facto public officials, which is an excessive government entanglement. The Lemon Test has come under scrutiny in recent years, but when one considers its application to marriage, it addresses the religious and state conflicts quite well.

The Tradition Test was created when the Supreme Court ruled that the chaplaincy practice of the Nebraska legislature was constitutional.[16] Chief Justice Burger ruled that since the chaplaincy could be traced to the First Continental Congress, it had become "part of the fabric of our society." For those who argue that marriage is part of the fabric of our society, the fact is that marriage is an ever-evolving institution. If marriage were still patriarchal and permanent, if birth control were still illegal, if whites could marry only whites and African-Americans could not marry at all, then perhaps the Tradition Test would be valid. Just because something is a societal norm does not mean it is constitutional, especially given the fact that societal norms change.

When the Supreme Court ruled that a nativity scene could be displayed in a public area among other secular Christmas items, it created what is known as the Establishment Test. In *Lynch v. Donnelly* (1984), Justice O'Connor's seemingly contradictory concurring opinion noted, "Endorsement sends a message to non-adherents that they are outsiders, not full members of the political community, and an accompanying message to adherents that they are insiders, favored members of the political community."[17] By not granting a marriage license to same-sex couples, the government is endorsing a traditionally religious view of marriage. This forces couples not meeting the heterosexual requirement of marriage into same position as nonadherents. Same-sex couples wanting to marry are viewed as outsiders and therefore given fewer protections than other citizens.

In *Lee v. Weisman* (1992), the Supreme Court ruled that the principal of a public middle school could not invite members of the religious clergy to deliver invocations at graduation ceremonies. Justice Kennedy noted that "prayer exercises in public schools carry a particular risk of indirect coercion" by placing pressure on some to participate.[18] This Coercion Test has been used in interpreting the Establishment Clause, but it has less merit when applied to marriage. After all, nonreligious couples are not forced to have marriages solemnized by clergy. But my own experience proves that it has some relevance.

When I was first married, even though my husband and I were not affiliated with a religion, I felt the need to have a church wedding. The ceremony took place in the aforementioned Unitarian Universalist Church not because of my knowledge or belief in Unitarian Universalist values, but because it was the only church I found where a minister would solemnize our marriage. To me, a wedding officiated by a minister in a church was added validity to the union to not only those attending but also society at large.

The Supreme Court seems to be moving away from the belief in a strict interpretation of the separation of religion and state toward the concept of neutrality. According to Frank Ravitch, "the Court's formal neutrality is the notion that religion has no special status and thus there is no need to differentiate between religion and non-religion if the government is acting *neutrally*."[19] Therefore, if the court treats religion separately or differently, it is treating religion with hostility. Ravitch has proposed another test, the Facilitation Test, defined as, "government action that substantially facilitates or discourages religion violates the establishment clause."[20] By enforcing the Christian marriage characteristic of hetero-sexuality, the government is facilitating the advancement of a particular religion. Martha Nussbaum argues that because religions do not require same-sex marriages, these unions do not have protection under the First Amendment.[21] Yet if the state's objective in promoting marriage is to provide domestic stability through the creation of established households, denying same-sex couples the ability to marry does nothing to advance this goal. And since some religions support marriage for both hetero-sexual and same-sex couples, the government is not acting from a point of neutrality when it supports the formation of some marriages but denies others based on religious doctrine.

Filing for Divorce

Eighteen years after my first wedding, I was married in a different Unitarian Universalist Church. Many years after my first marriage failed, I moved to Philadelphia and began attending First Unitarian Church. It was there I met my present husband. On our wedding day sunlight did stream through stained-glass windows, and I did walk down a familiar aisle. Being married in a church of a faith I had come to embrace, to a partner who shared my beliefs, gave me a true understanding of the significance of religious marriage. Once again, the Commonwealth of Pennsylvania granted us a marriage license, and my husband and I enjoy the civil benefits it provides. It is my hope and intention that this union will last "until death do us part."

But should the long-standing union of church and state be allowed to continue or is it appropriate to initiate divorce proceedings? I believe that separating the civil and religious aspects of marriage would better allow both society and religion to more fully represent their intended purpose. Granting church and state a divorce would benefit all.

In accordance with Walker's three theolegal worldviews: *Separationists* would affirm that the civil benefits given to married couples should be pro-tected from religious influence. By separating civil and religious marriage, all citizens of the United States seeking the civil benefits and social status that marriage provides could obtain them without religious interference. *Integrationists* concerned with the free exercise of religion would be assured that religious marriage would remain in accordance to their core beliefs. Religions seeking to preserve their religious traditions would be assured that the sacrament of marriage would continue to be honored. Because religion would be taken out of the civil marriage application process, state registrars and justices of the peace would not be forced to deny their religious beliefs in order to perform their civil duties. *Pluralists* would respect the diversity of many types of religious marriages, but would be satisfied that one religious tradition would not be the basis for determining all civil marriages. Committed couples wishing to marry would not be denied on the basis of religious discrimination and would have an equal opportunity to participate in obtaining the civil benefit marriage provides. Those applying for and receiving state marriage licenses would be granted civil marriage benefits. Those wishing religious marriages would obtain them at the discretion of their religious organization.

There are those who argue that separating religious and civil marriage opens the door to a laissez-faire system of marriage. This would not be the case. If a state defines marriage as a union of two persons, then the possibility of group marriage is eliminated. And if religious beliefs were separated from civil marriage, much of the emotional charge in the debate over the heterosexuality characteristic would be removed.

Church and state should be granted a divorce. But, as firmly established as our system of marriage is as part of our culture, will it ever happen? It very well could. And when it does, the change will not be led, as we would expect, by progressive clergy and those who believe in the legitimacy of marriage equality. Rather, if the Supreme Court were to uphold legal marriage for same-sex couples, or the Defense of Marriage Act were repealed, conservative religious clergy and those who do not condone same-sex marriage will begin to see the necessity of separating religious convictions from the public benefits that civil marriage bestows. Then, those on the polar sides of the argument will come together and develop a new system advantageous to both.

Like the civil and religious benefits that were granted to me upon my birth, civil and religious marriage benefits should be separate and distinct, independent rather than excessively entangled. By granting the church and state a divorce, couples can choose to have a civil marriage—a civil right—and/or a religious marriage—a sacramental rite. Only then will marriage honor the First Amendment of our constitution, ensuring that love and justice will live happily ever after.

Notes

1. Christian New Testament, Matthew 19:5 King James Bible says, "For this cause shall a man leave father and mother, and shall cleave to his wife: and they twain shall be one flesh."
2. Witte, John Jr. *From Sacrament to Contract: Marriage, Religion, and the Law in the Western Tradition.* Westminster John Knox Press, Louisville, KY, 1997.

3. Ibid., p. 21.
4. Cott, Nancy F. *Public Vows: A History of Marriage and the Nation.* Harvard University Press, Cambridge, MA, 2000, pp. 9 and 10.
5. Nussbaum, Martha C. *Liberty of Conscience: In Defense of America's Tradition of Religious Equality.* Basic Books, New York, NY, 2008.
6. Witte, p. 38.
7. Cott, p. 18.
8. Cott, p. 25.
9. In *Loving v. Virginia*, 388 U.S. 1 (1967) the U.S. Supreme Court unanimously found Virginia's "Racial Integrity Act of 1924" was unconstitutional, thereby ending all antimiscegenation laws in the United States.
10. *Reynolds v. the United States*, 98 U.S. 145 (1878) found that religious duty was not a suitable defense to a criminal indictment.
11. Feldman, Noah. *Divided By God: America's Church-State Problem and What We Should Do About It.* Farrar, Straus and Giroux, New York, NY, 2005, p. 106.
12. *Katherine Varnum, et al., v Timothy J. Brien*, Iowa District Court for Polk County case number CV5965.
13. Kristin M. Perry et al., Plaintiffs, City and County of San Francisco, Intervenor-Plaintiffs, v. Arnold Schwarzenegger et al., Governor of California, etc., 704 F. Supp. 2d 921 (N.D. Cal. 2010).
14. Sayare, Scott, and Maia De La Baume (2010), "In France, Civil Unions Gain Favor Over Marriage." *New York Times*, December 16, 2010, p. A1.
15. *Lemon v. Kurtzman*, 403 U.S. 602 (1971).
16. *Marsh v. Chambers*, 463 U.S. 783 (1983).
17. *Lynch v. Donnelly*, 465 U.S. 668 (1984).
18. *Lee v. Weisman*, 505 U.S. 577 (1992).
19. Ravitch, Frank S. *Masters of Illusion: The Supreme Court and the Religion Clauses.* New York University Press, New York, NY, 2007, p. 16.
20. Ibid., p. 168.
21. Nussbaum, Martha C. (1998). *Cultivating Humanity: A Classical Defense of Reform in Liberal Education.* Harvard University Press, Cambridge, MA, 1998, p. 338.

Part 4

Theodiplomacy

He Said
by Katie Ford

that city needed a good cleaning he said
my buddy he's in the guard he said

there were things going on down there
the public doesn't even know about

what killings I said of citizens I said
don't worry he said not innocent ones

you should have heard my buddy he said

Editorial Preface

We open this section about U.S. officials' use of theolegal behavior in international affairs with defense attorney David McColgin describing his experience representing Guantánamo detainees. Described as theotorture, McColgin recounts how female government interrogators told Muslim detainees they were menstruating and spread red liquid on their faces, aware of the passages in the Quran that prevent male Muslims to pray if touched by a woman other than his wife. Such acts as these, including desecrating the Holy Quran, led to riots and suicide attempts. These examples of theotorture, where the theology of the religious minority is used to achieve a policy goal, represent the most extreme example of a theolegal nation.

As articulated in Chapter 13, when it comes to nuclear war, it matters what we believe. Douglas Shaw demonstrates the positive uses of theology as applied in the international arena. If the United States is to have any influence in affirming peace and human dignity, he argues, it will not hurt to engage in *theodiplomacy*. He examines how the development, use, spread, and defense against nuclear weapons pose unusually devastating moral challenges. He explains that theology is but one diplomatic tool used by political, military, faith, and scientific leaders. In this way, theolegal rhetoric became a tool to affirm and promote peace for the common good. Could the same be applied to universal human rights?

William Shultz, former president of Amnesty International, USA, illustrates how the discourse on human rights has become the secular equivalent of a global religious faith. When religion concerns itself with universal values, he states, and expands its concern worldwide, it can become a tremendous force for human rights. However, when religion limits its concerns to a narrow segment of the world population, it fails to live up the universal human rights ideal. One of the most esteemed human rights is religious freedom, discussed in the closing chapter by three-time Nobel Peace Prize nominee, Joseph Grieboski.

Grieboski stresses the importance of ensuring freedom of religion as the foundation for security, stability, and democracy. Based on the understanding that religious freedom is more than a religion-state issue,

Grieboski explores ways to protect humankind's most fundamental right: freedom of religion and belief. This is achieved when a theolegal democracy allows citizens to use their beliefs in the public arena while guaranteeing that no one religion, or no single cluster of dominant beliefs, are used to erode the rights of religious minorities. In turn, laws allow for religious expression while simultaneously preventing religious discrimination, persecution, and tyranny. This final chapter outlines successful ways to create and strengthen legal, business, academic, media, and other systems within countries—and internationally—to protect religious freedom so that such abuses do not occur. By doing so, nations can ensure freedom of belief as the foundation for a healthy, safe, and prosperous democracy.

12

The Theotorture of Guantánamo[1]

David L. McColgin

It was winter when they brought Mohammed to Bagram Airforce Base, Afghanistan. The soldiers would drench him and leave him outside in the cold until his clothing froze to his body and he was shivering violently. Then they would bring him inside for questioning. Hours and hours of interrogations: sometimes 10 hours at a stretch. Afterwards, they would stop him from sleeping. Soldiers would bang on his cell. Up to a week would go by like that.

It was not working, though. The interrogations did not turn up the information they wanted. So they hung him by his wrists.

Later, after he had been moved to Guantánamo Naval Base, Cuba, interrogators would "short shackle" him—his hands bound to his ankles and clipped to a bolt in the floor. They would leave him trussed like a turkey. Sometimes they turned up the air conditioning while he shivered. Sometimes they left him, chained to himself like that for hours, until he could no longer keep from shitting himself.[2]

Mohammed is a farmer from Afghanistan. I am an American, a lawyer. In 2006, I sat in a cell, listening to Mohammed recount these things. I wondered: how could the United States allow soldiers to treat anyone like this? What had become of our respect for the Geneva Conventions and the Convention Against Torture, both of which we helped write? What was so different about this Afghan farmer that the United States would abandon core principles of fairness and humane treatment?

The people who did these things to Mohammed are my countrymen. An informant said he was with the Taliban, or Al Qaeda. The informant's name is secret, as are his motives. Did the informant do it for the large cash bounties the U.S. military was offering? Who knows.

Mohammed was not abused by a few rogue soldiers. Authorization for the use of "enhanced interrogation techniques" came from the highest levels of my government. And I have since learned that the abuse Mohammed suffered was mild in comparison to what was done to others at Guantánamo. The prisoners came from different backgrounds and countries. They had different life experiences. They spoke different languages. They shared only one thing in common.

Every one of them was Muslim.

As Nathan C. Walker argues, the United States is a theolegal democracy. The predominantly Christian religious views of the public and of the politicians we elect exert tremendous influence over the policies our government adopts. This influence intensified during the eight years of the Bush administration. George W. Bush told a televangelist prior to his first term that he thought "God wants me to run for president," and he viewed his election as an act of God's grace.[3] A born-again Christian, President Bush brought many like-minded evangelical Christians into positions of power. A wide range of faith-based policies followed—federal aid to church groups to perform social services ("faith-based initiatives"), promotion of "abstinence-only" programs in schools, and advocacy for the teaching of so-called "intelligent design."[4]

The theology of the Bush administration also inevitably influenced how the administration responded to the attacks by Al Qaeda on the World Trade Center and the Pentagon on September 11, 2001. A crusade-like mentality prevailed within the administration, and the "War on Terror" was seen in biblical terms as a battle of Good versus Evil. This theology created an environment in which the abuse and torture of Muslim detainees could seem justifiable.[5]

The extraordinary policies discussed in this chapter—the unprecedented refusal to apply the Geneva Conventions and the unprecedented issuance of legal memoranda authorizing torture—were born of this environment. Guantánamo demonstrates how the theology of our leaders can give rise to policies that would otherwise seem abhorrent in a democracy historically committed to human rights. Guantánamo likewise illustrates the use of the theology of subordinates to implement such policies. Those charged with implementing the administration's Guantánamo policies were plainly influenced by their anti-Muslim theology, as evidenced by their mistreatment of both Muslim detainees *and* Muslim service members.

The widespread nature of this abuse at Guantánamo also reflects a belief-system throughout the United States in which, post 9/11, Muslims as a group are viewed with heightened suspicion and as not deserving humane and lawful treatment. The incidence of anti-Muslim violence in the country rose 700 percent after 9/11.[6] Polling in the nation also demonstrated a marked rise in anti-Muslim sentiment, with 4 in 10 Americans admitting in 2006 that they harbor prejudice against Muslims and about the same proportion favoring more rigorous security measures for Muslims than for non-Muslims.[7]

This chapter examines the Guantánamo detention policies as an extreme example of how the theolegal nature of our democracy can permit the country to drift from its core principles in its treatment of a religious minority.

A Holy War

Following the attack of 9/11, President Bush declared a global "war on terror" and told the country that it would be a new kind of war, unlike any we had fought before.[8] The president and his staff cultivated the idea that the country was engaged in a holy war.[9] One week after 9/11 the president told the nation, "We will rid the world of evil-doers," and he described the war on terror as a "crusade."[10] His spokesman later apologized for his use of the word "crusade" after criticism from Muslim leaders in the United States.[11] Bush insisted that the war on terror was not a war on Islam,[12] yet a crusade-like mentality prevailed and members of his administration continued to use religious terms to describe the war on terror.

Attorney General John Ashcroft made the theolegal nature of the war on terror explicit. A Pentecostal, he held daily prayer meetings for his staff and viewed the wall between church and state as a "wall of religious oppression."[13] Ashcroft described the war on terror as "a conflict between good and evil," adding that "as President Bush has reminded us . . . God is not neutral between the two."[14] Ashcroft once said that America has "no King but Jesus," and he described Islam as "a religion in which God requires you to send your son to die for him," and Christianity as "a faith in which God sends his son to die for you."[15] Under Ashcroft, the Department of Justice used the newly passed PATRIOT Act[16] in the two months following the 9/11 attack to target the Muslim community, detaining over 1,200 predominantly Muslim and Arab foreign nationals and holding many of them without charges under harsh conditions.[17]

The theolegal nature of the war on terror was also evident through the views of a senior Pentagon intelligence officer who espoused openly anti-Muslim views. Lt. General William Boykin, an evangelical Christian, gave a speech while dressed in full uniform saying that Muslims worship an "idol" and not "a real God." He described the battle with Muslim radicals as a fight against "Satan," saying that Islamists attacked America "because we're a Christian nation." In another speech he mentioned a

Muslim fighter in Somalia, saying that "my God was bigger than his." While President Bush said these statements did not represent the views of the administration, his Secretary of Defense, Donald Rumsfeld, declined to criticize the general, instead praising his "outstanding" military record.[18] General Boykin gave similar talks at least 23 times, usually dressed in uniform. The controversy surrounding his anti-Muslim views did not hurt his career in a theolegal nation. Instead, President Bush promoted him in October 2003 to the position of deputy undersecretary of defense for intelligence and put him in charge of finding Osama bin Laden.[19]

For a time in 2003, even the Pentagon's World Intelligence Update— a top-secret digest of military intelligence delivered daily only to the president and top Pentagon leaders—reflected the crusade-like nature of the war on terror. At the direction of Major General Glen Shaffer, a Christian and a director of intelligence in the Pentagon, the cover sheets for these updates mixed biblical passages with images of U.S. troops at war.[20] One such cover had pictures of combat troops, tanks, and a fighter jet under a quote from Joshua 1:9: "Have I not commanded you? Be strong and courageous. Do not be terrified; do not be discouraged, for the Lord your God will be with you wherever you go."[21]

Emblazoned on another cover was a quote from Isaiah 6:8: "Whom shall I send, and who will go for us?" The response appears under a picture of soldiers praying: "Here I am, Lord. Send Me!"[22] At least one Muslim analyst was offended, but when colleagues complained to Shaffer, he responded that "my seniors"—referring to the president and Rumsfeld—appreciated the biblical quotes.[23]

The New Paradigm

The theolegal nature of the war on terror created an environment in which policies allowing for the unlawful abuse and torture of the Muslim detainees held at Guantánamo could seem justifiable. The implicit logic was that as God was on the side of a theolegal nation in its crusade against evil, its theolegal officials should not let legal niceties such as the Geneva Conventions and the Convention Against Torture get in the way.

Shortly after 9/11, Vice President Dick Cheney ominously explained, "We'll have to work sort of the dark side, if you will. We've got to spend time in the shadows in the intelligence world . . . [I]t's going to be vital for us to use any means at our disposal basically, to achieve our objectives."[24] Bush administration lawyers then set about creating a legal doctrine, known as the "new paradigm," which sought to accord the president near unilateral powers to wage war.[25] They included within this doctrine an unprecedented system of detention and interrogation designed to operate outside of any legal restrictions. And they chose as a location for the detention of enemy combatants a place they thought would be completely beyond the reach of U.S. laws and courts—the U.S. Naval Station at Guantánamo Bay, Cuba. (Ultimately, the Supreme Court in *Rasul v. Bush*[26] rejected the Bush administration's position, holding that federal courts do have jurisdiction to hear challenges to detention in Guantánamo.)

The first and most momentous step of the Bush administration under the new paradigm was to nullify the protections of the Geneva Conventions, making the United States the first signatory nation ever to do so.[27] The protections of the Geneva Conventions reflect well-established American values dating back to the Revolutionary War. George Washington, despite the brutality of the British Army, ordered that British soldiers be treated humanely and housed in conditions no worse than American soldiers. The "Leiber Code" adopted during the Civil War established strict rules regarding humane treatment of prisoners. This code became the model for conduct during war that was adopted by two international diplomatic conferences in The Hague at the turn of the century.[28]

The United States helped write the First Geneva Conventions in 1929 as well as the new Geneva Conventions in 1949. The latter were meant to ensure that all categories of people involved in international conflicts were protected from abusive and inhumane treatment. The United States followed the Geneva Conventions during all conflicts, including the Vietnam War even though the Viet Cong did not.[29]

Yet, with no public discussion, the Bush administration cast aside the doctrine of adherence to the Geneva Conventions. In early 2002, White House Counsel Alberto Gonzales wrote his now infamous memo to the president, stating, "As you have said, the war against terrorism is a new kind of war . . . In my judgment, this new paradigm renders obsolete Geneva's strict limitations on questioning of enemy prisoners." He described the requirements of the Conventions as "quaint." President Bush then signed an order on February 7, 2002, stating that the Geneva Conventions did not apply in the conflict with Al Qaeda, but that as a matter of policy the military would treat detainees humanely, as long as it was consistent with "military necessity."[30] It was not until four years later in *Hamdan v. Rumsfeld*[31] that the Supreme Court, in a complete rejection of the Bush administration's strained logic, would rule that the Geneva Conventions do apply to the detainees held in Guantánamo.

The denial of the protections of the Geneva Conventions had two critical consequences for the detainees ultimately held in Guantánamo. First, it meant that the so-called Article 5 tribunals, required under the Conventions to separate the combatants from the civilians, would not take place. The military had used such Article 5 tribunals with great success in the first Gulf War and determined that three-quarters of those seized were innocent refugees and should be released.[32] Detainees being shipped to Guantánamo, however, would have no opportunity to confront the evidence against them to show they were innocent bystanders. Second, the denial of Geneva Conventions' protections meant that the prohibition against abusive interrogation would not apply.

But dispensing with the Geneva Conventions was not sufficient. The second step the Bush administration took under the new paradigm was to nullify the United Nations Convention Against Torture,[33] which the United States helped draft and ratified in 1994, as well as the War Crimes Act, which criminalizes "torture" and "other cruel and inhumane treatment."[34] In their now notorious "torture memo" of August 2002, Office of Legal Counsel attorney John Yoo and Assistant Attorney General Jay S. Bybee set out to accomplish this task. They did so by defining "torture" so as to make it nearly impossible to commit.

"Torture" is defined in the Convention Against Torture as "severe pain or suffering, whether physical or mental." Yoo and Bybee added to this definition the requirement that there be an intent to inflict suffering equal in intensity "to the pain accompanying serious physical injury, such as organ failure, impairment of bodily function, or even death." Mental suffering had to "result in significant psychological harm" lasting for "months or years." In addition, to be guilty of torture, the interrogator had to have the "precise objective" of inflicting pain. Thus, an interrogator whose "precise objective" was merely to get information would not be guilty of torture, even though he or she was fully aware of the detainees' pain. Yoo and Bybee also argued that the president could simply make torture legal by authorizing it.[35]

On the basis of this legal advice, Secretary of Defense Rumsfeld issued two memos authorizing a range of "enhanced interrogation techniques" that went far beyond what the military authorized in its Army Field Manual. The newly approved techniques included "hooding," "exploitation of phobias," "stress positions," "deprivation of light and auditory stimuli," environmental manipulation, sleep adjustment, and extended isolation.[36] As Alberto Mora, the General Counsel of the Navy, said when he saw the first of Rumsfeld's memos, what it permitted was "torture."[37]

In their public statements, members of the Bush administration sought to justify the unprecedented decisions regarding the treatment of detainees at Guantánamo by describing the detainees as combatants unlike any others. Rumsfeld described them as "the worst of the worst,"[38] and claimed they were "among the most dangerous, best-trained, vicious killers on the face of the earth."[39] General Richard Myers, Chairman of the Joint Chiefs of Staff, claimed that if given the opportunity, they would "gnaw through hydraulic lines in the back of a C-17 [military plane] to bring it down."[40] These hyperbolic claims, which resonated with the anti-Muslim sentiment prevalent throughout the post-9/11 climate of a theolegal nation, masked the extent to which the new policies would allow for an unthinkable degree of officially sanctioned torture.

Enhanced Interrogation Techniques

Detainees began arriving in Guantánamo in January 2002. Ultimately, 779 Muslim detainees from 49 different countries would be held at the detention facilities there, most for a period of years. As of November 2010, most of the detainees had been released and 171 remained.[41]

Rumsfeld's description of the detainees as the "worst of the worst" proved to be woefully inaccurate. Out of the 56 detainees whose cases challenging their detention had been resolved as of November 2010, 37 (66%) were found by federal judges *not* to have been enemy combatants and to have been unlawfully detained.[42]

Without the screening mechanism of Article 5 tribunals under the Geneva Conventions, the U.S. military had no fair or effective way to screen out those who were uninvolved in Al Qaeda or the Taliban. One study found "that the large majority of detainees never participated in any combat against the United States on a battlefield," and only 8 percent could be characterized as Al Qaeda fighters. Only 5 percent were captured by U.S. forces. Most had been captured by Pakistani or Northern Alliance forces (Afghan resisters of the Taliban's rule) and then handed over to U.S. custody, often in exchange for large cash bounties the United States was offering.[43]

Similar conclusions were reached by a senior CIA intelligence analyst who was fluent in Arabic and was sent to Guantánamo in 2002 to find out why so little valuable intelligence was coming from the detainees. After interviewing a random sample of detainees, he concluded in a top-secret report that about one-third of all the detainees did not have any connection with terrorism. There was little intelligence to be gained because the detainees knew little to nothing. The commander in charge of Joint Task Force Guantánamo, Major General Michael Dunlavey, agreed, estimating that half of the detainees never should have been brought to Guantánamo. The CIA analyst was concerned about the effect of imprisoning innocent Muslims for an indefinite period without legal review. As he told Jane Mayer, "I thought we were going to lose a whole damn generation in the Arab world."[44]

However, the Bush administration turned a deaf ear to the concern that the detainees had little intelligence value. Instead, Rumsfeld and others became convinced the problem was that the interrogation techniques were too soft and so approved enhanced interrogation techniques to extract more information.[45] Rumsfeld also placed a new commander in charge of Guantánamo, Major General Geoffrey Miller, to introduce a harsher regime in November 2002.

General Miller professed himself a devout Christian. He had strong feelings about Muslims. As he explained to Chaplain James Yee, he felt a deep anger toward "those Muslims" who attacked on 9/11 because several of his friends and colleagues had been killed in the attack. His anger was so strong that he had sought counseling to deal with it.[46] General Miller's innovation at Guantánamo was to merge the functions of the guards and the interrogators, so that the guards would "set the conditions" for the interrogations by controlling the detainees' environment.[47] Under his watch, the incidents of abuse by interrogators and guards became widespread and rarely, if ever, resulted in disciplinary action.[48]

Freed from the constraints of the Geneva Conventions and the Convention Against Torture, interrogators and guards at Guantánamo began using a range of chillingly abusive techniques on many of the detainees. Over half of the detainees surveyed in one study reported abusive interrogation techniques. These included leaving the detainee short-shackled in painful stress positions for hours—a technique approved in one of Rumsfeld's memos. FBI agents witnessed a number of detainees held in this manner, and several agents saw the technique combined with cold temperature, loud music, and flashing lights.[49] A former guard at Guantánamo reported escorting detainees to an isolation room where the detainee would be kept in the room, which was extremely cold, for more than 10 hours: "And they're shackled by their hands and feet to the floor so that they are in a constant crouching position without being able to really put their ass on the floor, like sit down or anything."[50]

FBI agents saw detainees chained in a fetal position to the floor for "18, 24 hours or more," and noted that most urinated and defecated on themselves.[51] One agent saw a detainee locked in an unventilated room with the air conditioning turned off. The temperature was "over 100 degrees" and the detainee "was almost unconscious on the floor with a pile of hair next to him (he had apparently been pulling it out throughout the night)."[52] Agents saw dogs used to intimidate detainees by having them growl, bark, and show their teeth.

Interrogators also used sleep deprivation in what became known as the "frequent flyer" program—the detainee would be moved every few hours from one cell to another and not permitted to sleep more than a couple hours a night.[53] In one case, fully documented by a detailed interrogation log, a detainee was not allowed to sleep more than four hours a night for 48 of 54 days. During this time period he was also forced to strip naked, wear a leash, perform dog tricks, and wear a bra and thong underwear on his head, and was not allowed to use a toilet after being force-fed liquids intravenously.[54] Judge Susan Crawford, the chief judicial officer for the Military Commissions at Guantánamo, later concluded that the treatment of this detainee "met the legal definition of torture" and that the harsh techniques had been authorized by Secretary of Defense Rumsfeld.[55]

As a theolegal policy decision, many of the abusive techniques sought to exploit and degrade the Muslim faith of the detainees. Chaplain James Yee witnessed the degradation first-hand. Yee was a graduate of West Point who converted to Islam and became a military chaplain. He was assigned to be the Muslim Chaplain at Guantánamo in 2002. As Yee explained, "because religion was the most important issue for nearly all the prisoners [at Guantánamo], it became the most important weapon used against them."[56] The religion of the detainees became a tool by which to try and elicit intelligence.

Female interrogators were used to sexually humiliate detainees and mock their devotion to Islamic teachings that strictly bar physical contact between unrelated men and women. FBI agents observed female interrogators touching and acting in a sexual manner toward detainees, "whispering in their ears and generally invading the detainee's personal space."[57] One female interrogator, for example, was observed placing her knee in the detainee's crotch area, applying lotion to his arms, bending his thumbs back and grabbing his genitals. The agents saw the detainee turn his head away and grimace in pain. This occurred during the Muslim holy month of Ramadan: Muslims believe that if a male is touched by a woman not his wife, he is considered unclean and cannot pray. The agents reported this abuse to General Miller, but he merely replied, "Thank you, gentlemen, but my boys know what they're doing."[58]

Eric Saar, an army military intelligence linguist who provided English-Arabic translation for interrogators, witnessed a similar incident. A female interrogator told a detainee that she was having her period, asking him how he would feel about her touching him. She then slipped her hand into her pants and pulled it out with a red liquid smeared on it meant to look like menstrual blood. She showed her hand to the detainee and then wiped it on the detainee's face. The detainee screamed at the top of his lungs, began shaking, sobbing, and yanked his arms against his handcuffs. The interrogator explained to Saar that the detainee would now feel too dirty to pray and that she would have the guards turn off the water in his cell so he would not be able to wash the red substance off. "What do you think your brothers will think of you in the morning when they see an American woman's menstrual blood on your face?" she said as she left the cell.[59]

Abuse of the Quran and interference with prayer were also common tactics, used by both the interrogators and the guards. An FBI agent saw one interrogator squat over a Quran during interrogation and another saw a bearded and long-haired detainee gagged with duct tape covering much of his head because he had been chanting the Quran nonstop.[60] Chaplain Yee frequently saw guards mocking detainees during prayer, stepping on the Quran during cell searches, breaking the bindings and dropping the Quran on the floor. Such incidents inevitably caused the worst riots, which would in turn result in beatings of the detainees by guards.

In one such incident, a guard threw a Quran on the floor, stepped on it, and kicked it across the room. This resulted in an attempted mass suicide by the detainees. Every 15 minutes a detainee would try to hang himself with a sheet. Guards would rush in, release the detainee, and call the medics and then another detainee would be found hanging from a sheet. Twenty-three detainees tried to hang themselves that day.[61]

On another occasion, a Muslim interpreter who complained to a commander about an incident of Quran abuse was told angrily to leave the prison block. When a riot broke out later over the Quran abuse, he was called back to help out by another officer and tried to calm the situation by talking with the detainees. The commander again yelled at him to leave, charged him with disobeying an order, and then punished him by having him demoted and fined.[62]

The anti-Muslim abuse was not aimed only at the detainees. Muslim service members were also targeted and found themselves watched and suspected of being terrorist sympathizers simply because of their religion. Non-Muslim service members were uncomfortable with them praying together on Friday afternoons in a service led by Chaplain Yee and referred to them as the "Muslim clique" and "Hamas."[63] One Muslim chaplain reported in a memo to the command that the working environment there was "very hostile toward all Muslims," and that "[m]any military troops of the Muslim faith hide the fact that they are Muslim in fear of some sort of retribution."[64]

Chaplain Yee, after complaining repeatedly about the abusive treatment of detainees, was himself arrested while on leave and accused of spying. He was held in solitary confinement for 76 days before ultimately being cleared of all charges. A Muslim interpreter, Ahmad al-Halabi, was imprisoned for nine months, also on charges of spying. Most of his charges were ultimately dismissed, and he pleaded guilty to minor offenses for a sentence of time-served. A third Muslim service member, Ahmed Mehalba, was arrested for spying and imprisoned for nearly 20 months before being released.[65]

Conclusion

What happened at Guantánamo thus demonstrates how the theology of our country's leaders can create an environment in which policies allowing abuse and torture can seem justifiable and how the theology of subordinates can be used to implement those policies. These same theolegal characteristics, however, can also allow citizens of the United States and citizens of the world to step back and acknowledge how abuse and torture, in general, and specifically in the name of religion, is a fundamental betrayal of human rights. The experience of one prosecutor, Lt. Col. Darrel Vandeveld, illustrates the point well. Vandeveld was assigned to prosecute Jawad, a juvenile detainee at Guantánamo who was charged with throwing a grenade at a jeep in Afghanistan containing two U.S. Special Forces soldiers and their interpreter. Vandeveld initially thought Jawad was guilty because he had confessed to being solely responsible. But as he began to investigate the case, he learned Jawad's confession was probably false, that Jawad had been subjected to systematic abuse, including the "frequent flyer" program at Guantánamo, and that field reports suggested he was innocent. Vandeveld ultimately became convinced Jawad should not be prosecuted, but his supervisors refused to let him drop the charges.

Vandeveld had a crisis of conscience. After consulting with his Jesuit priest, Vandeveld ultimately concluded he should not "cooperate with evil" by furthering the unjust prosecution. As a positive example of a theolegal decision, Vandeveld chose to resign and became a witness for the defense. As he explained:

> No one who has fought for our country and its values has done so to enable what happened in Guantánamo. We did not sacrifice so that an administration of partisan civilians, abetted by military officers who seemed to have lost their moral compass, could defile our Constitution and misuse the law.[66]

The military war crimes case against Jawad ultimately fell apart, and a federal judge later ordered him released after finding that the evidence against him was "riddled with holes."[67]

My client Mohammed was released in November 2007 after spending four years in Guantánamo. He has returned home to his family in Afghanistan. I speak with him by phone from time to time. He never fails to express his gratitude for the efforts of our legal team in working for his release. He seems to hold no anger towards the United States for his arrest on false charges and for the torture he endured. I suspect that Mohammed, a devout Muslim, has like Vandeveld found his strength in his faith.

Notes

1. This chapter benefited greatly from the editing and comments provided by the following people: Keith M. Donoghue, Ian McColgin, Ahmed M. Soliman, Brett G. Sweitzer, and Sabin P. Willett.
2. Cleared notes of interview, Nov. 21, 2006, M. Q. file, David McColgin.
3. Stephen Mansfield (Charisma House, 2003). *The Faith of George W. Bush*, p. 109 (2003); Michael Duffy, "Marching Alone" *Time* (Sept. 9, 2002).
4. Garry Wills, "A Country Ruled by Faith," *The New York Review of Books* (Nov. 16, 2006).
5. It is beyond the scope of this chapter to assess what is, or is not "Christian." It is impossible to square torture, for example, with the injunction in Matthew's gospel to suffer, rather than respond to wrongdoing, Matthew 5:39, and to love, rather than hate one's enemy, Matthew 5:44. Nevertheless, "Christianity" is the claimed religious faith of the American majority, and among many professed "Christians" are those who see Islam (which, ironically, recognizes Jesus as a prophet) as the creed of the enemy.
6. Human Rights Watch, "We Are Not the Enemy: Hate Crimes Against Arabs, Muslims and Those Perceived to be Arab or Muslim after September 11, 2001," p. 17 (Nov. 2002).
7. Lydia Saad, "Anti-Muslim Sentiments Fairly Commonplace," Gallup News Service (Aug. 10, 2006), available at www.gallup.com/poll/24073/antimuslim-sentiments-fairly-commonplace.aspx.
8. President George W. Bush, "Address to a Joint Session of Congress and the American People," (Sept. 20, 2001), available at http://www.september11news.com/PresidentBushSpeech.htm (accessed Jan. 13, 2011).
9. Esther Kaplan, *With God On Their Side, George Bush and the Christian Right.* The New Press, New York. p. 18 (2004).
10. Manual Perez-Rivas, "Bush vows to ride the world of 'evil-doers,'" CNN (Sept. 16, 2001), available at http://archives.cnn.com/2001/US/09/16/gen.bush.terrorism/ (accessed Jan. 13, 2011).
11. Kaplan, supra note 9, p. 18.
12. Bush, supra note 8.
13. Kaplan, supra note 9, p. 34.
14. Ibid., p. 19.
15. Ibid., pp. 19, 34.
16. Provide Appropriate Tools Required to Intercept and Obstruct Terrorism (PATRIOT) Act of 2001.
17. "The Status of Muslim Civil Rights in the United States 2005," Council on American-Islamic Relations (CAIR) 7, available at http://www.cair-net.org/PDF/2005CivilRightsReport.pdf (accessed Jan. 13, 2011).
18. "Bush Renews Rebuke of Boykin," *The Washington Times* (Oct. 28, 2003); "Rumsfeld Praises Army General Who Ridicules Islam as 'Satan,'" *New York Times* (Oct. 17, 2003).
19. Michelle Goldberg, *Kingdom Coming: The Rise of Christian Nationalism*, pp. 163–164 (W. W. Norton & Co., 2006).

20. Rober Draper, "And He Shall Be Judged," GQ (June 2009), available at http://www.gq.com/news-politics/newsmakers/200905/donald-rumsfeld-administration-peers-detractors (accessed Jan. 13, 2011). AP, "Pentagon Briefings No Longer Quote the Bible" (May 19, 2009) (Pentagon spokesman confirms that daily intelligence briefings used to include biblical quotes).
21. Draper, supra note 20 (slide-show of Worldwide Intelligence Update cover sheets).
22. Ibid.
23. Ibid.
24. Jane Mayer, *The Dark Side*, pp. 9–10 (Doubleday, 2008).
25. Ibid., pp. 51–52.
26. *Rasul v. Bush*, 542 U.S. 466, 483 (2004).
27. Mayer, supra note 23, p. 9.
28. Ibid., pp. 84–85.
29. Ibid., 121; Joseph Margulies, *Guantánamo and the Abuse of Presidential Power*, pp. 72–83 (Simon & Schuster, 2006).
30. Mayer, supra note 24, pp. 123–125.
31. *Hamdan v. Rumsfeld*, 548 U.S. 557, 629 (2006).
32. Mayer, supra note 24, p. 121.
33. United Nations Convention Against Torture and Other Cruel, Inhuman, or Degrading Treatment or Punishment, G.A. Res. 39/46, U.S. GAOR. 39th Sess. Supp. No. 51, *entered into force* June 26, 1987, U.S.n Doc A/Res/39/46.
34. 18 U.S.C. § 2441.
35. Mayer, supra note 23, pp. 151–152.
36. Ibid., p. 220; Laurel E Fletcher, Eric Stover; "Guantánamo and Its Aftermath" (Human Rights Center & International Human Rights Law Clinic, University of California, Berkeley) pp. 11–12 (Nov. 2008).
37. Mayer, supra note 24, p. 223.
38. Katherine Q. Seelye, "Threats and Responses" *New York Times*, Oct. 23, 2002.
39. "Rumsfeld Visits, Thanks US Troops t Camp X-Ray in Cuba," American Forces Press Service, Jan 27, 2002.
40. Andy Worthington, *The Guantánamo Files: The Stories of the 774 Detainees in America's Illegal Prison*, p. 127 (Pluto Press, 2007).
41. Center for Constitutional Rights, "Guantánamo Habeas Scorecard," (Nov. 2, 2010), available at http://ccrjustice.org/GTMOscorecard (accessed Jan. 10, 2011).
42. Ibid.
43. Margulies, supra note 29, p. 69; Mark Denbeaux, Joshua Denbeaux, "Report on Guantánamo Detainees: A Profile of 517 Detainees through Analysis of Department of Defense Data," (Feb. 2006), available at http://law.shu.edu/publications/GuantánamoReports/Guantánamo_report_final_2_08_06.pdf (accessed Jan. 13, 2011).
44. Mayer, supra note 24, pp. 183–184.
45. Ibid., pp. 185–196.
46. James Yee, *For God and Country* (Public Affairs, 2005) pp. 124–125.
47. Worthington, supra note 40, pp. 191–192.

48. Ibid., p. 192.

49. Fletcher & Stover, supra note 36, p. 42 (Nov. 2008).

50. Ibid., p. 43.

51. "Guantánamo Bay Inquiry" Federal Bureau of Investigation (Dec. 21, 2006), available at http://foia.fbi.gov/Guantánamo/122106.htm (accessed Jan. 13, 2011).

52. Ibid.

53. Worthington, supra note 40, pp. 196–197.

54. Mayer, supra note 24, pp. 206–207.

55. "Detainee Tortured, Says U.S. Official," *The Washington Post* (Jan. 14, 2009), p. A1.

56. Yee, supra note 46, p. 110.

57. *A Review of the FBI's Involvement in and Observation of Detainee Interrogations in Guantánamo Bay, Afghanistan, and Iraq,* U.S. Dept of Justice, Office of Inspector General, pp. 188–189 (Oct. 2008) (hereinafter DOJ/OIG Report), available at http://www.usdoj.gov/oig/special/s0805/final.pdf (accessed Jan. 13, 2011).

58. Ibid. pp. 175–176, 188.

59. Erik Saar, *Inside the Wire,* pp. 226–227 (The Penguin Press, 2005).

60. DOJ/OIG report, supra note 57, pp. 56, 83, 191–192.

61. Yee, supra note 46, pp. 110–116.

62. Ibid., pp.117–118.

63. Ibid., p. 131.

64. Ibid., p. 118.

65. Ibid., p. 217.

66. Darryl J. Vandeveld, "I Was Slow to Recognize the Stain of Guantánamo," *The Washington Post* (Jan. 18, 2009), available at http://www.washingtonpost.com/wp-dyn/content/article/2009/01/14/AR2009011402319_pf.html

67. William Glaberson, "Obama Faces Court Test Over Detainee," *The New York Times,* July 29, 2009.

13

Theolegal Nuclear Weapons Policy

Douglas B. Shaw

The development, use, spread, and defense against nuclear weapons pose unusually devastating moral challenges for humanity and the American polity specifically. Nuclear weapons create the possibility of instantaneous, push-button destruction on a scale that would otherwise require enormous logistical resources over substantial time—a scale so large that the most likely scenarios for the use of nuclear weapons imply at least tens of thousands of civilian casualties. This awesome capacity was offered to President Franklin D. Roosevelt by Albert Einstein and other leading scientific minds out of the grim realization that it might otherwise fall into the hands of Nazi Germany, and it was used by President Harry Truman to bring the war with Japan to an immediate conclusion. The immediacies of the development and use of nuclear weapons weighed against the destruction of Hiroshima and Nagasaki shape an emotionally charged debate across a large and growing number of dimensions of nuclear weapons policy. Reverend Francis X. Winters asks in a 2009 book, *Remembering Hiroshima: Was it Just?*[1] Why does the United States retain nuclear weapons today? Is nuclear deterrence stable in the evolving world order? What should the role of nuclear weapons be? Under what circumstances would the United States use nuclear weapons? How many nuclear weapons should the United States have? How quickly and flexibly should U.S. nuclear weapons be kept ready for use? Is effective nuclear nonproliferation possible? Is nuclear disarmament desirable and achievable?

American answers to these political questions shape the technical possibilities for promptly ending millions of lives or even human life altogether. Given these tremendous moral implications of U.S. nuclear weapons policy, one might expect assumptions about the nature of God and the interconnectedness of mankind to be very near the surface public discourse about U.S. nuclear weapons policy, but they are not. This chapter asks what role theological assumptions play in the development of U.S. nuclear weapons policy and argues for a more inclusive dialogue on the moral implications of nuclear weapons policy choices.

The unique character of nuclear weapons invites the use of religious metaphor to describe their effects and strategies for their use. However, separationist impulses and the logically required assumptions underlying deterrence theory tend to exclude authentic religious perspectives from public policy discourse related to nuclear weapons. Paradoxically, this exclusion sets the stage for the strong influence of religious perspectives over nuclear weapons policy as the cases of former President Ronald Reagan's dream of a world free of nuclear weapons, former Senator Mark Hatfield's proposal of legislation supporting a "freeze" in U.S. nuclear weapons, and the potential of the 1983 U.S. Conference of Catholic Bishops Pastoral Letter on War and Peace suggest. Unfortunately, absent coherent integration of these theological perspectives into deterrence theory, the former could inadvertently undermine the latter and the stability believed to be based upon it. Finally, I argue that a more explicit and careful integration of the moral consequences and theological implications of nuclear weapons policy could benefit strategic nuclear stability and global security.

Religious Metaphor

Discourse about nuclear weapons is rife with religious metaphor. This does not mean that theology determines policy, but it does confuse and obscure the role of actual theology in public policy discourse. Former commander-in-chief of the U.S. Strategic Command, General Lee Butler (USAF-ret.) refers to a "nuclear priesthood" who make prospective life and death decisions through obscure mathematical models about millions of human beings they will never know.[2] Renowned deterrence theorist Professor Lawrence Freedman refers to the "canonical status" of Mutual Assured Destruction.[3] Perhaps most famously, the father of the atomic bomb J. Robert Oppenheimer reflected on the first detonation of a nuclear explosive by quoting the Bhagavad Gita, "I am become Death, the shatterer of worlds."[4]

The use of religious metaphor with regard to nuclear weapons reflects the uncompromising and mysterious nature of their role in world politics. Nuclear weapons are at once humanity's salvation and damnation. Nuclear weapons are a salvation because, as Kenneth Waltz and others have observed, they eliminate speculation with regard to the outcome of unrestrained war among states that possess nuclear weapons.[5] By transmuting war from an instrument of politics to an act of national suicide, nuclear weapons have been argued to have prevented war among the major powers since the bombing of Nagasaki.[6] Nuclear weapons are a damnation because they have placed the destruction of human civilization and all living creation within the easy technical reach of frail and fallible human beings. Even a limited, regional use of nuclear weapons could have global climate effects.[7] Since we do not know which one of these capacities of nuclear weapons will be validated by our future, our debates over whether we should have none, some, or a very large number of these weapons have a decidedly uncompromising and mysterious character.[8]

Practical Exclusion

In the absence of globally shared certainty that nuclear weapons are inherently dangerous, religious perspectives are systematically excluded from policy debate about nuclear weapons as irrelevant or even dangerous. Religion is anathema to contemporary nuclear deterrence theory. It drives preferences that are not reducible to a maximizing rationality and assigns significant authority over human behavior to interests other than those of the state.

The dissociation of morality from the workings of deterrence begins with the high moral purpose of deterrence: the prevention of war and the preservation of human civilization. At the start of the nuclear age, Bernard Brodie observed that "[t]hus far the chief purpose of our military establishment has been to win wars. From now on its chief purpose must be to avert them. It can have almost no other useful purpose."[9] If one accepts that either the dangerous nature of human beings or the anarchic structure of international politics make conflict likely, and further that conflict in the nuclear age has become unthinkable, then the temptation is strong to understand the end of avoiding nuclear war as justifying almost any means.

The second step in the dissociation of morality from deterrence is the assignment of causality for the absence of nuclear war to specific and obscure practices of nuclear deterrence. As Henry Kissinger observes, "[t]he nuclear age turned strategy into deterrence, and deterrence into an esoteric intellectual exercise."[10] Deterrence requires its subject to credibly hold at risk something its object values more than the potential fruits of the action to be deterred.[11] Theory animates this project, because it is theory that tells us that in the presence of a shared rational framework between object and subject, a credible, effectively communicated, and sufficiently fearsome threat will yield stable deterrence. Scholarly articulation of the particulars of these assumptions and conformance of human reality to them sustains considerable differences of opinion.[12] Unfortunately, scholarly confusion cannot be translated directly into effective nuclear weapons policy; the U.S. Government routinely makes discrete choices about nuclear weapons acquisitions, posture, and doctrine in the absence of certainty about how these choices align with the theoretical requirements of deterrence. The sum of these particular choices is a nuclear arsenal of specific technical description that the U.S. Government *further assumes* creates the physical capability to meet the theoretical requirements of assumptions that underpin deterrence.[13] In other words, the U.S. Government assumes that its particular nuclear weapons policy choices meet the physical requirements—which are subject to considerable expert debate—of the assumptions theoretically required for nuclear deterrence. The alternative to these two heroic logical leaps would be apoplexy in nuclear weapons policy, admittedly very dangerous in the context of the prospect of nuclear war. However, they further obscure the inherent morality of specific nuclear weapons policy decisions through an assumed causal linkage to war prevention.

A final step in the dissociation of morality from the practice of deterrence occurs as the U.S. Government acquires and deploys nuclear weapons to embody a nuclear deterrent strategy. As a practical matter in the United States, contemporary deterrence involves thousands of people building and maintaining thousands of nuclear weapons at a cost of billions of dollars annually.[14] Deterrence theory requires that all of these moving parts act as a unified whole. Individual moral uncertainty would undermine the logical construct on which deterrence depends.

The intervention of religious authority is unwelcome at each of these steps. Conceptually, the existence of nuclear weapons is argued to make deterrence unavoidable and therefore immune from moral critique. For example, even in the act of articulating the goal of eventual nuclear disarmament, President Barack Obama conceded that "as long as these weapons exist, the United States will maintain a safe, secure and effective arsenal to deter any adversary, and guarantee that defense to our allies."[15] Theoretically, deterrence depends on assumptions about the nature of states and how they make decisions; there is no room for religious authority in this discussion, either. Finally, the acquisition, deployment, and use of weapon systems is a technical military matter about the performance of men and machines, and as Bishop John J. O'Conner observes, "nuclear weaponry is not an area of episcopal expertise."[16] The result is that when former Seattle Archbishop Raymond Gerhardt Hunthausen called a Trident nuclear ballistic submarine missile base "the Auschwitz of Puget Sound," he could be dismissed as speaking outside his area of expertise.

This failure of clerical preparation extends to every other source of authority and scholarly discipline outside the relatively small community of practicing deterrence theorists, the military, and the occasional physicist or wayward lawyer. Orthodoxy is enforced by threatening unimaginable danger if the conceptual basis of peace through terror, the theoretical assumptions of rationality and credibility, or the association of particular machines with those assumptions is undermined by sentimentality. In this context, sentimentality includes the perspectives of not only the religious authorities in whom vast numbers of human beings invest their faith but also medical doctors, psychologists, anthropologists, behavioral scientists, and many others with undeniable expertise in the materially observable interactions of people and nuclear explosives.

For example, in the March 2008 announcement of a bipartisan Congressional Commission on the U.S. Strategic Posture chartered to provide an "outside examination" of U.S. nuclear weapons policy, then Chairwoman Ellen Tauscher of the Strategic Forces Subcommittee of the U.S. House Armed Services Committee described four physicists, four scholars of international relations, two lawyers, an engineer, a mathematician, and an economist as "uniformly and exceptionally well-qualified to conduct the analysis we called for."[17] These are the types of expertise the U.S. Congress views as relevant to nuclear weapons policy—religious authorities need not apply.

Paradoxical Importance

The absence of authentic religious perspectives from nuclear weapons policy debate may obscure rather than prevent the intrusion of theological considerations into nuclear weapons policy. In some important cases, the opacity of this dynamic may give religious perspectives a paradoxical importance in the development of nuclear weapons policy by protecting them from effective critique, asserting the relevance of the question: whose God rules U.S. nuclear weapons policy? A few examples illustrate this possibility and its potential dangers.

Reagan's "Personal Religious Mission"

John Lewis Gaddis argues in his 2005 *The Cold War: A New History* that Ronald Reagan was "the only nuclear abolitionist ever to have been president of the United States."[18] Daniel Ellsberg argues that President Ronald Reagan is the only U.S. president from World War II until 2007 not to "discuss internally or to direct serious preparations for possible imminent U.S. initiation of tactical or strategic nuclear warfare."[19] Paul Lettow observes that Ronald Reagan pursued a "dream" of "a world free of nuclear weapons" as "a personal religious mission."[20] A senior political advisor to President Reagan observed that "[t]his was a guy who believed in pre-destination, who believed that there was a purpose for everybody's life and we had to fulfill it. And that was his purpose . . . He was running for president because he believed he was destined to do away with nuclear weapons."[21] Reagan "was convinced that it was his mission to avert a nuclear holocaust."[22]

President Reagan's religious motivations for seeking a world free of nuclear weapons were obscured from public debate about his ideas. "As a politician," Lettow observes, "Reagan was famously reticent regarding his own religious beliefs."[23] Campaign advisers downplayed this issue because, in former Reagan White House Deputy Chief of Staff Michael Deaver's words, "as soon as you put Reagan and nuclear weapons in the same sentence, people would go up a tree."[24]

While many Americans may have been alarmed by the combination of nuclear weapons and President Reagan's swaggering style, his moral opposition to nuclear weapons may have had a less obvious but exponentially more important implication for U.S. nuclear weapons policy. It seems possible he did not believe that participation in nuclear deterrence to be morally permissible. This would be a much bigger problem for deterrence theory than his well-established but abstract vision of a world free of nuclear weapons, because it means he might not have "pushed the button" to retaliate in the event of a Soviet nuclear attack on the United States.[25] For deterrence theorists, this is so unthinkable in a president of the United States that it may be dismissed as irrelevant. But what if the commander-in-chief is not the only American with nuclear weapons duties whose religious convictions secretly but effectively undermine their willingness to carry out those duties? If large numbers of human beings refuse to accept additional personal moral responsibility for killing the world upon learning that the world is already doomed, these individual religious commitments may mean that nuclear deterrence is not functioning at all the way the experts specify it must. The implication being that if religious perspectives *can* endanger the validity of assumptions necessary for deterrence stability, then they probably already *do*, and national and global security do not benefit from denying this circumstance.

Hatfield's "Evangelical Progressivism"

Former Republican Senator Mark Hatfield of Oregon provides another example of a strong intrusion of religious motivations into nuclear weapons policy debate. In the Senate, Hatfield regularly opposed the funding of nuclear weapons and related systems.[26] Unlike President Reagan, Hatfield openly shared his religious motivations for a wide variety of policy positions. However, the prevalence of religious metaphor in discussion of nuclear weapons policy may have obscured or diluted the impact of the authentic religious convictions he expressed.

As a U.S. Navy officer long before his election to the Senate, Mark Hatfield inspected first-hand the destruction caused by the atomic bombing of Hiroshima.[27] Biographer Lon Fendall recalls that "from that time forward, 'never again' seemed imprinted on his moral consciousness."[28] So, when Senator Hatfield referred to U.S. nuclear weapons policy as "morally bankrupt," called President Reagan's Strategic Defense Initiative "the next 'great plague,'" and referred to his effort to stop the arms race by saying "[t]his was the apocalypse we were fighting," it seems likely he meant these religious references literally rather than metaphorically.[29]

The distinction is not subtle; Hatfield was at war with the "experts" whose views were not religiously informed. Few rival former Senate Armed Services Committee Chairman Sam Nunn in acceptance as experts in deterrence and arms control, but Hatfield could say, "I hate what he stands for, absolutely, but I don't hate him."[30] Over funding for the neutron bomb, Hatfield recalls that the two "fought with each other for hours, coming up with nothing but ash."[31] Hatfield believed that "the U.S. refusal to rule out the first use of nuclear weapons in later years completely violated just-war criteria."[32] In introducing a resolution supporting a unilateral freeze in the U.S. nuclear arsenal, Hatfield proclaimed:

> For the first time in the history of nuclear terror, control is shifting away from the secret cult of strategists, engineers, scientists, and other so-called "experts" who have held the globe hostage to their theories.[33]

In Mark Hatfield, actual religious theology confronted the metaphoric "theology" of nuclear deterrence and he could accept or give no quarter.

Hatfield won a convert to the opposition of nuclear weapons in Billy Graham.[34] He worked on the Nuclear Freeze with groups including the Fellowship of Reconciliation, Clergy and Laity Concerned, Sojournors, and Pax Christi.[35] Hatfield recalls an episode during the debate over his Nuclear Freeze resolution in which he had fellow Republican Senator Orin Hatch of Utah paged from the floor by impersonating a bishop of the Church of Jesus Christ of Latter Day Saints over the telephone and demanding to know why Hatch would not support the Freeze.[36]

Hatfield's position on matters of nuclear weapons policy was religiously determined, but he instrumentalized arguments of deterrence theory to defeat his opponents. He recalls answering concerns about Soviet parity in missiles by observing a U.S. advantage in launchers, and concerns about Soviet parity in launchers by observing a U.S. advantage in warheads, and concerns about Soviet parity in warheads by observing a U.S. advantage in accuracy.[37] While each argument has arguable merit within the context of deterrence theory, Hatfield mustered each for the same religious reasons unrelated to deterrence theory. In a prominent American lawmaker, this suggests that theological undercurrents may be more relevant to the development of U.S. nuclear forces and policy than the surface of public debate suggests.

Bishops, Bombs, and Possible Betrayal?

The 1983 Pastoral Letter on War and Peace of the U.S. Conference of Catholic Bishops, "The Challenge of Peace: God's Promise and Our Response," makes three points with regard to the use of nuclear weapons:

1. *Counter Population Use:* Under no circumstances may nuclear weapons or other instruments of mass slaughter be used for the purpose of destroying population centers or other predominantly civilian targets. Retaliatory action that would indiscriminately and disproportionately take many wholly innocent lives, lives of people who are in no way responsible for reckless actions of their government, must also be condemned.
2. *The Initiation of Nuclear War:* We do not perceive any situation in which the deliberate initiation of nuclear war, on however restricted a scale, can be morally justified. Nonnuclear attacks by another state must be resisted by other than nuclear means. Therefore, a serious moral obligation exists to develop nonnuclear defensive strategies as rapidly as possible. In this letter we urge NATO to move rapidly toward the adoption of a "no first use" policy, but we recognize this will take time to implement and will require the development of an adequate alternative defense posture.
3. *Limited Nuclear War:* Our examination of the various arguments on this question makes us highly skeptical about the real meaning of "limited." One of the criteria of the just-war teaching is that there must be a reasonable hope of success in bringing about justice and peace. We must ask whether such a reasonable hope can exist once nuclear weapons have been exchanged. The burden of proof remains on those who assert that meaningful limitation is possible. In our view the first imperative is to prevent any use of nuclear weapons and we hope that leaders will resist the notion that nuclear conflict can be limited, contained, or won in any traditional sense.[38]

The letter makes plain the Bishops' view that there are religious implications of behavior involving nuclear weapons and attempts to guide the faithful in both avoiding wrongdoing and in the development of policy alternatives. In issuing the Pastoral Letter, the Bishops argued that they acted not only as religious authorities, "but also as a body of persons exercising a respected role in public debate."[39]

The Bishops' Pastoral Letter may have opened minds to private reflection and raised public awareness of the moral and physical dangers of nuclear war. It also led to less predictable concerns, such as those expressed by former U.S. Air Force officer Matthew Murphy in his book *Betraying the Bishops*, about how its message was taught.

Murphy faults many of those who undertook to teach from "The Challenge of Peace: God's Promise and Our Response" for failing

> to point out that the opposition to counter-population use is morally binding, while their two principles concerning the use of nuclear weapons [the impossibility of moral justification for the deliberate initiation of a nuclear war and the improbability of a limited nuclear war] are prudential judgments.[40]

Confusion about such a seemingly complex and obscure point might be easily forgiven among "nonexperts" intervening in what is understood to be a highly technical field. But Murphy argues for a more careful and, incidentally, permissive interpretation of the Bishops' letter in the context of grave moral consequence: authoritative observation of an obligation that would be morally binding on Roman Catholics. A church whose leaders have publicly imposed discipline on its members with regard to other morally significant public policy issues like abortion could demand more than reflection from the faithful who actively participate in nuclear deterrence.[41]

Without the distinction that Murphy observes, the Bishops could be understood to be condemning elements of current U.S. Government policy as morally unacceptable. Religious authority did not in this case directly challenge the authority of the state or the law, policies, and legal orders governing the behavior of faithful citizens and members of the Armed Services. However, the combination of historic good fortune and the caution of the U.S. Catholic Bishops play a larger role in explaining this outcome than any reliable theological grounding for the morality of nuclear deterrence.

In developing the "just war" tradition in response to the reality of the nuclear arms race, the Bishops raise a complicated and evolving question. As Rev. J. Bryan Hehir observes, "[r]educed to its bare essentials, the moral tradition holds that morally legitimate use of force must be limited use, and limits are to be imposed on purposes, methods, and intentions."[42] In the late 1970s, Carl Sagan and other leading scientists investigating the potential global climate effects of a nuclear war discovered the distinct possibility that it might lead to a "nuclear winter" extinguishing all human life. Following the 1997 discovery that even a limited, regional use of nuclear weapons would lead to global climate effects, a meaningfully "limited" use of nuclear weapons is harder to imagine than ever, while the moment when authorities from one or more religious traditions directly challenge the morality of involvement with plans for the use of nuclear weapons is increasingly easy to imagine.[43]

Theology Ignored, Deterrence Denied?

The presumed exclusion of religion from U.S. nuclear weapons policy is delicate and uncertain. It may also be counterproductive. There are reasons to hope that the conscious and plural inclusion of diverse religious perspectives may offer transformational potential for better policy and greater national and human security. First, the rigorous requirements of rationality for deterrence demand that all relevant motivations be predictable to the other side. Second, the explicit inclusion of religious perspectives in public debate over nuclear weapons policy can help us reclaim responsibility for the ethical implications of our policies, respond to the uncertainties that the resurgence of religion in international politics and the intrusion of religious values into deterrence theory have created, and create a plural environment in which no religious community feels targeted by U.S. nuclear weapons.

The insights of contemporary international relations theory suggest that systemic causes, particularly the absence of a higher power to organize and enforce rules among states, account for many outcomes of interest in international politics, particularly the prevalence of conflict. These insights, including those of deterrence theory, have enabled stabilizing policy choices that have reduced the risk of nuclear war as well as reduced the risk of the theft or diversion of nuclear weapons and materials. However, these theoretical insights do not absolve leaders of responsibility for their actions, which religious authorities observe to be significant with regard to nuclear weapons.[44]

Undisturbed, "faith" in deterrence and nuclear weapons ensnares us in an indefinitely repeated gamble that machines and systems designed and operated by fallible human beings will always perform infallibly.[45] The ethical vigilance that religious perspectives suggest with regard to nuclear weapons may prove a grain of sand in the oyster of deterrence theory. Pope John Paul II and other religious authorities have emphasized that even if we do not see an alternative today, we cannot morally rely on deterrence forever.[46]

Deterrence theorists lament the difficulty of adequately describing what religiously motivated terrorists might hold dear (and the consequent further difficulty of threatening with explosives rewards located in the distant future or even the afterlife). Some have suggested that these different sorts of values leave religious believers "undeterrable" because they hold "transcendental value inventories"—what they hold most dear is safe from any bomb. However, religious values also open the door to conflict resolution options not available to states. Edward Luttwak describes one dimension of this peacemaking potential:

> in the degree that the involved authority of religion has internal political validity for the parties, warranting a deference that neither side may show the other, religiously based conflict resolution can ameliorate the objective circumstances of the conflict and not merely operate within unchanging constraints.[47]

Luttwak may suggest a lighter side to "transcendental value inventories." What we cannot threaten to explode may be also ours to claim through dialogues of inclusion based on shared respect for human life and dignity. This may sound like nonsense to traditional deterrence theorists, and that may be a reason they should not control nuclear weapons policy by themselves.

Finally, explicit inclusion of plural religious perspectives in the debate over nuclear weapons policy can ameliorate fear that U.S. nuclear weapons exist to threaten certain religious groups. Deterrence theorists may dismiss these fears as irrelevant; in light of Congressman Tom Tancredo's 2005 suggestion that the United States should be prepared to "take out their holy sites" if radical extremist Muslims take part in a future act of nuclear terrorism against the United States, it is possible to understand how some might arrive at these fears.[48] Careful, respectful, plural theological consideration of the meaning of nuclear weapons for human existence may lead to heavy moral criticism of those who build, maintain, and plan to use nuclear weapons, which is an issue of concern for the United States, not only because our government seems mute today in its own defense against such criticism, but also because nuclear weapons pose a unique danger to our national security and mustering religious condemnation against their use also protects us, and if experts like Graham Allison are right about nuclear terrorism being "the ultimate preventable catastrophe," we need all the help we can get.

Notes

1. Francis X. Winters, *Remembering Hiroshima: Was it Just?* (Burlington, VT: Ashgate, 2009).

2. General Lee Butler, "The Risks of Nuclear Deterrence: From Superpowers to Rogue Leaders," Remarks delivered at the National Press Club, February 2, 1998, transcript available at: http://www.nuclearfiles.org/menu/key-issues/ethics/issues/military/butler_risk-nuclear-deterrence.htm. General Butler extends this metaphor, observing that "[t]his abiding faith in nuclear weapons was inspired and is sustained by a catechism instilled over many decades by a priesthood who speak with great assurance and authority. I was for many years among the most avid of these keepers of the faith in nuclear weapons, and for that I make no apology."

3. As referenced by Paul Lettow, *Ronald Reagan and his Quest to Abolish Nuclear Weapons* (New York: Random House, 2006), p. 23.

4. As referenced by Gerard J. DeGroot, *The Bomb: A Life* (Cambridge, MA: Harvard University Press, 2005), pp. 64–65. Less famously, Oppenheimer preceded this remark with another passage from the *Bhagavad Gita*: "If the radiance of a thousand suns; Were burst into the sky, That would be like; The splendor of the Mighty One—." The use of religious metaphor in nuclear weapons policy discourse continues today. For example, in February 2009 Dr. Clark Murdock advocated for the development of a more reliable nuclear warhead requiring fewer hazardous materials in its manufacture by arguing, in part, that "[t]he question of 'new' and what constitutes 'new' is an important theological discussion." As referenced by Jeffrey Lewis, "Did Congress Define 'New' Nukes," blog post at www.armscontrolwonk.com February 18, 2009; available at: http://www.armscontrolwonk.com/2171/did-congress-define-new-nukes. The property of "newness" is not theological in character; but those who believe that a nuclear weapon would only be "new" if it has new properties related to its destructiveness or deliverability find no common ground for discussion with those who believe that international legal nonproliferation undertakings to work toward nuclear disarmament would be undermined by the development of any nuclear explosive device of a new design.

5. For example, Waltz argues "nuclear weaponry makes miscalculation difficult because it is hard not to be aware of how much damage a small number of warheads can do" in Scott D. Sagan and Kenneth N. Waltz, *The Spread of Nuclear Weapons: A Debate Renewed* (New York: W. W. Norton, 2003), p. 44.

6. Ibid.

7. Owen B. Toon, Alan Robock, Richard P. Turco, Charles Bardeen, Luke Oman, and Georgiy L. Stenchikov, "Consequences of Regional-Scale Nuclear Conflicts," *Science*, March 2, 2007, Vol. 315, pp. 1224–1225.

8. As Janne Nolan has observed, the number of nuclear weapons any particular commentator thinks the United States should have says more about the commentator than it does about nuclear weapons.

9. As referenced by J. Bryan Hehir, "The Moral Measurement of War: A Tradition of Change and Continuity," in John D. Carlson and Erik C. Owens, eds.,

The Sacred and the Sovereign: Religion and International Politics (Washington, DC: Georgetown University Press, 2003), p. 47.

10. As referenced by Lawrence Freedman, *Deterrence* (Cambridge: Polity Press, 2004), p. 12. See also Martin van Creveld's collection of Thomas Schelling's articulations of "'the diplomacy of violence,' 'the art of commitment,' 'the manipulation of risk,' and 'the dialogue of competitive armament,'" in Martin van Creveld, *Nuclear Proliferation and the Future of Conflict* (New York: The Free Press, 1993), p. 60.

11. "Deterrence as a strategy, however, depends on the assumption that the behavior of potentially hostile others can be manipulated through issuing timely and appropriate threats . . ." Freedman, supra note 10, p. 30.

12. See, for example, Jeffrey Lewis, "Minimum Deterrence," *Bulletin of the Atomic Scientists*, July/August 2008, Vol. 64, No. 3, pp. 38–41.

13. For example, see United States Air Force Doctrine Document 2-12, "Nuclear Operations," May 7, 2009, p. 19: "The day-to-day purpose of nuclear weapons is to deter; to create desired political effects without actually employing nuclear weapon kinetic effects. Deterrence is a political tool which can be postured to effect the desired outcome. Civilian leadership can send strong messages to assure our allies and dissuade our adversaries through strategic messaging, generation of forces, posturing the forces, deployment of forces, and limited strikes to show our resolve and/or provide escalation control."

14. "In policy-making circles it was still extremely difficult to think of ways to assess the size and composition of nuclear arsenals except by reference to the assumed requirements of actual exchanges, as evidenced in numerous debates in Washington over new weapons systems, these debates eventually required a routine quality." Freedman, supra note 10, p. 18.

15. President Barack Obama, Remarks delivered in Prague, Czech Republic, on April 5, 2009; full text available at: http://www.huffingtonpost.com/2009/04/05/obama-prague-speech-on-nu_n_183219.html

16. Matthew F. Murphy, *Betraying the Bishops* (Lanham, MD: University Press of America, 1987), p. 13.

17. This effort is not a minor critique or course correction, as Congresswoman Tauscher explains: "We need this commission to get our nuclear policy back on track. For too long we have missed the forest for the trees, and I am hopeful this commission will encourage a vital national discussion that is both open and transparent about the appropriate role of nuclear weapons in our national security strategy," available at: http://armedservices.house.gov/list/press/armedsvc_dem/hascpr031908.shtml

18. John Lewis Gaddis, *The Cold War: A New History* (New York: Penguin, 2005), pp. 226–227. According to Gaddis, Reagan "insisted" that "the ultimate purpose of [the Strategic Defense Initiative] . . . was not to freeze nuclear weapons, but rather to render them 'impotent and obsolete.'" This last theme reflected something else about Reagan that almost everybody at the time missed: he was the only nuclear abolitionist ever to have been president of the United States. He made no secret of this, but the possibility that a right-wing Republican anticommunist pro-military chief executive could also be an antinuclear activist

defied so many stereotypes that hardly anyone noticed Reagan's repeated promises, as he had put it in the "evil empire" speech, "to keep America strong and free, while we negotiate real and verifiable reductions in the world's nuclear arsenals and one day, with God's help, their total elimination."

19. Daniel Ellsberg, "Roots of the Upcoming Nuclear Crisis," Chapter 4 in David Krieger, ed. *The Challenge of Abolishing Nuclear Weapons* (New Brunswick: Transaction, 2009), p. 51. Ellsberg does go on to note that Reagan did maintain plans to use nuclear weapons in foreseeable contingencies and "did not experience a crisis of comparable challenge."

20. Lettow, supra note 3, p. 6.

21. Ibid., pp. 30–31.

22. "While there is little evidence as to when Reagan first adopted that conviction, both Cannon and Morris state that he mentioned it to evangelical clergymen, to his advisers, and to a few others, in the late 1960s and continuously thereafter." Ibid., p. 21.

23. Ibid., p. 8.

24. Ibid., p. 39.

25. "Some of Reagan's presidential advisers were almost certain that he would not retaliate in the event" of a Soviet nuclear attack." Ibid., p. 35.

26. Lon Fendall, *Stand Alone or Come Home* (Newberg, OR: Barclay Press, 2008), p. 81.

27. Ibid., pp. 73–74.

28. Ibid., p. 79.

29. Mark O. Hatfield as told to Diane N. Solomon, *Against the Grain: Reflections of a Rebel Republican* (Ashland, OR: White Cloud Press, 2001), pp. 190–193.

30. Ibid., p. 191.

31. Ibid., p. 190.

32. Fendall, supra note 26, p. 77.

33. Hatfield, supra note 29, p. 193.

34. Fendall, supra note 26, p. 80.

35. Edward M. Kennedy and Mark O. Hatfield, *Freeze!* (New York: Bantam, 1982), p. 116.

36. Hatfield recalls telling Hatch, "I'm calling long distance from Salt Lake City . . . We've just held a council meeting of the elders of the church. And I want to report to you we're all terrible disappointed you have not yet supported Senator Hatfield's Nuclear Freeze measure . . . If you have any questions we would be happy to answer them from a doctrinal point of view." Hatfield, supra note 29, p. 193.

37. Hatfield, supra note 26, p. 192.

38. U.S. Conference of Catholic Bishops, "The Challenge of Peace: God's Promise and Our Response," A Pastoral Letter on War and Peace by the National Conference of Catholic Bishops, May 3, 1983, p. 2.

39. Murphy, supra note 16, p. 8.

40. Murphy, supra note 16, p. 10. The implication being that: "[t]he faithful are morally bound to oppose a policy that bases deterrence on the direct, intentional taking of non-combatants' lives; but the faithful are free to decide in

conscience whether to oppose policies based on the premise that not all uses of nuclear weapons will inevitably escape control, or on the premise that effective deterrence of Soviet attack against NATO requires that NATO retain the option to use nuclear weapons first." Murphy, supra note 16, p. 21.

41. For example, His Holiness Pope Benedict the XVI, then as Cardinal Joseph Ratzinger, prefect of the Vatican Congregation for the Doctrine of the Faith, directed that "the minister of Holy Communion may find himself in the situation where he must refuse to distribute Holy Communion to someone, such as in cases of a declared excommunication, a declared interdict, or an obstinate persistence in manifest grave sin. Cardinal Joseph Ratzinger, "Worthiness to Receive Holy Communion. General Principles," Letter to U.S. Bishops as published in L'Espresso, June 2004, available at: http://www. catholicculture.org/culture/library/view.cfm?id=6041&CFID=19769110&CF TOKEN=60351160.

42. The just-war tradition "denies the central claim of the modern doctrine of sovereignty—the right to declare war purely on the basis of national interest interpreted by the state—by establishing tests of 'just cause,' 'right intention,' and 'last resort.'" Hehir, supra note 9, p. 45. The just-war "tradition therefore is not 'realist' in the sense of insulating sovereign power and strategic discourse from moral analysis, but it is realist in the sense that it seeks to understand, engage, and even complement the state in its role of defending the political community up to and including the use of force." Ibid., p. 46.

43. Toon, Robock, Turco, Bardeen, Oman, and L. Stenchikov.

44. "We are being, increasingly, swept along the current towards accepting war as a master, with a dynamism of its own, to which our standards of right and wrong are not applicable, a process which enslaves those who partici-pate in it and subdues them to its purposes, much in the same way as does a totalitarian state." R. A. Markus, "Conscience and Deterrence," in Walter Stein, ed., *Nuclear Weapons and Christian Conscience* (London: Merlin Press, 1961), p. 87.

45. For reasons for skepticism, see, for example, Scott Sagan, *The Limits of Safety: Organizations, Accidents, and Nuclear Weapons* (Princeton: Princeton University Press, 1993); and Shaun Gregory, *The Hidden Cost of Deterrence: Nuclear Weapons Accidents* (London: Brassey's, 1990).

46. U.S. Conference of Catholic Bishops (1983), p. 2.

47. Edward Luttwak, "The Missing Dimension," in Douglas Johnston and Cynthia Sampson, eds., *Religion, the Missing Dimension of Statecraft* (New York: Oxford University Press, 1994), p. 18. Luttwak observes that this potential is not unlimited: "To be sure, the quasi diplomacy of religious leaders, religious institutions, and religiously motivated lay figures, all lacking in the instru-mentalities of state power, can only function within the context created by the relevant balances of power; it may therefore be argued of these as of all conflict-resolution efforts, that they can only yield results already pre-ordained by the balance of power." Ibid., p. 17.

48. Associated Press, "Tancredo: If they Nuke Us, Bomb Mecca," July 18, 2005, available at: http://www.foxnews.com/story/0,2933,162795,00.html

14

Theology and Human Rights

William F. Schultz

"You philosophers are like blind men looking in a dark room for a black cat that is not there," a theologian once remarked. "Yes," retorted a philosopher, "and if we were theologians, we would find the cat."

Philosophers rarely agree with other philosophers; theologians rarely agree with other theologians; and the two almost never agree with each other. That is why it was both courageous and quixotic when in 1947 the United Nations Educational, Scientific and Cultural Organization convened a group of both types of thinkers under the title *Committee on the Philosophic Principles of the Rights of Man*. The job of the committee was straightforward, if not daunting: as a prelude to the drafting of a Universal Declaration of Human Rights (UDHR)—sometimes referred to as the "international bill of rights"—it was to survey the world's great thinkers from a wide variety of traditions, religious, philosophical, political, scientific, in order to distill common assumptions about the theoretical basis for human rights and the fundamental rights that all people shared. Needless to say, though the committee managed to enumerate a fair number of rights that it regarded as agreed upon universally, beginning with the "right to a life that is free from the haunting fear of poverty and insecurity," it had a far harder time describing the *theoretical* basis for those rights.[1]

As a result the UDHR fudges the question. Its first Whereas clause refers to "recognition of the *inherent* dignity and of the equal and *inalienable* rights of all members of the human family" and Article 1 affirms that "All human beings are . . . *endowed* with reason and conscience," all three italicized words being interpretable as referring implicitly either to some form of deity or at least to natural law. But the Declaration also cites a host of pragmatic reasons for respecting human rights—it deters rebellion; it promotes friendly relations between nations; it promotes social progress.

The UDHR is actually a remarkably fluent document considering that it was designed to appeal to those who hailed from traditions secular and religious, communist and capitalist, Western and Eastern, and that it was written by a committee.

The Roots and Rationale of Human Rights

Nonetheless, the truth is that in the Western tradition at least common notions of rights emerged in good measure out of the conviction, derived largely from Judaism and Christianity, that human beings are made in the "likeness of God" and that the human spirit is a reflection of God's own.[2] Indeed, in these traditions, as well as the Islamic, human dignity—the fundamental basis of human rights—is so intrinsic to one's humanity as a creature of God that to deprive a human being of dignity through humiliation or torture, for example, is quite literally to seek to deprive God of God's dignity, to humiliate and torture God.[3] It is not surprising, then, that the rationale for the defense of human beings' "inherent" dignity and "inalienable" rights and hence the very grounds for human rights themselves has often been a religious one.

Such a rationale of course is not without its problems. At the most fundamental level, if rights are intended to be *universal*, then the rationale for rights will need to be one that is universal too, in the sense that it transcends particular traditions or cultures and speaks to people from a wide variety of backgrounds. A religious rationale hardly meets this criterion not only because there is an abundance of different faiths in the world—by one count at least 22 major faith traditions with half a million or more members[4]—and not only because within each of those traditions there are an uncountable number of sects, to say nothing of the myriad cults that claim no relation to any of those traditions, but also because of the millions of people who do not truck with any form of religion at all.

Those who fall into this latter category may therefore be more comfortable understanding human rights as, in Elie Wiesel's phrase, the secular equivalent of a global religious faith.[5] Michael Ignatieff has descried that description but has called them "the *lingua franca* of global moral thought" and Nadine Gordimer has dubbed them "the creed of humanity."[6] Such appellations provide no help in determining the theoretical grounding for human rights, but they do have the advantage of signaling that human rights transcend particular religious incarnations and appeal to some common human experience, for example, reason, pity, or suffering. Indeed, the historian Lynn Hunt has argued that it was not until human beings developed the capacity to empathize with one another—a social development she attributes to the emergence of certain eighteenth-century novels—that modern notions of human rights were possible.[7]

This division between those who understand human rights to be essentially a religious enterprise and those who see it in purely secular terms has been especially prevalent within an American context. Most major human rights groups—Amnesty International USA; Human Rights Watch; Human Rights First, et cetera—are decidedly secular organizations, which is not to say that they do not make alliances with religious groups or welcome members who bring strong religious convictions to their human rights work but that both their policies and the rationales for those policies are framed in largely secular terms.

Those for whom human rights is first and foremost a religious calling may, in turn, be roughly divided between believers who regard their faith as requiring support for human rights as a means of making manifest the Kingdom on earth and those American exceptionalists who, hearkening back to the founding of the country, believe that the United States has a special God-given responsibility to protect and promote the "divine gift of freedom" around the world. Within the first group will be found activists of both a so-called "liberal" stripe, such as Roman Catholics who abhor the death penalty or evangelicals devoted to ending poverty, and a "conservative," such as those antiabortionists who defend "the rights of the unborn."

The second group, American exceptionalists, would be comprised in good measure of political neoconservatives, the imperatives of whose faith former President George W. Bush put succinctly in his Second Inaugural Address when he said, "From the day of our Founding, we have proclaimed that every man and woman on this earth has rights, and dignity, and matchless value, because they bear the image of the Maker of Heaven and Earth . . . Advancing these ideals is the mission that created our Nation . . . So it is [today] the policy of the United States to seek and support the growth of democratic movements and institutions in every nation and culture, with the ultimate goal of ending tyranny in our world."[8]

Such a view reflects the epitome of theolegalism—not a claim that one particular sectarian faith ought to take precedence over all others, but that from its beginning the existence of America (or, to be more precise, the presence of European settlers on the American continent) has been characterized by a special relationship with "the Maker of Heaven and Earth" —what more than 40 years ago the sociologist Robert Bellah called "civil religion," which he described as "a genuine apprehension of universal and transcendent religious reality as seen in or . . . revealed through the experience of the American people."[9] Moreover, that special relationship has placed certain political and even policy demands upon the country and its people. Be it at the time of the American Revolution, the Civil War and the abolition of slavery, the Spanish American War, the First and Second World Wars, the civil rights movement or the 2003 Iraq War, those demands have frequently been seen as manifest in a defense of (human) rights.

The Consensualist Requirement

While all these groups, secularists, traditional believers, and American exceptionalists, understand themselves to be supporters of human rights, their notions of what human rights mean and which human rights deserve support may differ notably. Whether abortion is a violation of human rights, for example, may divide people within religious camps just as readily as it can religious from secular. Most human rights activists who take a primarily secularist orientation and some people of faith will oppose the death penalty—a position likely to be at odds with other traditional believers and most neoconservatives. And the role of the United States in both promoting human rights and abiding by them is highly controversial.

In his analysis of American civil religion, Bellah noted that "at its best, it has neither been so general that it has lacked incisive relevance to the American scene nor so particular that it has placed American society above universal human values."[10] But Bellah's words "at its best" constitute an important caveat for American theolegalism has all too often prompted a narrow, American-centric view of human rights—the notion that that nation endowed with a special relationship with God must also be best equipped to define what rights God has bequeathed to His children. This is evident in the frequency with which the United States takes reservations to international human rights treaties, insisting that their provisions are only operative to the extent to which they conform with the latest U.S. Supreme Court interpretation of relevant provisions of the U.S. Constitution. It is evident in the general resistance to understand social and economic needs in terms of human rights. It is evident in the refusal of even some of the greatest self-professed champions of human rights—I think, for example, of the late Congressman Tom Lantos, the only survivor of the Holocaust to serve in Congress and the co-founder of the Human Rights Caucus in the House of Representatives—to admit that the death penalty as practiced in the United States was a violation of human rights. Theolegalism and its offspring, American exceptionalism, has fostered an attitude of "my way or the highway" when it comes to delineating and defending human rights.

But fortunately there exists an independent yardstick against which to measure any particular nation's posture toward human rights. For regardless of their origin or rationale, be they religious or not, human rights do not "become" rights until they are recognized as such by the international community in the form of treaties, covenants, international legal jurisprudence, decisions of the UN Security Council and actions and rulings by international human rights bodies, such as the UN Human Rights Council, UN treaty bodies, or regional human rights entities.

In this sense an individual is certainly free to believe that torture or the death penalty is a violation of human rights because it is an affront to one who is made in the "likeness of God," and another individual to oppose those abuses because they are an affront to human dignity as determined by natural law but, until torture and the death penalty are declared violations of human rights by broad-ranging international consensus, as they have been, one cannot say that the right not to be tortured or subjected to state execution is a universally recognized human right. The lack of international consensus around the issue of abortion is exactly why that act is *not* understood to be a violation of internationally sanctioned human rights, strongly as some people may feel it ought to be. This consensualist requirement, then, is what prevents any one religious or philosophical tradition from imposing its own views on everyone else in the name of universal human rights.

And it is also what precludes any one nation, no matter how powerful, from claiming with any legitimacy that it alone can interpret the meaning of human rights and the actions that flow from that interpretation. The Geneva Conventions, prohibitions on torture and international rules regarding the treatment of prisoners, describe the rights accorded to persons in custody—rights that generally cannot be ignored or suspended unilaterally, even in circumstances of national emergency. Everything from the laws of war (sometimes called international humanitarian law) to the emerging doctrine of the "responsibility to protect," for example, describe the circumstances under which nations may take military action (*casus belli*) and the type of action they may take.[11] The American government's departure from these internationally recognized, consensus-driven principles in its treatment of prisoners held in connection with the "war on terror" and its declaration of the Iraq War is precisely what accounted for the significant decline in respect for the United States as a human rights leader around the world between 2001 and 2006.[12]

The importance of the consensualist requirement for our purposes therefore is simple: it is a bulwark against the excesses of a narrowly theolegal approach to human rights. To be sure, resistance to the subordination of American predilections to global law and opinion has been abundant. In the early 1950s, for example, Senator John Bricker (R-OH), fearing infringement of international law on U.S. sovereignty, tried repeatedly to circumscribe the president's ability to sign human rights treaties. Still today leading figures such as Supreme Court Justice Antonin Scalia disparage reference by the court to international law, describing it as "meaningless" but "dangerous" dicta.[13] Resolutions have frequently been introduced in Congress in recent years that would prohibit judges from citing international law in their decisions and in some cases would impeach them if they do.[14]

But, robust as such opposition has been, it has in fact been American leadership that has advanced the notion that human rights acquire their salience from a global imprimatur. The Atlantic Charter (1941), with its commitment to "freedom from fear and want" as one of the organizing principles of a postwar world was an initiative of Franklin Roosevelt and Winston Churchill and was subsequently endorsed by the governments of Belgium, Czechoslovakia, Greece, Luxembourg, the Netherlands, Norway, Poland, the Soviet Union, Yugoslavia, and representatives of General Charles de Gaulle, leader of the Free French. The Universal Declaration Human Rights (1948)—the bedrock instrument upon which modern human rights claims rest—was shepherded by Eleanor Roosevelt and adopted without dissenting vote by the United States and 48 nations, 9 standing in the Islamic tradition, 3 in the Buddhist, and 1 in the Hindu. The United States under Democratic and Republican presidents alike has, with the exception of the administration of George W. Bush, been an active participant in UN human rights mechanisms, an implicit acknowledgment that enforcement of human rights is a global responsibility.

Some years ago when the state of South Carolina banned video poker, one aficionado of the practice was heard to remark, "Why, it's practically Communist. It's like they're taking away our damn rights." But unfortunately for him, there is no global consensus—yet—that playing video poker is a human right and, thanks to American leadership, that is what it takes. Short of such agreement, that poor man is out of luck.

Case Study: Religious Freedom

Deeply involved as religious people have long been in the struggle for social justice and human rights—one thinks immediately of nineteenth-century efforts to abolish slavery; of the Catholic Worker Movement, of the civil rights movement; of opposition to the death penalty—those religious communities that have traditionally been regarded as "conservative" in both their theology and politics, had until the 1990s largely refrained from engaging in human rights struggles, active as they may have been on such issues as abortion, prayer in schools, and vouchers for private education.

In 1997, however, prompted by a Statement of Conscience the previous year from the National Association of Evangelicals pledging "to do what is within our power to the end that the government of the United States will take appropriate action to combat the intolerable religious persecution now victimizing fellow believers and those of other faiths";[15] the formation by the World Evangelical Fellowship of the International Day of Prayer for the Persecuted Church[16]; and two popular books, Paul Marshall's *Their Blood Cries Out: The Worldwide Tragedy of Modern Christians Who are Dying for the Faith*,[17] and Nina Shea's *In the Lions Den: Persecuted Christians and What the Western Church Can Do About It*,[18] the conservative Christian community began to mobilize around legislation in Congress to establish a U.S. Government Office of Religious Persecution Monitoring. Known initially as the Wolf-Specter bill, the legislation would have imposed automatic sanctions on any country engaged in a pattern of religious persecution. Though Congress had held hearings on religious discrimination abroad in 1996 and adopted any number of resolutions on violations of religious freedom over the years, including the previous year condemning the persecution of Baha'is in Iran,[19] this was the first legislation that would have institutionalized that particular concern and one of the few that mandated sanctions for any human rights violation.

Needless to say, the proposal ran into staunch opposition. The business community and Clinton administration balked at the provision of automatic sanctions. Some academics criticized as chauvinistic the popular notion that religious freedom was the "first freedom" because it was the first amendment to the constitution and worried that the bill was an attempt to foist American notions of church-state separation on the rest of the world. And secular human rights organizations criticized the privileging of one violation over many others, concerned that the establishment of a separate and dedicated office would undermine the work of the Office of the Assistant Secretary of State for Democracy, Human Rights and Labor (colloquially known as "the Human Rights Bureau") with its broad and inclusive agenda. Some also were suspicious (in light, no doubt, of the origins of the initiative) that attention to the travails of Christians would take precedence over persecution of those of other faiths though the legislation itself was quite clear that it applied to denial of anyone's religious freedom, not just that of Christians.[20]

After more than a year of hearings, revisions, negotiations, and a surprise substitution of a new bill in the Senate, the International Religious Freedom Act of 1998 (IRFA) was finally passed by both houses and signed into law by President Clinton on October 27, 1998. No longer containing automatic sanctions, IRFA created an Office of Religious Freedom within the State Department headed by an ambassador-at-large and an independent nine-member Commission on International Religious Freedom charged with issuing reports on the status of religious freedom around the world and the designating of the worst offenders as "countries of particular concern" (CPCs). It outlined 15 possible actions the president can take in relation to those CPCs though it allowed for the waiver of action if it "would further the purpose" of IRFA or was required by "an important national interest."

More than a decade has now passed since IRFA became law. Implementation has been far from perfect, but few, if any, of the critics' concerns have been realized.[21] The ambassador and the commission have been careful to respect the traditions of the countries they criticize while pulling no punches about violations of religious freedom that justifiably warrant condemnation. Concern about persecution of Christians has not precluded attention to abuses against other faiths. The existence of an Office of Religious Freedom within the State Department has not diminished the role of the Human Rights Bureau. And in a few cases at least the IRFA-sanctioned mechanisms appear to have had a positive impact. After it was named a CPC in 2004, for example, Vietnam negotiated a "binding agreement" with the United States promising to open previously closed "house churches," end forced renunciations of faith, and release religious prisoners.[22]

Perhaps most strikingly, however, success in their efforts to pass legislation advancing religious freedom led conservative and evangelical religious communities to engage around a variety of other human rights issues. They were instrumental in the passage in 2000 of the Trafficking Victims Protection Act and the establishment of an Office to Monitor and Combat Trafficking in Persons in the State Department with a corresponding ambassador-at-large. Outraged by the Sudanese government's attacks on southern Sudanese Christians and animists, evangelicals pushed for the Sudan Peace Act of 2002 and the designation of a high-level U.S. emissary, both of which contributed to the ceasefire in South Sudan in 2003 and the peace treaty in 2004. What accounts for this new-found activism? As one observer put it succinctly, ". . . a strong belief that the U.S. is involved in a continuing international struggle between good and evil. While in the 1980s this struggle was defined by the Cold War, from the mid-1990s evangelical concern focused centrally on human rights issues."[23]

Theolegal Lessons

What does all this tell us about theolegal democracy in the United States? In the first place, there is no question but what human rights issues that conservative and evangelical advocates have focused on have generally been ones related to their religious faith and communities. This is obvious in the cases of religious freedom and perhaps sex trafficking. In the case of south Sudan too, many of the victims of atrocities were Sudanese Christians who had suffered at the hands of the Islamic government.

What is also obvious is that the responsiveness of legislators to these concerns, especially that of religious freedom, reflects the powerful role religion has played in shaping of the American experience. It is highly unlikely that a European government, for example, would have singled out religious freedom for special attention and a discrete ambassadorship. Moreover, the designation of religious freedom as the "first freedom" (because it is the first right listed in the American Bill of Rights) with the implication that it is therefore the *most important* right also carries with it the assumption that the United State's history reveals a theolegal hierarchy of values that are somehow normative for the rest of the world.[24]

Nonetheless, both these circumstances have had in these instances largely positive ramifications. There is nothing wrong with any community advocating on behalf of human rights victims from that community. The LGBT community, for example, quite appropriately advances concerns about the mistreatment of LGBT folks, and expatriates from countries overseas are often the most powerful advocates in the United States for their sisters and brothers in their native lands. This is often the way people are drawn into the broader human rights movement: through an initial concern for their own. Indeed, the late philosopher Richard Rorty argued that it was impossible to feel "solidarity" with "human beings as a whole"; that "our sense of solidarity is strongest when those with whom solidarity is expressed are thought of as 'one of us' where 'us' means something smaller and more local than the human race." Only by identifying first with "us" and then "extend[ing] our sense of 'we' to people whom we have previously thought of as 'they,'" primarily through the sharing of stories about "their" suffering, he said, could we begin to see traditional differences as unimportant and hence our common claim to rights as legitimate.[25]

Nor is there anything inherently wrong with a government giving special attention to particular rights as long as those rights are internationally recognized, as the right to religious freedom surely is, and that attention does not distract from concern for other rights about which the government could have a positive influence. Some governments are better placed than others to affect change. The United States, for example, can have far less impact on the military dictatorship in Burma (Myanmar) than the ASEAN nations can. The fact that European governments may not expend much energy on combating religious persecution could be a strong argument in favor of the United States "taking up the slack."

Where problems can arise is when an exclusivist focus threatens to undermine the indivisibility of human rights. Human rights are not like a cafeteria from which one can pick and choose as one likes, much as the

United States would like to think they are as it takes one reservation after another to provisions of human rights treaties it has ratified. The Universal Declaration of Human Rights contains 30 articles and, when the United States voted for its adoption in 1948, it voted to adopt all 30! The genius of consensualism is that it signals those human rights values about which the international community has reached broad—not perfect or unanimous necessarily, but broad—agreement and hence those values that constitute the indivisible human rights regimen as a whole.

On some issues, such as whether LGBT persons may claim the right to marry, that consensus does not yet exist. On others, it has long been established. With regard to the latter, international law is no different from domestic law. An embezzler cannot claim to be a law-abiding citizen simply because he obeyed the law against armed robbery and no one was killed in the course of his crime. A country either obeys international human rights law as a whole or fails to. If it fails to, it cannot be considered an international human rights leader. International law, for example, precludes sentencing children to life without parole. The United States was, until recently, the only country in the world that continued that practice. No matter how robust the U.S. fair trial system may be; no matter how often the defeated candidate at the polls peacefully turns over his or her office to the victor; no matter how many religions may practice their faiths in this country without fear of persecution, the United States could not have claimed to be a true human rights exemplar as long as it defied international consensus and sentenced children to life without parole. Human rights are indivisible.

Admirable as the engagement of certain religious communities has been around religious freedom, trafficking, and peace in south Sudan, with notable exceptions those communities as a whole have been slower to embrace other human rights causes, such as condemnation of the use of torture by the United States or the Muslim-on-Muslim conflict in Darfur. No one can say for sure what is in the hearts of those who resist a broader human rights agenda—though it was eminently clear when the vice president of the National Association of Evangelicals, Richard Cizik, was dismissed for saying he was changing his mind about the prohibition on civil unions for same-sex couples[26]—but to the extent that that relative silence is motivated by a narrow religious consciousness, it does a disservice to the human rights ideal.

Similarly, the Bush administration often pointed with pride to its pursuit of religious freedom—indeed, to its larger "freedom agenda" —and claimed that that entitled it to assume the mantle of Human Rights Defender, despite its gross abuses of human rights at Abu Ghraib, Guantanamo Bay, Bagram Air Force Base in Afghanistan, and the secret prison sites around the world. The human rights plumb line established through consensualism and the indivisibility of human rights that flow out of it are the best defense against such misplaced claims.

Conclusion

Absent consensualism with its insistence that religious freedom be extended to all faiths, it is possible that some might have sought to privilege Christianity over other religious traditions in the U.S. Government's action against religious persecution. Should that have happened, it would have represented theolegalism at its worst. That it did not means that not only a serious human rights abuse—religious persecution—has been countered, but also a new community has become engaged in a greater number of human rights battles than they might otherwise have been. One can only hope that that new-found engagement will eventually result in an expanded sense of "we" embracing an even wider circle of those previously thought to be "they."

Ultimately, of course, whether that happens is more a function of the religious sentiments themselves than the legal or political systems in which they operate. A religion that addresses universal values and extends its care to the world at large can be a powerful force for human rights. Religion that limits its affections to a narrow segment of the world citizenry or a small range of human rights issues is in the end bound to find itself at odds with what human rights are all about, grounded as they are in a sense of the common misery of humankind and a vision of the common good.

That vision of the common good, as we have seen, is derived in good measure from the best of the American tradition, theolegalistic though that tradition be. It reflects what Nathan C. Walker describes as the pluralist approach "when participants . . . express their views in universal terms [and] defend the rights of people other than themselves." Couple that with a global sense of human values and the result is a marriage that can truly save the world.

Notes

1. Lauren, P. G. *The Evolution of International Human Rights*. Philadelphia: The University of Pennsylvania Press, 1998, pp. 219–225.
2. Hebrew Scriptures, Genesis 5:1.
3. Imam Feisal Abdul Rauf and William F. Schulz, "The End of Barbarism? The Phenomenon of Torture and the Search for the Common Good," in Steenland, Sally, et. al., eds., *Pursuing the Global Common Good: Principle and Practice in U. S. Foreign Policy*," Center for American Progress, Washington, DC, 2007.

4. http://www.adherents.com/Religions_By_Adherents.html.
5. http://www.pbs.org/eliewiesel/resources/millennium.html.
6. Michael Ignatieff, *Human Rights as Politics and Idolatry* (Princeton, NJ: Princeton University Press, 2001), p. 53.
7. Lynn Hunt, *Inventing Human Rights: A History* (New York: W. W. Norton & Co, 2007).
8. http://www.bartleby.com/124/pres67.html.
9. Bellah, Robert, "Civil Religion in America" *Dædalus, Journal of the American Academy of Arts and Sciences,* from the issue entitled, "Religion in America," Winter 1967, Vol. 96, No. 1, pp. 1–21.
10. Ibid.
11. In 2005 the United Nations unanimously adopted the doctrine of the "Responsibility to Protect" (often referred to as "R2P") that delineates a nation's responsibilities to its own citizens and the obligation of the international community to intervene, even militarily, to protect those citizens if the government is unable or unwilling to do so.
12. http://www.worldpublicopinion.org/pipa/articles/btjusticehuman_rightsra/229. php?lb=bthr&pnt=229&nid=&id=k.
13. *Lawrence v. Texas,* No. 02-102, slip op. at 14 (June 26, 2003) (Scalia, J., dissenting).
14. https://secure.acslaw.org/files/Keitner%20ACS%20issue%20brief.pdf.
15. Nina Shea, "The Origins and Legacy of the Movement to Fight Religious Persecution," https://www.rfiaonline.org/archives/issues/6-2/204-origins-and-legacy.
16. http://www.persecutedchurch.org/about/index.cfm.
17. Dallas: Word Publishing, 1997.
18. Nashville: Broadman & Holman, 1997.
19. H. R. Con. Res. 102, 104th Congress, 1996.
20. For a summary of various criticisms and a reply to them, see T. Jeremy Gunn, "A Preliminary Response to Criticisms of the International Religious Freedom Act of 1998," *Brigham Young University Law Review,* 2000, pp. 841–865.
21. For a critique of that implementation by the chair of the commission and a description of where U.S. policy should go from here, see Felice Gaer, "Echoes of the Future? Religious Repression as a Challenge to U.S. Human Rights Policy," in William F. Schulz, ed., *The Future of Human Rights: U.S. Policy for a New Era* (Philadelphia: University of Pennsylvania Press, 2008), pp. 193–214.
22. https://www.rfiaonline.org/archives/issues/6-2/203-international-religious-freedom-act.
23. https://www.rfiaonline.org/archives/issues/6-2/196-religion-and-human-rights-culture.
24. Op. cit., Shea.
25. Richard Rorty, *Contingency, Irony and Solidarity* (Cambridge: Cambridge university Press, 1989), pp. 190–192.
26. http://www.blackchristiannews.com/news/2009/01/homosexual-marriage-still-linchpin-issue-for-evangelicals.html.

15

Religious Freedom

Joseph K. Grieboski

Religious freedom is a principal reason for the success of the American republic. It is the "first freedom" of the Bill of Rights, the first 16 words of which—by guaranteeing free exercise and banning establishment—were designed to encourage the religious enterprise.

The American First Amendment is based on the conviction that believers can and will do good things for themselves, their coreligionists, and their country, and that they should be encouraged to do so. Most important, however, the First Amendment also protects the rights of those who choose not to believe. The American Founding Fathers did not see religion as a "private matter" with no relationship to society or government. Rather, they saw religion and religious people as the cornerstone of the American democracy and representative of the vitality of a nation.

Religious liberty, in the full sense of the term, is the first human right. It is, therefore, a liberty that should not be confined to the private sphere only. The famous American clergyman John Witherspoon—the only cleric to sign the Declaration of Independence—stated in a May 1776 sermon what may be considered a philosophy of religious purpose in America: "It is in the man of piety and inward principle, that we may expect to find the uncorrupted patriot, the useful citizen, and the invincible soldier. God grant that in America true religion and civil liberty may be inseparable and that the unjust attempts to destroy the one, may in the issue tend to the support and establishment of both."

Religions play an integral role in contemporary global affairs and are increasingly being perceived with a sense of urgency. Open fora bringing together representatives of religious groups to discuss the centrality of the role of religion take a great importance. Good things happen in history when the will of believing people is channeled and directed toward the ideals of freedom, justice, and equality for all.

Human rights and religious freedom need to be the basis of a new political ideology of respect and mutual understanding, which needs to take shape and become the energizing concept for public action in this twenty-first century.

In Central Asia, China, the Indian subcontinent, the Middle East, and elsewhere, the actions of religious leaders and institutions serve to empower radicals by encouraging threatening behavior. For this reason, incidentally, it is vitally important that governments around the world nurture environments of free expression so that moderate views may predominate.

Where freedom of religion and belief is protected by governments, promoted by religious believers and institutions, and valued by citizens, religion-based violence, repression, and terrorism will not take root. In this sense, freedom of religion is an antidote to terrorism, especially religion-based terrorism, because it encourages a theological and political awareness of the need to accept the "other." To discriminate against religious beliefs, or to discredit religious practice, is exclusion contrary to respect for fundamental human dignity that will eventually destabilize society by creating a climate of tension, intolerance, opposition, and suspicion not conducive to social peace.

A religion's recognition of the necessity of freedom of religion and belief indicates the theological centrality that every individual has value and worth. In truth, religious freedom is at the heart of the basic beliefs and theologies of every major global faith.

For a body of faith to be defined as a religion—rather than as a belief system or spiritual system—it must claim to hold a monopoly on Truth and Salvation. As the Roman Catholic Church has stated, *Extra Ecclesiae Nulla Salus*—"Outside the Church there is no salvation." If a religion believes—as they all do—that Truth exists, they must also recognize that in order to grasp that Truth, an individual must be free to pursue it. Without the theological freedom to pursue Truth according to the dictates of one's heart, mind, and conscience, an individual is the victim of religious tyranny and not of true religious devotion or fervor.

All men are bound to seek the Truth, especially in what concerns God and His Mandate to Man, and to embrace the Truth they come to know. It is upon the human conscience that the obligations fall and exert their binding force. The Truth cannot impose itself except by virtue of its own truth, as it makes its entrance into the mind at once quietly and with power. Religious freedom, in turn, which men demand as necessary to fulfill their duty to worship God, has to do with immunity from coercion in civil society.

The human person has a right to religious freedom. This freedom means that all men are to be immune from coercion on the part of individuals or of social groups and of any human power, in such wise that no one is to be forced to act in a manner contrary to his own beliefs, whether privately or publicly, whether alone or in association with others, within due limits.

The right to religious freedom, as enunciated by the Second Vatican Council, "has its foundation in the very dignity of the human person as this dignity is known through the revealed word of God and by reason itself." This right of the human person to religious freedom is to be recognized in the constitutional law whereby society is governed, and thus it is to become a civil right.

It is in accordance with their dignity as persons—that is, beings endowed with reason and free will and therefore privileged to bear personal responsibility—that all men should be at once impelled by nature and also bound by a moral obligation to seek the truth, especially religious truth. They are also bound to adhere to the Truth, once it is known, and to order their whole lives in accord with the demands of Truth.

However, men cannot discharge these obligations in a manner in keeping with their own nature unless they enjoy immunity from external coercion as well as psychological freedom. Therefore, the right to religious freedom has its foundation not in the subjective disposition of the person, but in his very nature. In consequence, the right to this immunity continues to exist even in those who do not live up to their obligation of seeking the truth and adhering to it, and the exercise of this right is not to be impeded, provided that just public order be observed.

Freedom of religion is arguably the right most intimately connected to human dignity. Human beings are characterized by the capacity to reason, by a conscience formed through intellect and experience, and by the power to act on reason and conscience. As such, every person is "hard wired" with a thirst to know the truth about the origin, nature, purpose, and destiny of mankind.

Accordingly, to protect religious freedom is to protect the right to seek that truth, and the right to peacefully live and worship in accord with it, both individually and in community with others. (Religious freedom also protects those who believe the search for truth, and the moral imperatives that ensue, involve not only rights but also binding obligations.) Religious freedom goes to the core of what it means to be human and what it means to say (as does, e.g., the Universal Declaration of Human Rights) that human beings possess an intrinsic and inviolable dignity.

A guarantee of religious freedom also supports the other fundamental rights necessary to all human persons: because it is grounded in the universal dignity of the human person, religious freedom encourages other related rights. A government that denies the right to freedom of religion and belief is far more likely to deny other rights central to human dignity, such as freedom from torture or murder. The reverse is also true. Freedom of religion and belief is also closely connected to other civil and political rights necessary to democracy.

Without freedom of conscience, there is no freedom of speech, as believers cannot communicate among themselves about their most fundamental beliefs; there is no freedom of assembly, as like-minded believers cannot meet to share their beliefs and worship their Creator; and there is no freedom of the press, as believers cannot print and share their beliefs with others. Religious individuals and groups need and deserve freedom of speech, freedom of assembly, and the right to be secure in their homes from unwarranted government intrusion.

In many countries with religious minorities, the most that is thought to be achievable is a commitment to religious tolerance. True religious freedom, however, is more than mere tolerance. It constitutes an embracing of universal human dignity because of—rather than in spite of—one's religious convictions.

The great project of the twenty-first century is to encourage and empower religious communities—especially Muslims—who have this view, that is, adapting to non-Muslim religions within Islamic societies is not a compromise of Islam but a deepening and clarifying of it. Islam wields a sword. Shall it be only the sword that thrusts outward to cut off the ears of its perceived enemies, or the sword that pierces inward to cut out that which tears at the truth of Islam?

The great tragedy is that the torch of sacrifice and truth in Islam—and I dare say all faiths—has been snatched from the hands of those who should bear it aloft, and is instead carried high by the enemies of truth and freedom. The so-called "fires of apostolic zeal" alive and well in all faiths has been stolen from the altars of God and now burn as an inferno in those who grind the altars into dust. We are, in fact, destined for another war, but not the clash of civilizations to which is so often incorrectly referred. We are destined for a war against false freedoms—civil and religious—that endanger our true and divine freedom.

This cannot, however, be limited exclusively to Islam, as other religious traditions are susceptible to the kinds of intolerance that lead to violence. We see this, for example, in the recent rise of Hindu nationalism in India, and growing religious tensions in Eastern Europe and Central Asia.

We see before us an ongoing regression and devolution of religious rights globally. Most dangerously, we are sadly observing many former havens of freedom and religious expression becoming new and subtle arenas for religious discrimination. A bill passed by the French National Assembly to ban the wearing of religious garb is an example of this new and potentially dangerous trend.

Similarly, the creation of blacklists of minority religious and spiritual movements by the French and Belgian parliaments severely restricts the rights of members of such groups and all religious communities, since such lists—no matter how misconceived and steeped in misinformation—have been and continue to be considered authoritative by both government and private sector bodies.

European democracies such as France, Belgium, and Germany ought and must be models for states seeking to develop into full-fledged democracies; instead we find China citing France's actions against minority faiths as a justification for its own treatment of the Falun Gong and Christian and other groups. Germany, in the wake of 9/11, has enacted amendments to its Association Law that give the government full discretion to simply shut down religious organizations that it considers a threat to national security, without due process. Governmental actions of this kind by European democracies limit and restrict the rights of all people from practicing their beliefs according to the dictates of their consciences, and serves as a dangerous model for other states worldwide.

The exercise of the right of religious freedom cannot be considered a dispensation granted by the state to its citizens or residents. Additionally, the assurance of this right cannot be deemed an exception. Therefore, it is atypical that more limiting legal or administrative procedures should be implemented with regard to religious beliefs and institutions than those for which the juridical system provides its organization in general.

Rejection of religious freedom also places a prodigious—and perhaps even fatal—obstacle in the way of successful democratic governance, a point closely related to the internal stability and sustainability of a given nation. The danger is greatest with new and aspiring democracies, but cannot be ignored in established polities. For example, the continued political success of India—the world's largest democracy—is contingent in part on overcoming the threat posed by Hindu extremists to that country's tradition (if 50 years can make a tradition) of religious tolerance. Nor can the problem of Kashmir be treated exclusively (by India, Pakistan, or the United States) as a politico-strategic issue, without taking into account the need to address the crucial matter of Hindu-Muslim intolerance.

In new and aspiring democracies, the stakes are even higher. We are witnessing a struggle over the value of religious freedom today in Afghanistan and many of the post-Soviet nations of Central Asia. Each is lurching at one speed or another in the general direction of democracy, but all are in danger of assuming that democracy amounts to little more than a sterile proceduralism of party organization and secret ballots. In fact, as long experience in the West has shown (and, indeed, may need to be relearned in Western Europe), democracy requires a moral framework of universal principles in which it can operate. If that framework is an intolerant interpretation of Islam, democracy will come aborning just as surely as it will flounder from a framework of secular intolerance.

It is very important to emphasize that freedom of religion must not be confused with freedom from religion. A policy of secularism should not be promoted in any way as a cover for unintentional intolerance and atheism as a state policy. Moreover, protecting religious freedom presents a foundational challenge to governments that, for whatever reason, seek to ally with a particular religious tradition in order to suppress others. Overcoming this problem, as much as any economic, ethnic, or political factor, will determine the success or failure of Russian democracy, as Russian leaders struggle with the temptation to suppress non-Orthodox religious minorities in seeking the political support of the Russian Orthodox Church. The same dilemma assails leaders in Ukraine, Belarus, Georgia, and most other European countries that languished under the Communist thumb during the Soviet period.

Other "lingering-Communist" countries, such as China and Vietnam, in which no particular religious tradition underpins culture, view with alarm the growth of religious observance that appears to attend and hasten the demise of Communist institutions. The result is often harsh repression as those governments try to manage and control religious fervor and even alter faith traditions perceived as "foreign" and therefore threatening, such as Roman Catholicism in China. Both China and Vietnam have used the heightened international (and especially American) concern over terrorism to justify attacks on "splittists" and other erstwhile security threats such as Protestants in the Vietnamese Central Highlands, the Buddhists of Tibet, and Uighur Muslims in Northwest China.

National Security

Promoting freedom of religion and belief globally is vital to the national security of each and every state in the world, as well as to international security, in two ways. First, it promotes democracy and therefore strengthens internal and regional stability, and encourages economic prosperity. Second, it helps fight the war on religion-based terrorism. I am not aware of a single regime in the world that both respects religious freedom and poses a security threat to the United States or any other state.

Pluralism and Freedom

It is indeed a fine and fragile balance that needs to be maintained between a state's secular nature and the positive role of believers in public life. To avoid such a twist is as necessary as it is to prevent the misuse of the concept of freedom. This corresponds, among other things, to the demands of a healthy pluralism and contributes to the building up of authentic democracy.

As Pope John Paul II stated, "When States are disciplined and balanced in the expression of their secular nature, dialogue between the different social sectors is fostered and, consequently, transparent and frequent cooperation between civil and religious society is promoted, which benefits the common good." A systematic and systemic discrimination and persecution of any minority, particularly a religious minority, create security, economic, and social consequences for itself, its neighbors, and the international community. The estrangement of one sector of a state's population by the government, or by another segment of the population with the government's active or passive support, establishes resentment and alienation among those groups.

Religion-based discrimination and persecution by a government, actively or passively, serve to create a security dilemma for said state among its neighbors, and may escalate to raise the attention of other interested states and international organizations. Social and political tensions and conflicts created by feelings of inadequacy potentially lead to coercive measures and imposition of tougher laws. One such law is now in place in France, and is under consideration in Germany, Belgium, and other states as well. There could be no real power in laws that so many religious believers will resent or will try to circumvent. Alienating people and making them feel unwelcome is not the solution. The government has a responsibility for the common good, social peace, and coexistence within the state. Consequently, it has the duty and responsibility to guarantee these rights and benefits by respecting pluralism.

Such feelings of isolation, separation, and inadequacy—created by inequitable social, economic, educational, and other standards based solely on differences in religion—in addition to actual incidents of state-sponsored or supported persecution, are cause for entire migrations of targeted peoples. Such migrations create internal displacement and potential refugee issues for neighboring states.

Mass movements of populations across borders potentially become a security threat to states neighboring a religiously repressive state. This can grow to be a true security dilemma if the religiously repressive regime chooses to use force against religious minorities. While the situation in North Korea is horrific all the way around, the treatment of North Korean refugees by Chinese authorities provides an adequate example of concern for such an issue.

The security dilemma caused by a lack of religious freedom is amplified when religious repression and lack of religious freedom serve as an impetus for acts of violence and even terrorism by targeted religious minorities. These acts against the government are not and can never be justified, but may seem to the perpetrators as the only recourse to a regime that represses their fundamental rights. Denial of the fundamental right of religious freedom can indeed directly impact the state's own security. The respect of every expression of religious freedom is, therefore, an effective means for guaranteeing security and stability within a state.

In today's world, where terrorism is the new evil empire and religious extremism *the* threatening political ideology, these words of President Ronald Reagan hold as true as they did when he spoke them in his March 8, 1983, speech to the National Association of Evangelicals: "The real crisis we face today is a spiritual one; at root, it is a test of moral will and faith . . . the source of our strength in the quest for human freedom is not material but spiritual, and because it knows no limitation, it must terrify and ultimately triumph over those who would enslave their fellow man."

Conclusion

Edwin J. Greenlee and Nathan C. Walker

The most contentious social policy issues in the United States are those that are most often the object of religious—usually conservative religious—political attention. In cross-cultural comparisons of policies on access to abortion, restrictions on stem cell research, and the movement to restrict the definition of marriage to one that can exist only between one man and one woman, we see that even the selection of these issues as points of major political contention reflects the dominance of conservative Judeo-Christian religious beliefs in American society.[1] Before the first figurative volley is fired in a debate on any of these issues, conservative religious discourse selects the issues and often frames the debate. Other topics, which could also be seen as valid objects of religious concern, like homelessness, poverty, unemployment, and underperforming elementary and secondary schools, never generate anywhere near the level of heated religious-political discourse and action that same-sex marriage and abortion produce in the United States.

With the issue of abortion, William LaFleur, in *Liquid Life*,[2] notes how modern Japanese society, which has a much larger number of abortions than does America, leaves the question of abortion up to the choice of a patient and her physician. Abortion has been legal in Japan since 1952, and lacks the religious and political uproar that surrounds this issue in the United States. This is in part because of the difference in religious beliefs that exist between American Christians and Japanese Buddhists. With its emphasis on reincarnation, Buddhists in Japan interpret the meaning of having an abortion differently than do say, many theologically conservative American practitioners. Rather than look for an outward, political solution, Japanese Buddhists look to religious solutions that are personal and individual and draw upon a Japanese emphasis on apology and ritual. A fairly new Japanese ritual, referred to as *Mizuko Kuyo*, has become a popular way to help Japanese Buddhist women who have had an abortion deal with some of the religious and psychological impacts. Again, this shows that even basic principles and beliefs of Americans and how they understand phenomena like abortion or same-sex marriage are closely linked to dominant religious beliefs in American culture.

The way in which unrestricted access to abortion services is said to reflect a culture of death, or the creation story in Hebrew Scriptures is combined with elements of science to come up with intelligent design, the impact of dominant American religious beliefs shape the sociopolitical world in which we engage in the twenty-first century, as well as its vocabulary and discourse. Too often, these beliefs, which are historically and culturally limited, are polemically presented by participants in theolegal discourse and practice as universal and unvarying through time. In assessing the impact of religious and political understandings in American democracy, it is important to acknowledge and appreciate historical and cross-cultural differences, as demonstrated by the diverse authors presented in this publication.

The purpose of *Whose God Rules?* has been to introduce the notion of a theolegal democracy. We began by exploring the relationship between religion, law, and social policy in terms of American constitutional law. We then looked at the connection between religion and key participants in the legal and political systems, including legislators, judges, and presidents. Following that discussion we applied the theory of theodemocracy in specific instances such as stem cell research, intelligent design, and marriage. We closed the book with an examination of theodiplomacy, looking at the use of theology in international affairs including discussions of torture, nuclear nonproliferation, human rights, and religious freedom.

One way of applying the theolegal theory is to use the three schools of thought as conceptual lenses: the separationist, the integrationist, and the pluralist worldviews. We conclude by responding directly to each of these perspectives.

To the separationists, we commend the vigilance it takes to preserve the ideal of the separation of religion and state. The preservation of religious fairness in our society has been one of the country's great accomplishments, ensuring both the nonestablishment of a state religion and preserving the free-exercise of belief. However, this ideal is just that. In many of the specific examples reviewed in this book, we find an increasing use of religious rhetoric in political discourse about selected social policy issues. The problem is not the involvement of religion in politics, but rather the use of the religious beliefs of a particular predominant ideology to make, apply, and administer law. Secular values cannot be exclusively used to successfully challenge the beliefs of religious conservatives; progressive religious groups are often allies of science and reason in public discourse and in defending universal principles of equality and justice. Progressive religious discourse more effectively balances conservative religious discourse than secular arguments alone, as noted by Steve Shiffrin[3] and Robert P. Jones.[4] When progressives, whether secular or religious, appeal to the shared value of religious liberty, religion itself is no longer viewed as the enemy.

As sympathizers with separationists, we caution all, including ourselves, to be just as diligent in looking for shared values as we are in promoting the value of a liberal democracy. The purpose in doing so would be to find commonalities with communities of faith rather than shutting down when hearing "God talk."

We admire the attempts of integrationists to authentically balance their religious views with their professional obligations in the public square. For far too long, there has been a false divide between individual beliefs and public roles and responsibilities. Appreciative of this approach, we recommend that integrationists not be too insular in their understandings and assumptions. For example, when public officials hide their religious affiliations, they practice covert theolegal practices resulting in public distrust. It is therefore critical to be public about one's standpoint without diminishing the rights of others to do the same. The responsibility resides with the individual to be aware of the potential for bias when dealing with those of differing beliefs. It is necessary that integrationists not only affirm codes of professional practice that aim at preventing bias, but also support changes in the political and legal systems that will institutionalize mechanisms for eliminating prejudice.

Pluralists are right to celebrate a multicultural, religiously diverse democracy where all citizens are given a voice. They are also aware that over time groups with varied beliefs gain power, ensuring that no single actor rules indefinitely. However, as supporters of a pluralistic democracy we too must not assume that every group, particularly minorities, will have equal access to resources and power in order to effectively mobilize. The truth remains: there is an ongoing tension between preserving the integrity of the majority's decisions with that of the rights of minorities. We must also prevent ourselves from romanticizing pluralism as the highest ideal, which can result in failing to see the very differences we seek to celebrate. When pluralists quickly conflate all people into general statements, they take away the particularities that inform each tradition. To idealize groups into one sweeping category prevents the celebration of the unique differences that each community brings to the public arena.

In this spirit, we hope the pluralists, integrationists, and separationists will celebrate their unique beliefs while simultaneously learning the language of one another's worldviews. In doing so, we are less likely to judge and react to difference. We come to respect the unique wisdom that each worldview brings to our society. We become aware of the limitations of our own perspectives. All of this results in taking shared responsibility for creating a culture based on respect, aware that we have more in common than we believe.

Notes

1. See the Pew Forum's discussion of stem cell research, abortion, and gay marriage around the world at http://www.pewforum.org. The various Pew Forum reports underscore that fact that industrialized countries around the world have differing policies from those in the United States and that American laws tend to be more restrictive or "conservative" when examined from a comparative perspective.
2. LaFleur, William R. *Liquid Life: Abortion and Buddhism in Japan*. Princeton: Princeton University Press, 1994.
3. Shiffrin, Steven, *The Religious Left and Church-State Religions*. Princeton: Princeton University Press, 2009.
4. Jones, Robert P., *Progressive & Religious: How Christian, Jewish, Muslim, and Buddhist Leaders Are Moving beyond the Culture Wars and Transforming American Life*. New York: Rowman & Littlefield Publishers, 2008.

Contributors

TONY BLAIR was prime minister of the United Kingdom from May 1997 until June 2007. He is currently working in the Middle East as Quartet Representative, helping the Palestinians to prepare for statehood as part of the international community's effort to secure peace. Tony Blair continues to advocate on issues involving Africa and climate change. He works on governance projects in Rwanda and Sierra Leone, advising President Kagame and President Koroma, respectively, on policy delivery and attracting investment, with a team of his staff working full-time with both countries. Having been the first major head of government to bring climate change to the top of the international political agenda at the Gleneagles G8 summit in 2005, Mr. Blair is now leading the Breaking the Climate Deadlock Initiative, through which he is working with world leaders to bring consensus on a new and comprehensive international climate policy framework. He has launched the Tony Blair Faith Foundation www.tonyblairfaithfoundation.org to promote respect and understanding between the major religions and to make the case for faith as a force for good in the modern world.

PAULA M. COOEY holds the Margaret Weyerhaueser Harmon chair in religion at Macalester College in Saint Paul, Minnesota. After receiving her PhD in religion from Harvard University in 1981, she taught for 18 years at Trinity University in San Antonio, Texas, before moving to Macalester in 1999. In addition to numerous articles in scholarly journals, she has published several books, among them, *Religious Imagination and the Body: A Feminist Perspective* (Oxford University Press, 1994) and *Family, Freedom, & Faith: Building Community Today* (Westminster John Knox Press, 1996). Her most recent book is *Willing the Good: Jesus, Dissent, and Desire* (Ausburg Fortress Press, 2006).

CHRISTINE CARLSON is a communications executive for a Philadelphia metro area real estate firm. Her interest in the relationship between church and state began with her dismay of the violence and intolerance incited by differing religious beliefs. Curiosity about the seeming intertwined components of marriage in the United States caused her to research how and why our system originated. She has delivered sermons on this and other topics at the First Unitarian Church of Philadelphia. She received her Bachelors in Science in music education from West Chester University.

ALAN DERSHOWITZ is a Brooklyn native who has been called "the nation's most peripatetic civil liberties lawyer" and one of its "most distinguished defenders of individual rights," "the best-known criminal lawyer in the world," "the top lawyer of last resort," "America's most public Jewish defender," and "Israel's single most visible defender—the Jewish state's lead attorney in the court of public opinion." He is the Felix Frankfurter Professor of Law at Harvard Law School. Dershowitz, a graduate of Brooklyn College and Yale Law School, joined the Harvard Law School faculty at the age of 25 after clerking for Judge David Bazelon and Justice Arthur Goldberg. He has also published more than 100 articles in magazines and journals, and more than 300 of his articles have appeared in syndication in 50 national daily newspapers. Professor Dershowitz is the author of 27 fiction and nonfiction works with a worldwide audience. His most recent titles include *Rights From Wrong, The Case For Israel, The Case For Peace, Blasphemy: How the Religious Right is Hijacking the Declaration of Independence, Preemption: A Knife that Cuts Both Ways, Finding Jefferson–A Lost Letter, A Remarkable Discovery,* and *The First Amendment in an Age of Terrorism.* In addition to his numerous law review articles and books about criminal and constitutional law, he has written, taught, and lectured about history, philosophy, psychology, literature, mathematics, theology, music sports—and even delicatessens.

KATIE FORD is the author of *Deposition* and *Colosseum* (Graywolf Press, 2002 & May, 2008) and a chapbook, *Storm* (Marick Press). *Colosseum* was named among the "Top 10 Poetry Books for 2008" by the *Virginia Quarterly Review* and was named the "Best Book of 2008" by *Publishers Weekly.* In 2008 Ford received a Lannan Literary Award, recognizing writers who have made significant contributions to English-language literature. Her poems have appeared in The New Yorker, *American Poetry Review,* the *Paris Review, Ploughshares, Partisan Review, Seneca Review, Poets & Writers, Pleiades,* and many other journals. She has taught poetry and literature at Loyola University, Reed College, and now at Franklin & Marshall College. Ford has graduate degrees in theology from Harvard University and in poetry from the Iowa Writers' Workshop. Her BA in English is from Whitman College. She has received awards and grants from the Academy of American Poets, the Pen American Center, and Prairie Lights. She was an Iowa Arts Fellow while at the Writers' Workshop, and received a scholarly award, the Hopkins Share Award, from Harvard University. Ford is at work on her third book of poems, a meditation on American violence and its theological correlatives. She lives in Philadelphia with her husband, the novelist Josh Emmons, and their infant daughter.

ROBERT P. GEORGE holds Princeton University's celebrated McCormick Chair in Jurisprudence and is the founding director of the James Madison Program in American Ideals and Institutions. He has served on the President's Council on Bioethics and as a presidential appointee to the United States Commission on Civil Rights. He is a member of the Council on Foreign Relations and a corresponding member of UNESCO's World Commission on the Ethics of Scientific Knowledge and Technology (COMEST). He was a Judicial Fellow at the Supreme Court of the United States, where he received the Justice Tom C. Clark Award. His other honors include the United States Presidential Citizens Medal and the Honorific Medal for the Defense of Human Rights of the Republic of Poland. He is the author of *In Defense of Natural Law, Making Men Moral: Civil Liberties and Public Morality,* and *The Clash of Orthodoxies: Law, Religion and Morality in Crisis,* and co-author of *Embryo: A Defense of Human Life* and *Body-Self Dualism in Contemporary Ethics and Politics*. A graduate of Swarthmore College and Harvard Law School, he received a doctorate in philosophy of law from Oxford University.

KENT GREENAWALT is a university professor at Columbia University Law School. Before joining the Columbia faculty in 1965, he was law clerk to U.S. Supreme Court Justice John M. Harlan and subsequently spent part of a summer as an attorney with the Lawyers Committee for Civil Rights in Jackson, Mississippi. From 1966 to 1969, he served on the Civil Rights Committee of the Association of the Bar of the City of New York. Greenawalt was a member of the Due Process Committee of the American Civil Liberties Union, deputy U.S. solicitor general, and president of the American Society for Political and Legal Philosophy. Publications include *Conflicts of Law and Morality; Religious Convictions and Political Choice; Speech, Crime, and the Uses of Language; Private Consciences and Public Reasons; Does God Belong in Public Schools?;* and *Religion and the Constitution I & II.*

EDWIN J. GREENLEE, CO-EDITOR, is the associate director for Public Services, Biddle Law Library of the University of Pennsylvania's School of Law. He is also an adjunct faculty member at the University of Pennsylvania Law School and at Drexel University, and a member of the Pennsylvania and New Jersey bars. He has a PhD degree in anthropology and a law degree, both from Temple University. He holds a Masters degree in library and information science from Drexel University and a Master of Liberal Arts degree from the University of Pennsylvania.

JOSEPH K. GRIEBOSKI is founder and chairman of the Board of the Institute on Religion and Public Policy, which has received three nominations for the Nobel Peace Prize. As a religious freedom and human rights expert, he has testified before the United States Congress, the Organization for Security and Cooperation in Europe, and many other legislative and international bodies. He currently serves as the chairman and CEO of Just Consulting; founder and secretary-general of the Interparliamentary Conference on Human Rights and Religious Freedom; founder and chairman of the International Consortium on Religion, Culture, and Dialogue; member of the Board of Advisors of the Military Religious Freedom Foundation; member of the Board of Directors of the Leadership Council for Human Rights; foreign news contributor for The Cutting Edge News. Grieboski has also served as a faculty member of the Boston University Institute on Religion and World Affairs (IRWA) Seminar "Religion and Democracy." Grieboski was inducted into the International Board of Sponsors of the Martin Luther King Jr. International Chapel at Morehouse College—Martin Luther King's alma mater—in April 2010. The award commemorates those who have made significant contributions to the civil and human rights nonviolence movement in the tradition of Martin Luther King. He holds a Bachelor of Science degree in foreign service and a Master's in national security studies from Georgetown University. In 2008, Joe received an honorary Doctorate of Humane Letters from Marywood University.

TED G. JELEN is professor of political science in the University of Nevada, Las Vegas, and earned his PhD from Ohio State University in 1979. His main research interests are in public opinion, religion and politics, feminism, and the politics of abortion. He has authored, co-authored and edited many books, including *To Serve God and Mammon: Church-State Relations in the United States* (Westview, 2000); *Between Two Absolutes: Public Opinion and the Politics of Abortion* (Westview, 1992); *Perspectives on the Politics of Abortion* (Praeger, 1995); and *Religion and Political Behavior in the United States* (Praeger, 1989).

DAVID L. MCCOLGIN is a criminal defense lawyer practicing in Philadelphia. He specializes in federal appellate litigation, and has argued cases in the Third Circuit Court of Appeals and the Supreme Court. Since 2006 he has been representing several detainees held at Guantánamo.

BRENDAN MORRIS is a graduate student at the University of Nevada, Las Vegas, and is working toward his PhD in political science. He has earned a Master's degree from the University of Nevada, Las Vegas, in political science with a concentration in comparative politics and a Bachelor's degree from Saint Joseph's University in Philadelphia, PA, with a major concentration in political science. His graduate research has focused on U.S. foreign policy for international security and foreign aid for developing countries.

MARTHA NUSSBAUM is the Ernst Freund Distinguished Service Professor of Law and Ethics, appointed in the Philosophy Department, Law School, and Divinity School of the University of Chicago. She is an associate in the Classics Department and the Political Science Department, a member of the Committee on Southern Asian Studies, and co-chair of the Human Rights Program. She is the founder and coordinator of the Center for Comparative Constitutionalism. She received her BA from New York University and her MA and PhD from Harvard. She has taught at Harvard, Brown, and Oxford universities. She received the Brandeis Creative Arts Award in Non-Fiction for 1990, and the PEN Spielvogel-Diamondstein Award for the best collection of essays in 1991; *Cultivating Humanity* won the Ness Book Award of the Association of American Colleges and Universities in 1998 and the Grawemeyer Award in Education in 2002. *Sex and Social Justice* won the book award of the North American Society for Social Philosophy in 2000. *Hiding from Humanity* won the Association of American University Publishers Professional and Scholarly Book Award for Law in 2004. *Frontiers of Justice: Disability, Nationality, Species Membership* won the Elaine and David Spitz Award of the American Political Science Association for the best book in liberal/ democratic theory in 2008. She is the author of the 2007 Supreme Court Foreword for the Harvard Law Review entitled "Constitutions and Capabilities: 'Perception' against Lofty Formalism" and *Liberty of Conscience: In Defense of America's Tradition of Religious Equality*, from which this chapter is based.

MARK J. ROZELL is professor of public policy at George Mason University and the author of numerous studies on the intersection of religion and politics in the United States, interest group politics, and the presidency. His latest book (co-written with Mitchel Sollenberger) is *The President's Czars: Undermining Congress and the Constitution* (University Press of Kansas, 2012).

WILLIAM F. SCHULTZ, president of the Unitarian Universalist Service Committee, served as executive director of Amnesty International USA from 1994 to 2006 and as president of the Unitarian Universalist Association of Congregations from 1985 to 1993. He is the author of two books on human rights, *In Our Own Best Interest: How Defending Human Rights Benefits Us All* (2001, Beacon Press) and *Tainted Legacy: 9/11 and the Ruin of Human Rights* (2003, Nation Books); and the contributing editor of *The Phenomenon of Torture: Readings and Commentary* (2007, University of Pennsylvania Press) and *The Future of Human Rights: US Policy for a New Era* (2008, University of Pennsylvania Press). The New York Review of Books said of him in 2002: "William Schulz . . . has done more than anyone in the American human rights movement to make human rights issues known in the United States."

DOUGLAS B. SHAW is associate dean for Planning, Research, and External Relations and assistant professor of International Affairs at the George Washington University's Elliott School of International Affairs as well as Senior Fellow for National Security Affairs at the Institute on Religion and Public Policy. He is an expert on weapons of mass destruction, terrorism, and international relations with more than a decade of professional experience in multilateral diplomacy and political communication. As a special advisor to the director of the Department of Energy's Nuclear Material Security Task Force for Russia, the New Independent States, and the Baltics, Mr. Shaw worked to secure plutonium and highly enriched uranium from theft or diversion in Ukraine. Mr. Shaw holds Bachelor's and Master's degrees from Georgetown University's School of Foreign Service and is a doctoral candidate in Georgetown University's Government Department. He has taught courses on weapons of mass destruction, terrorism, and international relations at George Washington and Georgetown universities.

STACEY L. SOBEL is an assistant professor and director of the Criminal Law Practice Center at Western State University College of Law and has held lecturer positions at the University of Pennsylvania Law School and George Washington University Law School. Her publications include *The Mythology of a Human Rights Leader: How the United States Failed Sexual Minorities at and Abroad* in the Harvard Human Rights Journal. She is the former executive director of Equality Advocates Pennsylvania (2001–2008). Prior to joining Equality Advocates, she was the legal director of the Servicemembers Legal Defense Network. Ms. Sobel has been invited to share her expertise with many groups, including the White House, members of Congress, the Department of Defense, attorneys, and universities. Ms. Sobel received her BA, cum laude, from the University at Albany, State University of New York and her JD from the George Washington University where she was a Dean's Fellow.

NATHAN C. WALKER, CO-EDITOR, is an ordained Unitarian Universalist minister and serves the First Unitarian Church of Philadelphia. He is currently a doctoral candidate in law, education and religion at Columbia University where he received his Master of Education and Master of Arts degrees. He also graduated from Union Theological Seminary with a Master of Divinity degree and from Emerson College with a Bachelor of Fine Arts. He is a mindfulness practitioner in the Zen Buddhist tradition led by Thich Nhat Hahn.

MICHAEL ZIMMERMAN is Vice President for Academic Affairs and professor of biology at The Evergreen State College in Olympia, Washington. He is also the founder and executive director of The Clergy Letter Project (www.theclergyletterprojct.org), an organization of clergy and scientists dedicated to demonstrating that religion and science need not be in conflict with one another. Zimmerman earned his PhD in ecology from Washington University in St. Louis. In addition to conducting research on aspects of pollination ecology, he has studied popular perceptions of the evolution/creation controversy. He has been elected a Fellow of the American Association for the Advancement of Science in recognition of his work promoting a broader appreciation of science literacy. In addition to numerous research papers and popular reports, he is the author of *Science, Nonscience, and Nonsense: Approaching Environmental Literacy* (Johns Hopkins University Press). His work appears regularly in the Huffington Post.

Index